THIS INFANT ADVENTURE

In 1788 Sir Joseph Banks wrote to Mr William
Devaynes, Chairman of the East India Company:
'The inhabitants of Canton . . . may be induced by the
offer of liberal terms . . . to embark their tea shrubs and all
their tools of culture and manufacture and migrate with
them to Calcutta, where they will find the Botanic
Gardens ready to receive them, twenty acres of which is
already prepared, and lying under very nearly the same
latitude as Canton could not fail to suit in every particular
THIS INFANT ADVENTURE'

THIS INFANT ADVENTURE

Offspring of the Royal Gardens at Kew

Christian Lamb

The following pictures in this book have been reproduced by kind permission of:
Sir James Mitchell: p 24 St Vincent Botanical Garden by Reverend Lansdown Guilding.
Linnean Society: p 61 Henry "Rubber" Ridley; p 68 Ridley's 'herring bone' rubber tapping;
Rafflesia Arnoldii; p 127 tea pluckers; p 129 tea carting – Ceylon.
Natural History Museum: p 15 *Camellia sinensis (thea)*; p 43 *Amazona guildingii* – St
Vincent parrot; p 65 *Tapir indicus*; p 162 Australian black swan; p 165 Dugong; p 169
Banksia coccinea; p 176 Merino sheep.
Royal Botanic Gardens, Kew: p 28 *Artocarpus incisa* – Breadfruit; p 82 The Royal Palm;
page 85 *Codiaeum pictum*; p 152 *Amherstia nobilis*.
Royal Horticultural Society: p 32 *Blighia sapida* – Akee fruit; p 94 *Vanilla planifolia*; p 122
Cocos nucifera – coconut; p 128 Ceylon tea growing areas; p 138 *Ficus benjaminus* – fig tree.

Infant Adventure
Offspring of the Royal Gardens at Kew

First published in 2010 by
Bene Factum Publishing Ltd
PO Box 58122
London
SW8 5WZ

Email: inquiries@bene-factum.co.uk
www.bene-factum.co.uk

ISBN: 978-1-903071-29-8
Text © Christian Lamb

A CIP catalogue record of this is available from the British Library

Cover and book design by Mousemat Design Ltd

Printed in Slovenia on behalf of Latitude Press Limited

CONTENTS

── Acknowledgments and Credits ──

Firstly I must thank Tim Smit CBE, creator of a modern and innovative botanic garden – The Eden Project, for writing such a notable and penetrating Foreword.

I also owe thanks to many people for helping me write this book. First to Mike Phillips without whose cheerful cooperation I could never control my computer. To Alan Wilkinson, Literary Consultant for his constructive criticism; Liz O'Brien for her professional editing and good advice; Neil Chambers, Research Curator of Banks' Archive at the Natural History Museum; Michelle Losse and Craig Brough for their guidance at the Archive and Library of the Royal Botanic Garden, Kew; Linda Brooks and Ben Sherwood for their help in the Linnean Library; and Dr Brent Elliott for his assistance at the Lindley Library. Anthony Weldon of Benefactum Publishing for his skills and accomplishment in putting it all together.

Acknowledgements also to the authors to whose books, letters, etc I have referred: Henry Cave *Golden Tips – Ceylon and its Great Tea Industry,* DM Forrest *A Hundred Years of Ceylon Tea,* John Loadman *Tears of the Tree,* Joe Jackson *The Thief at the End of the World,* Fiammetta Rocco *The Miraculous Fever Tree,* Edward Kynaston, *A Man on Edge,* F. Bruce Lamb *Mahogany of Latin America,* Audrey Biggs *Family Recollections,* Robert Duncan *James Duncan and the Garden of Mauritius,* and Nicholas Courtney for introducing me to the Reverend Lansdown Guilding.

I have drawn practically all my material from sources contemporary to the time about which I am writing, and which used the original names of places. I appreciate that many names have changed. But for the sake of consistency, and to avoid confusion for the reader, I have stuck throughout the book to the older versions – for example Ceylon instead of Sri Lanka."

Christian Lamb, Cornwall 2010

With the passage of time the history of human endeavour often takes on many of the characteristics of comic strip heroism and in so doing enters the imagination of the present as a sort of mythology. It is too often presented as nostalgia for times that were better or more vivid than today. Or, alternatively, as a cautionary tale from which we can supposedly learn a great deal – with a bittersweet background voice that tells us that our tragedy is to never learn – we are destined to repeat our follies.

The world of botanic exploration has its own pantheon of heroes complete with a stage set of exotic locations, unimaginable bravery and hardships, and a narrative that tells of an obsession to bring back living things from around the world for the curiosity and economic benefit of the sponsors of the expeditions. These ranged from the great nursery ventures, supplying their privileged customers with novelties for gardens and estates, to the great institutions like the Royal Botanic Gardens at Kew. Kew was and remains without doubt the most famous and important botanical garden the world has ever seen.

However, our present day interests in gardens and plants is tempered by a cultural lens that sees botany as the preserve of academics and gardens as an accessory to our daily lives. This is a huge mistake. The importance of botany and the great plant hunters lie not in a heritage of wonderful landscapes and gardens, great though this is, these are a mere by-product. What Christian Lamb's important and enlightening book illustrates is that the new botanic gardens were the heartbeat of an empire. The plant hunters and their administrative colleagues should be seen as not eccentric adventurers – no, the proper context if one were to draw a parallel with the present day would be with the giants of silicon valley – such as Bill Gates, Steve Jobs and so on.

No group of people in history so transformed the economic, political and cultural landscape as the plant hunters and the great botanical gardens that acted as the hubs and planners for this great pursuit. Imagine a world without industrial amounts of rubber, quinine, tea, coffee, cocoa, spices and so on and without the great corporations and financial institutions that evolved on the back of them and you see a very different world.

These men literally created the foundations for global markets and historically the tragedy of their legacy is that their real importance is overshadowed by the mythology of exploration. The real genius lay in the organising of their discoveries into industrial packages that would shake the world we know today. This book , disarmingly presented as a miscellany of botanic garden histories reveals so much more than that – it shines a light on an extraordinary period of history and the people who made it, and, in so doing gives a powerful nod in the direction of suggesting a re-evaluation of the importance of "the godfather" of the botanic revolution, Christian Lamb's hero – Sir Joseph Banks.

What then is the lesson from history we can take from this? I would suggest firstly that it highlights our dependence on plants in a way that the modern world denies at its peril and secondly, while the imperial overtones may chime badly in the modern context, the scale of the operation and ingenuity of its participants demonstrate that industrial solutions to the supply of plant based products require a balance of skills in both production and conservation. It is this new balance that the botanic garden world now struggles to champion in the face of a global economy that fails to see this work as essential – preferring to characterise it as "charitable" activity. To go on believing this could be the greatest folly in humankind – now this is a lesson from history worth listening to.

Tim Smit
September 2010

Sir Joseph Banks, 1743-1820, President of the Royal Society and unofficial
Director of the Royal Gardens at Kew, painted by Sir Joshua Reynolds.

The Royal Gardens, Kew

It so happens that I 'collect' botanic gardens; but because you can't take them away with you and gloat over them it is not quite the same physical activity as for those who spend half their lives hunting for rare stamps or vintage cars. This book is a nebulous collection of a few chosen from the vast array available – the stars in their spheres – and even these must be confined to catching short periods in their lives – no garden stands still.

These *objets d'art* have swung into my orbit and become favourites for the unforgettable, but sometimes forgotten, brilliant young botanists who created them, for their romantic British Empire associations, for their stunning commercial success with such commodities as rubber and tea, and above all for giving us passionate plantsmen the delight of growing in our own gardens a plethora of the most exquisite and unique members of the vegetable kingdom.

The British Empire associations were not all romantic – the diplomatic, military and naval exploits are well recorded. Far less well-known are the contributions of 'my' gardens which, in their own unsung way, helped to underpin the Empire's commercial success and were also so instrumental in furthering botanical knowledge around the world.

Gathering their histories together is the perfect way to indulge in such a love affair, to research and travel, and in case anyone out there is interested, to write about them simply adds to the pleasure. My focus is on those offspring of the Royal Gardens of Kew which date back to my hero, Sir Joseph Banks (1743-1820) when he was instrumental in their formation and who unwittingly supplied my title '*This Infant Adventure*' perfectly describing the birth of a great botanic garden.

If only I could have interviewed the dedicated young naturalists who initiated these far-flung institutions, real people always being the best source of evidence with first hand information straight from the horse's mouth. There is no way I can question them directly so can only search for the answers, spending time in the vast botanic archives and libraries of the world, combing the many letters, articles, books, manuscripts and pamphlets (for some reason these are particularly exciting and revealing) produced over the last two centuries, which tell us what they found and did, and in particular, thought. Inevitably the author becomes an erstwhile reporter working in an age without modern communication aids. Excavating the origins of these entrepreneurs is the most intriguing aspect of my research, each of whom has left an indelible legacy, and whose writings have directed me towards their adventures and achievements, prompting me to bring them back to life and try to vivify their contribution to science in that amazing Age of Enlightenment and the prestigious Victorian era which followed.

My background of world travel has allowed me excellent opportunities for making my collection, luckily wandering round the globe at Her Majesty's expense, first with my father and then my husband, both in the Navy. Now that I am unencumbered I can make further explorations of a purely pleasurable kind, discovering exciting background stories and illuminating a few of the many pioneering plantsmen who have so far not been given enough of their well-earned limelight.

When my life was taken over by gardening, camellias were my first obsession. Finding out about their long history requires much study, and I have followed their progress from China and Japan westwards, investigating where they landed in the early seventeen hundreds onwards to the zenith of their popularity in Victorian days. But it was the surprise unravelling of their arrival in Australia (I return to this later) which first introduced me to Sir Joseph Banks, and this was via a man named Bligh. Surely not our old Bligh of the Bounty? But, in fact it was.

Aware that I was thinking of embarking on a new career, a good friend suggested I should take up lecturing. 'Any fool can do it,' she advised (knowing that I am rather voluble, have certain obsessions and can talk for ever about plants). 'All you need is a good beginning and a good end, because nobody listens to the middle.' I took her excellent advice and invented a talk on camellias. Not everybody knows that the camellia is the original tea plant, *Camellia sinensis,* and the tale of how our ingenious botanists made two thriving colonial industries out of it (in Ceylon and the Himalayas – more about these soon) is quite a saga. Many varieties of the *Camellia japonica* reached England when optimistic traders tried to import tea plants by clipper, direct from their native country, which the Chinese (correctly suspecting our intention of cutting them out of their monopoly) craftily substituted for this decorative species.

Camellia sinensis (also referred to as *Camellia thea*) – the Tea Plant, known as cha, originally from China. Its leaves were infused with hot water and drunk for perhaps three thousand years before its Western discovery.

Building my new career was not quite as easy as I had hoped, but I persevered, and was invited here and there, managing to get to various botanic institutions in America and Australia, eventually joining a rather prestigious organisation in England where my anxiety was always to camouflage my very amateur status.

It was necessary to think of economic but still enjoyable ways of visiting the countries of my botanic gardens. Cruises immediately came to mind, being not only my favourite form of travel but providing the opportunity for a few talks on board, thus boosting the exchequer – and by now I had added a talk on Sir Joseph Banks to my repertoire. It seemed a good idea to arrange a few solo lecture tours on my own, making sure the venues were adjacent to my present research subject. I also joined groups of like-minded people, such as the International Dendrology Society, and the International Camellia Society and various other organisations to which I belong, whose tours often ideally suit my interests.

Joseph Banks was the backbone of Kew Gardens for nearly fifty years. His father, a wealthy landowner in Lincolnshire, sent him to be educated at Eton, where he found the heavy classical curriculum unendurable, and so instead escaped to spend his time gathering plants as he wandered along the banks of the Thames. This was Banks' introduction to botany, a lifelong passion; it was also the start of his natural history collections. His father died when he was only twenty-one, and he inherited his ancestral home Revesby Abbey, near Lincoln, and a vast fortune which included thousands of acres of land. However, he continued his education in natural science at the British Museum in London, where two years later he was elected a Fellow of the Royal Society, of which he was to become the President at thirty-five and remain so for forty years, the longest ever incumbent.

After his first field expedition to Labrador and Newfoundland, travelling with the Navy, he heard about the proposed voyage of discovery to the South Seas, under the command of Captain Cook, and persuaded the Royal Society to arrange with the Admiralty to take him at his own expense so he could study the plants and wildlife of the countries visited. The voyage lasted three years, 1768-1771, and has been well documented, his adventures and successes legendary.

On their return King George III sent for Banks and from their first meeting they became lifelong friends, being much the same age with many scientific interests in common. Banks became the King's adviser on all such matters and unofficial Director of the Royal Gardens at Kew. The King made him a Baronet in 1781.

Ever since the first century when the Greek physician and herbalist Dioscorides compiled *Materia Medica,* botanists and gardeners have copied his ideas. All through the ages right up to the present day botany has been a thoroughly practical science, the aim of those who study it being to turn the resources of the vegetable kingdom to account for scientific as well as useful and commercial ends.

The first botanic garden in England was the Royal Garden at Hampton Court, founded by Queen Elizabeth, and liberally supported by Charles II, the founder of the Royal Society, and George III, both interested in science. Although a Royal Garden it has always been available for public advantage, and some of the oldest specimens of English botanical literature are the descriptions of rare plants grown at Hampton Court.

The origin of Kew as a scientific institution was entirely due to the intelligent tastes of the Hanoverian Royal family. The Princess Dowager of Wales, mother of George III, lived at Kew and began the botanical collections about the middle of the 18 C. George III enjoyed many happy years at Kew Palace, and very much increased these, receiving considerable scientific help from Joseph Banks. Kew has been a botanic garden ever since; that is, a place where collections of rare plants are grown, studied and exhibited.

Banks wanted Kew to be much more than a collection of exotics – it was to be a living encyclopaedia, the great exchange house of the Empire, testing plants for their acclimatisation and practical usage in horticulture, medicine and commerce. This was to be the starting point from which Banks helped to set up and encourage many of the early botanic gardens in our colonies and beyond.

Problems with Kew began when King George III and his protégé Sir Joseph Banks, the unofficial Director of the Royal Gardens, died within a few months of each other in 1820. The Gardens were dependent on their patronage and enthusiastic support, and the subsequent deterioration was a melancholy sight. Kings George IV and William IV were otherwise engaged, and it wasn't until Queen Victoria came to the throne in 1837 and took a personal interest in the Gardens that green shoots appeared again at Kew.

John Lindley, Professor of Botany at University College London and

Assistant Secretary to the Horticultural Society, was appointed by the Treasury in 1838 to enquire into the management of the Royal Gardens, aided by two members of Parliament. Without Lindley's vision it is doubtful that Kew would have survived what the Treasury proposed – a cost cutting exercise. But like his friend William Hooker he was a man of exceptional energy and stamina.

It is very probable that when William Hooker (1785-1865) was appointed Director of the Royal Gardens at Kew, it was the result of some pretty internecine skulduggery, but it certainly resulted in the salvation of the gardens. He had been the choice twenty years before, of Joseph Banks, one of whose last benevolent acts before he died was to recommend the impoverished Hooker to direct the botanic gardens in Glasgow. Hooker, just in time, extracted himself from this appointment, and aiming ambitiously at the Royal Gardens of Kew, managed, with a neat sleight of hand, even lobbying the young Queen Victoria (via a supportive Duke) and undercutting his rival (by accepting a smaller salary), to win himself his life's quantum leap. Then, after superintending Kew for the next quarter of a century, he was careful to arrange the succession in favour of his son Joseph Hooker (1817-1911), who carried on the tradition with his son-in-law, William Thistleton-Dyer (1843-1928).

William Hooker, as Director of Kew, succeeded in the course of a few years in laying the foundations of all the different departmental activities, which he saw were needed to make it perform the functions established by Dr Lindley, and as demanded of it by the Empire at large. These have gone along the same lines ever since, though enormously expanded. There were large collections of living exotic plants at Kew when it passed from the management of the Crown, which formed the basis of those which now exist.

An echo of Banks's imperialism sounds through the rhetoric of Lindley's justification for a National Botanic Garden - the destined umbilical cord of all colonial gardens which would come within its orbit: 'they should all be under the control of the Chief of the Garden, acting in concert with him, and through him with each other, reporting constantly their proceedings, explaining their wants, receiving their supplies and aiding the mother country in everything that is useful in the vegetable kingdom. Medicine, commerce, agriculture, horticulture, would derive considerable advantages from the establishment of such a system.' This goal would be diligently pursued by the dynasty – the two Hookers and Thistleton-Dyer – for the next hundred years.

CHAPTER 1

The St Vincent Botanic Garden

The huge mahogany tree, *Swietenia mahogoni,* standing proud in the Botanic Gardens of St Vincent in the West Indies, sowed the seed of the idea that gathering these old Colonial gardens together into a collection might be fun to write about. I was sun-seeking during the depth of our cold English winter, and had chosen the most perfect cruise ship – she might indeed have been designed for me – because, on her itinerary was a visit to this historic garden, which claims to be the oldest in the Western Hemisphere.

The *Sea Cloud,* a magnificent square rigger, was a particularly good choice, sailing between the many islands of the West Indies over which the English and French spent so much time fighting, during the early 1800s. I could vividly imagine this ship taking part in those colourful sea battles.

Sea Cloud was designed and built in 1931 (with money no object) for the financier EF Hutton and his cereal heiress wife Marjorie Merewether Post, to dazzle all who saw her. She featured unheard of technologies, such as watertight compartments, up until then only found in submarines. Yet towering above the teak decks and mahogany cabin structures was the nearly two hundred foot high rig of a late 19th C four-masted barque, one of the largest sailing ships that ever plied the tradewind routes.

She had a somewhat chequered career before becoming a cross between a luxury yacht and a five star cruise ship. The most expensive cabins came with vast double beds, marble bathrooms and antique furniture, each uniquely designed in what I call the bilges, but Marjorie chose this area where she and her husband were to live, knowing that it would have minimum roll. Now, at the end of each cruise, all the passengers, (sixty is the most she can

The four-masted barque *Sea Cloud* – originally privately built in 1931
and now a luxurious cruise ship.

accommodate), are invited to view the ten opulent apartments while sipping a glass or two of champagne. I preferred my much cheaper cabin on the upper deck, where I could sit over my breakfast in bed and gaze at the sea through a big square window, occasionally catching sight of flying fish or frolicking dolphins.

The sail setting procedure was explained to us: the furling and unfurling of sails is done in the rigging, the setting and dousing is handled from the deck, and evocative words paint the atmosphere, such as 'set the lower and upper topsails, set topgallants and royals, gibs and staysails and spankers'.

The Captain was American, his First Officer Russian, the catering officer Hungarian – a remarkable and successful coalition – and the Bosun and his mostly Filipino crew were always busy, dashing up and down the rigging, adjusting sails, polishing the bright work, and painting and maintaining the yards and stays. I regret to say that I have always been a fairweather sailor, so the West Indies is my idea of heaven; the wind blows mostly from the same direction so you never have to go about or jibe; indeed when I mentioned 'jibe' to the Bosun, he went a little pale – I gathered this is not something *Sea Cloud* does, and he explained what happened if this tactic became necessary, but he lost me very quickly.

The early explorers who opened the South Seas to the eyes of the world brought back seeds and living plants of exotics, as well as valuable crops of the Indies to the botanical gardens. As these plants could only be grown in hothouses in Europe, many were thus established and then reshipped to the colonies in the Western hemisphere. The introduction, development and exploitation of these useful articles of commerce were encouraged, and in 1758 the Royal Society offered 'a gold medal for the first person bringing mango seeds to England to be sent to the West Indies for planting'.

By 1760 special prizes had been offered by the Royal Society for such commodities as olives, opium, cinnamon, nutmeg, mace, sarsaparilla, indigo and cotton, as well as vanilla, cloves, pepper, camphor, quinine, various tinctorial plants and ornamental woods – all of which carried an economic premium in the European market and could be cultivated in the West Indies more easily and cheaply.

In 1763 the Windward Federation of Islands (Grenada, St Vincent, Dominica and Tobago) was ceded to Great Britain, and General Robert Melville was appointed as the first Governor. Touring his territory in 1765, Melville met Dr George Yonge, the principal Military Medical officer of St Vincent and an ardent horticulturist. Melville had the idea of establishing a Government botanical garden similar to the famous Kew Gardens for 'cultivation and improvement of many plants now growing wild and the importation of others from similar climates'.

Dr Yonge was enthusiastic and agreed to apply for crown lands for a plot for which he was assigned an area of woodland about a mile north of Kingstown, the island capital. The General had the land cleared at his own expense and Yonge was appointed Superintendent. By 1773 the garden was described as 'a place of beauty', and he was awarded a gold medal by the Royal Society for having '140 healthy cinnamon, mango and nutmeg trees and so on' in the establishment.

Joseph Banks, unofficial Director of the Royal Gardens at Kew, was involved in the affairs of the St Vincent Botanical Garden from its beginning until his death in 1820. There was a dependence on plants for medicine by troops in the Caribbean, garrisoned by the British Government in order to protect colonial interests and British nationals during intervals of war and peace. This created a substantial reliance on correspondents to supply the War Office, then responsible for the garden with information about plants and herbs that could be used to stem the mortality and morbidity rate of the troops in the Caribbean. Fevers and dysentery as well as other health conditions associated with warfare and the tropics, destroyed European troops at an alarming rate. The losses encouraged the establishment of temporary battalions, by colonial legislatures (largely comprised of planters and merchants) and the British Government personnel known as Ranger Corps. It is from the troops of Africans, led by commissioned white officers only, that the West India Regiments emerged.

During the 17th and 18th centuries there was an influx of Europeans who were physically unable to adapt to tropical conditions. The continual problem concerning health was resolved only by painstaking medical efforts, involving devastating losses and suffering.

There was another aspect of Banks' influence and activities relating to the St Vincent Botanic Garden: the site was not favoured by the 'plantocracy' of the Caribbean, nor their lobby in the British Isles. Every effort was made by the planters and merchants in St Vincent to prevent it from being successful in spite of its proven value. In fact it was seen by antagonists as land that should have been used for planting valuable sugarcane. Land and slaves were seen as essential to its profitable production.

A local revolution of the Caribs ended in the French taking over the island between 1780 and 1783, but by great good luck the French General was a friend of both Melville and Banks. He took a considerable interest in Dr Yonge and the garden which prospered during his care, even introducing plants from the French colonies overseas. St Vincent was given back to the British that year, and when Governor Melville returned to England with Dr Yonge, he was succeeded as Superintendent of the garden by Dr Alexander Anderson, who had worked with Yonge as medical doctor for the troops. Anderson was a most energetic man, and his subsequent account of how he dealt with 'the enemies of the garden' and finally won his battle, plus his diligent stewardship, paint an interesting contemporary picture. He established its fine reputation which lasts to this day.

Nevertheless the smouldering disapproval of the local sugarcane growers influenced the new Governor who was inexperienced in that part of the world, and who received advice and 'artful insinuations from illiberal and designing persons'. There had also been trouble since the beginning over the garrison land. Before the garden was envisaged, 50 acres of land had been purchased in 1764 by commissioners for the King for 'a garrison and other public uses that might afterwards appear necessary.' It was from part of what became known as this 'garrison land' that six acres were originally set aside for the garden. However, Anderson relates that 'the natural site of this garden being on a declivity, with scarcely any level surface, most of the soil is washed off, and it is with difficulty that young plants, particularly seedlings, can be reared in it.' He was therefore anxious to add some of the adjacent very level land to the garden, and this request was agreed by the Governor.

Commanding Officers viewed such occupation as an 'infringement of their prerogative', in spite of the fact that 'what yet remained of barrack ground was more than the garrison had occasion for', so when it turned out that this amount of land was quite inadequate for what was required of the garden another twenty acres were added. The Commanding Officer reacted with an armed force and prevented the enclosure of the allotted land and its cultivation. Luckily General Melville was still there, and the bounds between the garden and the barracks – as limited by him – were settled by the express order of the King in 1771. Tranquillity was for some time restored to the establishment.

After many vicissitudes during the following years and a period when Dr Yonge was away, the Governor took possession of the garden and turned it into pasture for his own cattle. He appropriated the buildings for a native woman and her children and refused to confirm Dr Anderson's appointment, obliging him to live in a tavern at his own expense for over six months. Anderson refused to give up hope, but although as he says in his account that 'the most disagreeable prospect was to quarrel with the representation of majesty', it wasn't until he heard the news that a packet was to sail for England in two days time that he finally went again to the Governor saying that he was determined to know whether he was to be given possession of the garden or not, 'as I was under the necessity of representing home, on which he got in a violent passion'. Anderson left the scene immediately, and that evening a letter came saying he could take possession of six acres. The very next morning he found the house empty and immediately occupied it – triumphantly writing, 'from this the chief point was gained for according to the common adage 'possession is 11 points of the law."

St Vincent Botanical Garden painted by the Reverend Lansdown Guilding 1797-1831.

However, the Governor's servants and slaves laughed at him and treated him with contempt, continuing to drive horses and cattle through every part of the garden, by now ruinously overgrown and missing most of the fences. Poor Anderson found his labours constantly harassed and obstructed.

He records: 'I was determined not to yield in the least from the mode of conduct I had fixed on,' and his resolution was rewarded when another packet arrived with letters from Dr Yonge and Lord Sydney for Governor Lincoln. Anderson was sent for and told that 'I might do with the whole of the lands as I thought proper and hire as many labourers as I judged requisite.'

Anderson had won at last. From that moment the Governor could not have been more helpful, paying him every possible attention, and even giving him useful advice about planning and arranging the new ground he was adding to the garden. Anderson adds: 'He studied by every means in his power to render my situation agreeable'. Things had certainly improved, although his description of how he achieved the actual work in the garden reveals what difficulties he faced.

He says: 'The only labourers must be slaves acquainted with no cultivation but that of the sugarcane, which is simple and without any variation in the mode of it, but in horticulture there are varieties of work, all different from what they are accustomed'. Anderson explains that it seemed impossible for a negro to learn the difference between plants which 'they were to preserve from those they were to destroy'; you had to actually show him how to do a task. He says 'before a native can perform a job he is unaccustomed, it must first be done before him. It is not by direction but by example only he can go on it.' As the old garden had been totally ruined, it all had to be redesigned and fenced, and a great deal of this manual labour devolved on the Superintendent. He notes: 'Such hard labour in a tropical climate few European constitutions are fitted for', but fortunately for him he had been well inured to the nature of the climate by the many hardships he had previously experienced.

Anderson passionately wanted to increase the variety of interesting plants: 'my early wish was correspondence with scientific men, particularly lovers of botany in every part to which a communication could be kept open. By punctual answers and liberal returns for seeds and plants received, the number of these received in the Garden increased fast'.

Anderson spent a great deal of time trying to find the best way of growing the clove and 'several varieties of cinnamon, which had been introduced from the French islands, to which they had been brought by their ships from Asia.'

'The clove' he says, 'is an elegant little tree: that in the garden, now bearing is about eight feet in height, and the stem near the ground is about two inches in diameter. That so small a tree should bear fruit I ascribe to its being raised from a layer. The nature of the plant is not yet well known in the West Indies. All the information I have heretofore received as to the culture of it has for the most part has been imparted from ignorance or from ill intentions, and consequently has led me into errors on that subject, by which I have often lost the individual: but I have always been so fortunate as to preserve an offspring or layers from it.' He read the *Herbarium Amboinense* of Rumphius and learned much helpful information from it, finding 'that he corroborates my idea respecting the nature of the soil.'

Every packet-ship that arrived from England brought parcels of East India seeds from Sir Joseph Banks and Sir George Yonge and by May 1786

Anderson decided the garden was sufficiently restored to be left for a month or two under the care of an overseer, leaving him free to explore any countries within range for some plant-hunting himself. After a short trip to Trinidad 'which appeared to me one of the most desirable and fertile fields perhaps in the world', he found the best place an Englishman could go were the Dutch colonies of Guiana.

'A fortunate occasion offered at the beginning of the year 1791 for the accomplishment of my design. Mr Lochhead of Antigua, a great enthusiast for natural history and as anxious for the expedition as myself, being then with me, having at his command a small schooner remarkably well fitted for the purpose, we soon determined on a visit to Guiana.'

They set off for the colonies of Berbice, Demerary and Essequibo which had been very little visited by naturalists, agreeing that 'the large rivers inter-secting them facilitates the penetrating into their interior parts.' He gives a lively description of what they found: 'We departed the 6th March touching at Barbados to gain information as to the navigation of that low and dangerous coast. The only method of penetrating into the country is by boats and Indian canoes on the rivers and creeks until about 200 miles from the sea. Every moment was precious by presenting something new. The uncommon appearance of the watery surface of the country with mud beds surrounding it, its sea coast with trees literally growing in the water; further up the river, notwithstanding the watery surface of the rest are vast extent of the most dry and arid plains, entirely level, some extending as far as the eye can see; inter-spersed here and there, as if planted by the hand of man for ornament, were clumps of small trees, beautiful and rare shrubs as well as herbaceous plants nowhere else found.' They were able to travel higher up the river than any sailing vessel had gone before, and found it a great advantage 'having always a comfortable home at night and every convenience for arranging and preserving our seeds and plants.'

At about 200 miles from the sea the country became mountainous and dry so they had to explore further into the forests, 'but not less dangerous from the number of tigers which haunt them, we fortunately saw only their tracks.'

Having travelled about 300 miles up the River Demerary, while luckily the dry weather held, the Indian guides now absolutely refused to enter the territory of the warlike Caribs and obliged them to return, much against their instincts.

The Dutch colonists had been extremely kind in putting them in touch with European inhabitants on the river, and helping with pilots, Indian guides and local knowledge. Anderson's party had hoped to continue the journey down the River Essequibo, but they did not find the same welcoming hospitality and the river was very dangerous without a pilot.

Anderson recounts: 'There is no ascending it above 50 miles; the channels are frequently so close to the islands that we made use of poles to keep the side of the vessel from rubbing on the land. It is the most remarkable and romantic river in this part of the continent. Many of the islands are large, all covered with tall trees, with the winding channels that separate them forming such a variety of beautiful scenes is surpassed perhaps by few rivers in the world.'

It was now the end of June and the dry season was coming to an end; 'frequent lightning and rolling thunder in the interior parts clearly pointed out the rainy season was commencing and time for us to bid adieu to the continent.'

In the middle of July they arrived in St Vincent and Anderson concludes: 'although I had left the continent with regret yet I was very anxious to see the Garden again. What I expected I found, too true, the Garden much neglected and out of order by the ignorance and inattention of my assistant at that time.' The most famous and historically important plant to be grown in St Vincent was undoubtedly the breadfruit *Artocarpus altilis.* The idea of transplanting it from the East Indies to the West Indies had been discussed for many years; William Dampier, pirate and explorer, first describes the fruit in 1688 as 'soft and yellow when ripe with a sweet and pleasant taste. The natives gather it when it is green and hard and bake it; the inside then becomes soft and tender and white like the crumb of a penny loaf'. Captain Cook spoke enthusiastically of the tree which supplied the islanders of Tahiti with bread throughout the year – nine months with fresh fruit, and three months with paste preserved in leaf-lined holes in the ground. Dr Solander, who was with Banks on his voyage with Captain Cook in HMS *Endeavour,* describes the fruit in a letter, 'which was by us for several months daily eaten as a substitute for bread, was undeniably esteemed as palatable and as nourishing as bread itself. No one of the whole ship's company complained when served with breadfruit in lieu of biscuit'.

It was in 1771 that Valentine Morris, planter and West Indian Governor of St Vincent, keen gardener and a friend of Joseph Banks, made the first practical proposal to transplant the breadfruit. Most of Great Britain's sugar came from the West Indies, with the labour performed by slaves from Africa. Hurricanes during the last five years had wrecked the harvest of their staple diet (the expensive and difficult to grow plantain and maize) and the American War of Independence had prevented supplies reaching them from America, resulting in 15,000 slaves dying of starvation. King George III backed the plan, and the Royal Society offered a Gold Medal to the first person who conveyed six plants of one or both species in a growing state.

The breadfruit does not produce seeds, so living plants had to be transported. Banks was intimately involved in the planning of the expedition,

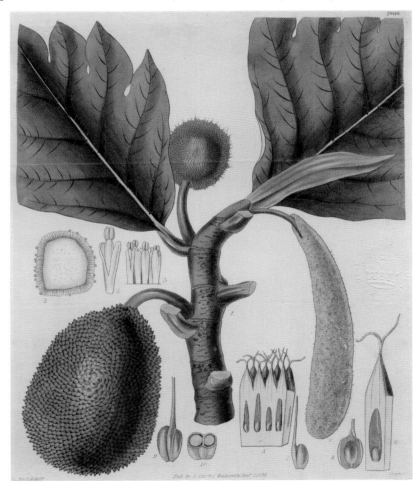

Artocarpus altilis – the Breadfruit Tree

arranging the alterations to the ship HMS *Bounty* for taking the plants in pots. There was now not enough room in the small ship to allow accommodation for marines who could have prevented the mutiny. Although the story of the expedition has been told many times, Bligh is usually the villain of the piece. He was of course involved in two other full scale mutinies, one at the Nore in 1797, the other at the Rum Rebellion in 1808 in Australia (I come to this later). He was also the subject of at least two most damaging Courts Martial, not to mention many public rows. Yet Bligh was a real paradox of a man and – contrary to what one might expect – a Commanding Officer who cared intensely for the wellbeing of his men. Also little known is his contribution to horticulture and the Gold Medal he was awarded by the Royal Society for conveying the breadfruit from Tahiti to St Vincent and Jamaica on the second voyage.

Bligh sailed with Captain Cook on his third and fatal (for Cook) expedition to the South Seas, and it was from him that he learnt not only his consummate skill as navigator and cartographer, but the vital importance of the health of his crew. He served with renown at the battles of Camperdown and Copenhagen with Nelson who personally thanked him. His many friends held him in high esteem, not the least of whom and ever his champion included Sir Joseph Banks. None of his many detractors ever attacked his moral character, and he was a devoted husband and father, (he had five daughters, his twin sons having died in childbirth) – a figure both admired and respected.

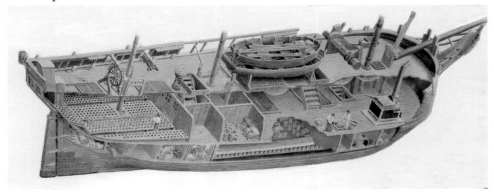

Cut-away view of His Majesty's Armed Transport *Bounty* (better known as HMS *Bounty*), the ex-merchant ship and commissioned for the botanical breadfruit expedition to the South Pacific in 1787.

Lieutenant William Bligh (1754-1817) (later Captain and subsequently Vice-Admiral) appointed to command HMS *Bounty* in 1787 and to procure and convey breadfruit trees 'to the West Indian islands'.

He was described by one of his junior officers as 'A very choleric man, at the same time a very just man'; he was justifiably proud that the care of his crew was his prime consideration and he had a supreme contempt for those Commanders who arrived in port with half their men sick with scurvy fever.

In his log (in HMS *Bounty)* he says: 'I fed them hot breakfasts of ground wheat and sugar, portable [sic] soup (a kind of vegetable concentrate) and krout equal to cabbage made a valuable meal; pease mixed with the former two articles was equal to the greatest dainty. I supplied half their salt meat by giving them flour and raisins in lieu.'

On five closely written pages he describes the measures he took throughout the voyage to make his men cheerful and comfortable, lighting fires between decks to dry out their clothes and the ship; he made his fiddler play from 6-8pm every evening when 'their fun in attempting to dance on the forehatch kept them in health and spirits. He adds, 'I am satisfactorily repaid for all my trouble by bringing all here (the Cape) without a single complaint.' Another optimistic quotation from his log: 'We are all in good spirits. My officers and young gentlemen are all tractable and well disposed and we now understand each other so well we shall remain so the whole voyage'!

Knowing that fresh fruit and vegetables were the secret of health on long voyages, Bligh planted fruit trees everywhere he went, with future (his own as well as other seamen's) visits in view; he stocked up at the Cape and took apple tree saplings, all sorts of seed from corn to lemons and oranges for Mr Nelson (the gardener of the voyage) to plant on their travels round the Pacific, taking the greatest botanical interest in anything that might improve his men's diet.

In his log Bligh notes 'Got no observation of the sun, it never being once out in 24 hours'. Only Cook and one or two intrepid adventurers had ever sailed these seas before and he kept a scrupulous record of everything sighted including the birds that flew along with them – blue petrels, shearwaters, pintadas and albatrosses. In spite of the difficulties of taking observations, Mewstone Rock, Tasmania hove to in sight, exactly as he predicted, at 2pm 19th August – 6,000 miles from the Cape. Bligh was a peerless navigator.

They found the east side of Adventure Bay where the soil looked good and at Nelson's recommendation Bligh says: 'I fixed on the most proper situation for planting some of the fruit trees which I had brought from the Cape of Good Hope and planted three fine young apple trees, nine vines, six plantain trees, and a number of orange and lemon-seed, cherry-stones, plum, peach and apricot stones, pumpkins and all sorts of Indian corn and apple and pear kernels. Near the watering place, likewise, we planted on a flat, which appeared a favourable situation, some onions, cabbage roots and potatoes.' He then collected about 70 valuable plants to take on to Tahiti (some of which would be destined for Kew) where they arrived in early October.

Unfortunately, and unknown to all, it was too early in the season to propagate the breadfruit which had not finished fruiting; thus it took the five fatal months to establish the 1,000 or so suckers and prepare the plants for their long journey. Bligh's comment, 'Eating the lotus by day on that fair isle where it always seemed afternoon, the weeks slipped easily away', about sums it all up.

Bligh's punishments were known to be mild and few, so give or take the usual number of floggings for insubordinate behaviour, things seem to have gone moderately well. But when they set sail from Tahiti on 30 March 1789 with 1,015 breadfruit plants 'in a very fine state' Fletcher Christian (the Mate) in particular, and others to a lesser degree, suffered such withdrawal symptoms from the seductive life of Tahiti that their relationships shattered, with Bligh's

Blighia sapida, the Akee fruit, introduced to Jamaica by Captain Bligh in 1793
(after his second voyage to Tahiti).

violent accusations against Christian, hitherto his 'darling' who could do no wrong. The injustice of these triggered off an act of rebellion unparalleled in naval history.

The row erupted over the theft of Bligh's coconuts; Bligh staged the same sort of inquisition as Captain Queeg at his most paranoid, portrayed in the film *The Caine Mutiny*. Christian must have smouldered over night because it was next dawn that he seized Bligh at bayonet point and forced him over the side into a small boat. Seventeen unwilling companions went with him, their touching faith in his seamanship fully justified.

Christian meanwhile heaved the breadfruit over the side and disappeared beyond the horizon in what he hoped would be the continuation of interrupted bliss, but which ended in total disaster for them all.

Bligh achieved the impossible, saving all 17 their lives. His 23 ft long boat, water lapping within seven inches of the gunwales, sailed from Tofua to Timor in 41 days, 3,618 miles through uncharted waters, tempestuous

The Mutiny on the *Bounty* – the epic moment when Lieutenant Bligh and fourteen seamen were cast adrift in April 1789 – contemporary print after a painting by Robert Dodd.

weather and attacks by savages. He even managed to note in his precious log the whereabouts of an island which they called Restoration Is which he says was covered in 'Manchineal trees and some palm trees from the tops of which he found a soft interior which was very palatable in a stew.' Some fern roots were also valuable in allaying thirst.

Bligh will always be an enigma if one reads only about his stormy career, but his own descriptions of those 41 days in the open boat show such professional skill and ingenuity with the meagre provisions that they somehow underline the good points in his character. A few words from his account are worth repeating as an example of the sufferings of his men. On Saturday 9th May he writes : 'In the morning a quarter of a pint of cocoa-nut milk and some of the decayed bread was served for breakfast; and for dinner I divided the meat of four cocoa-nuts with the remainder of the rotten bread which was only eatable by such distressed people. In the afternoon I fitted a pair of shrouds for each mast and contrived a canvas weather cloth round the boat and raised the quarters about nine inches, by nailing on the seats of the stern sheets, which proved of great benefit to us.

The wind had been moderate all day, in the south east quarter with fine weather; but about nine o'clock the clouds began to gather and we had a prodigious fall of rain with severe thunder and lightning. By midnight we caught about twenty gallons of water. Being miserably wet and cold, I served to the people a teaspoonful of rum each to enable them to bear with their distressed situation. The weather continued extremely bad and the wind increased; we spent a very miserable night, without sleep, except for such as could be got in the midst of rain. The day brought no relief except light; the sea broke over us so much that two men were constantly baling and we had no choice how to steer being obliged to keep before the waves for fear of the boat filling. As there was no prospect of getting our clothes dried I recommended to everyone to strip and wring them through the salt water, by which means they received a warmth, that while wet with rain they could not have.' He continues: 'On Sat 16th. In addition to our miserable allowance of one 25th of a pound of bread and a quarter of a pint of water, I issued for dinner about an ounce of salt pork to each person. Hitherto I had issued the allowance by guess, but I now made a pair of scales with two cocoa-nut shells, and, having accidentally some pistol balls in the boat, 25 of which weighed a pound or 16 ounces, I adopted one as the proportion of weight that each person should receive of bread at the times I served it. I also amused all hands with describing the situation of New Guinea and New Holland and gave them every information in my power, that in case any accident happened to me, those who survived might have some idea of what they were about, and be able to find their way to Timor, which at present they knew nothing of, more than the name and some of them not even that.'

Bligh, having made it to Timor took the next ship for England to report the mutiny, where after a routine court martial he was exonerated and honourably acquitted.

A second voyage was promptly organised and Bligh, now promoted Captain was given command of HMS *Providence.* This time her crew included 20 marines, and she was accompanied by HMS *Assistant* as consort and tender, under the command of Lieutenant Porlock.

Bligh sailed for the second voyage in Aug 1791, following his previous route, and finding one apple tree still alive in Tasmania is considered the founder of the Tasmanian apple industry. He also continued his fruit tree planting with quinces, figs and pomegranates.

Arriving once more in Tahiti he collected twice the number of rooted plants in half the time, and reached St Vincent in January 1793.

Dr Anderson came on board from the garden next morning, and the 544 breadfruit plants were carried on the heads of natives the two miles from the dock to the botanic gardens. Bligh was also greeted by a deputation from the Council who waited on him royally and presented him with a piece of plate worth 100 guineas, a mark of their approbation and esteem. When Bligh sailed a few days afterwards with the remainder of the breadfruit plants for Jamaica, he took with him from the St Vincent Garden 465 of 'botanic plants' for His Majesty's Gardens at Kew. These plants Anderson had carefully prepared for the voyage and in spite of delays at Jamaica, reports indicate that all the plants arrived in good condition in England.

It is interesting to read Sir Joseph Banks' personal letter (dated 25th June 1791) of instructions to James Wiles, the gardener of this second voyage; these suggest in remarkable detail the care Banks took to avoid some of the problems that beset the *Bounty* expedition, and also show his own considerable knowledge and experience of plant travel.

He says: 'The principal enemy to the health of plants in long voyages is the spray of the sea, which seldom fails to rise into the air at such times as the wind is high enough to turn over the tops of the waves into what the seamen call 'white caps' and to fall in the form of a white dew on everything it meets with. If the leaves of a plant are wetted with this dew, the salt contained in it crystallises upon their surface as they become dry, and unless it is speedily washed off with fresh water the plant infallibly perishes; Monkeys, Goats, Dogs, Cats – (Banks is known for his eccentric capital letters) and in short every animal that is not confined is to be dreaded as the smell of the earth is very attractive even to those that do not eat vegetables and tempts them to scratch. It is to be hoped that none of the first two will be permitted on board, as however cautiously they are looked after they may, if they escape destroy the whole garden in half an hour. Rats, Mice and cockroaches are the natural enemies of Plants on board a Ship. They destroy by gnawing the bark and young buds, which you must constantly examine in order to be aware of their mischief before any great progress is made'.

James Wiles carried out his instructions to the letter and was rewarded on his arrival at Jamaica by being offered the job of Superintendent of the Government Botanic Gardens there, which he accepted and where he was able to continue to care for the many plants he had brought safely through their sea journey.

Anderson was extremely proud of his new breadfruit plants and conscientiously reported to the Royal Society on their growth. In one communication he states: 'In June 1793 of the original plants, fifty were reserved in the garden to yield future supplies for different islands; in October 1794 some began to produce fruit – in March following all of them. At present most of the trees are about thirty ft high, the stem two ft from the ground, from three to three and a half ft in circumference.

The fruit comes out in succession the greater part of the year; from November till March fewer than at any other time. But as there are six varieties of the tree and fruit in the garden, some kinds are loaded, whilst there is scarcely any fruit on the others, so that some of them is almost always in fruit. The number one tree produce is very great, often in clusters of five or six, bending the lower branches to the ground. According to different varieties, the fruit is of various shapes and sizes, in weight from four to ten pounds, some smooth-skinned others rough and tuberculated.

The fruit is in its greatest perfection about a week before it begins to ripen; at that period it is easily known from the skin changing to a brownish cast and from small granulations of the juice. When it is ripe it is soft and yellow, in smell and taste like a very ripe melon.

From the first appearance of the fruit (when of the size of an egg) it is three months before they are full or fit for eating. Having no formation of seeds the tree produces its progeny by suckers from its roots, at the time it begins to yield its fruits, and a numerous young family arises at the distance of from three to thirty ft from the parent stem. For two years past several hundreds of them have been transported to the different islands. Independent of its utility, the tree is one of the handsomest, and for ornament it is anxiously sought after in any country. It is hardy, a tough wood and resists the severest gusts of wind'.

Dr Anderson wrote many reports to the Royal Society, but continually complained of the lack of support he received from the 'plantocracy' – 'certain ranks among the military and others who sought the demise of the garden'.

He was disappointed to find that very few plants had been raised from the quantities of seed he had dispersed among them; 'plantocrats' were not really interested in anything but sugarcane, and the most valuable breadfruit was neglected and despised by most of them. He adds: 'They say that negroes do not like it, and will not eat it if they can get anything else; but this is not really the case, as I know, and can declare from experience, that the very reverse is the fact, when once they are a little accustomed to it. The fact is that the planters hate giving it a place on their estates, as they regard it as an intruder on their cane land and they dislike any other object but canes.'

Such a detailed description of its habit must have been fascinating to the President of the Royal Society, Sir Joseph Banks – who was of course among the few to have seen it growing and eaten it from the tree – and other members who would have been involved in the long and anxious business of arranging its journey from Tahiti. Hearing of Anderson's devoted industry in growing these arduously acquired plants, his efforts in trying to establish them all over the islands must have been music to Banks's ears. It would be good to believe that he lived long enough to know that eventually in spite of the local planters' discouragement, the inhabitants took to eating the breadfruit three times a day.

I am tempted to think of Banks as being totally immersed only in his scientific interests, but in 1792 he was clearly distracted by horrific world events and, after King Louis XV1 was executed and war was declared with France, he wrote to a friend: 'the French nation are certainly in a state of canine madness, very desirous of biting all mankind & by that means infecting them with the disease they themselves are vex'd with, I conceive them like a pack of mad foxhounds who cannot be confined to their kennel and feel sometimes a kind of horror lest they should infect too many of the quiet animals feeding around them.'

His friend replied with sombre agreement that the French conduct was a disgrace to human nature and that 'if freedom had at once been granted to the slaves of Jamaica and St Domingo they could not act more shockingly' – a revealing note on the social perspectives of the times.

Anderson's chief interest was the prospering of the many plants he had introduced. His excitement is illustrated by his obtaining two nutmeg plants from Cayenne which were thriving, and his anxiety that they should be male and female; one can only sense his anguish when he wrote: 'I am grieved to inform you that I lost one of my nutmeg trees, unfortunately the other which prospers luxuriantly turns out to be a male plant, consequently worth nothing. I blame myself in some measure for this loss by taking too much care of it, and not letting nature take her own way. Unluckily the war precludes any correspondence with Cayenne or I would have replaced it from thence.' He describes how the French Government took the trouble to send ships to the East Indies to collect spices and other useful plants, bringing them to the Ile de France, (Mauritius): 'nursing and increasing them there afterwards bringing them from thence in frigates to their West Indies colonies .....and I think it merits observation that although the British interest, extensive connections as well as territory, is far beyond any other European nation in the East, yet as far as my knowledge extends not a single live plant or seed of any of the East India commercial plants has ever been sent to the West Indies but by Sir Joseph Banks and Sir George Yonge. The French have been as anxious in preserving and processing them as the English have been remiss. Of the nutmeg they now have several plantations which annually produce.'

In 1806 Anderson updates the Royal Society, saying that 'war interrupts correspondence in Natural History as much as speculations in commerce' and reports his expectations 'of some useful plants from Mexico, and other Spanish colonies in that quarter, by way of Cuba; but from thence the transportation must be circuitous by North America and after that, subject to loss and interruption before they can reach St Vincent. I have therefore given up all hopes while the war continues.'

He goes on to describe the present state of the garden, transmitting a very important catalogue 'of the variety of plants it contained on 24th September last,' and adding : 'there are many more from different quarters received without names, or those that are known by the Aborigines, and I cannot arrange them till they flower.'

Dr Anderson had been the most dedicated and energetic Superintendent throughout his many years, devoted to the garden; he retired because of infirmity and died a few months later, in 1811.

Sir Joseph Banks maintained his immediate interest in the garden, and in 1816 he sent out George Caley as Superintendent. Caley had worked for Banks as plant collector in New South Wales for many years but was another of those who always fell out with everyone; indeed, continual complaints about his temperament followed him around. Nevertheless he was extremely competent at his work, while suffering the very same troubles as Dr Anderson with the plantocracy and sugar planters being continually antagonistic to the progress and stability of the garden.

With the death of the two great patrons of botany and natural history, George III and Sir Joseph Banks within a few months of each other in 1820, the work of the garden in St Vincent, as at Kew, started to decline. No-one trained in England, who took account of its valuable collection of plants and unique history had been assigned to the garden. Towards the end of this dormant period it was given the status of 'Botanic Garden' and considered instrumental in introducing a range of new productions that would be of economic value to the colonies and the 'mother country,' such as arrowroot, cocoa, tobacco, cotton and spices. The purpose of the 'new' botanical garden was not unlike that of the old establishment from which it emerged.

The Reverend Lansdown Guilding (1797-1831), garrison chaplain on the island, was best known for his works on the flora and fauna of St Vincent. He was born on the island, one of six children of Rector John Guilding and his wife Sarah. At five he went to England and spent the next fifteen years being educated, eventually taking his BA degree at Oxford and returning to St Vincent in 1817. He immediately began collecting animal specimens, illus-trating and publishing his work in the Zoological Journal and the Transactions of the Linnean Society between 1822 and 1837. These are preserved primarily in the collections at Kew and the British Museum (Natural History). Botanists remember him for '*An Account of the Botanic Garden in the Island of St Vincent*', privately published in 1825. This was severely criticised by J C Loudon, landscape gardener and horticultural writer of note, who reviewed the work in 1826, saying that although the illustrations are credited to the Rev L Guilding, 'one plate at least corresponds in all details to a description given by Anderson (mss. Linn. Soc.) of a drawing done for him by his artist, John Tylie, years before. Neither Tylie's drawing nor Guilding's scenes can be located.' Guilding's biographers R A and E S Howard, say of him: 'Guilding was a capable artist of plants and animals who prided himself on the accuracy of his work and use of colour. When his work was redrawn he criticised both the artist and the engraver, and he often objected to the reduction of his work.'

He carried on a correspondence with Sir William Hooker and supplied illustrations, specimens and notes for the latter's articles, his *Exotic Flora* and Botanical magazine.

Guilding was elected a Fellow of the Linnean Society when he was only 20 years old, and although there is no evidence that he attended any meetings, it is probable that his acquaintance with Hooker and his other distinguished correspondent AB Lambert began there at this institution. His biographers say of him: 'In view of the ages and positions of these older and established scientists, Guilding's letters are astonishing. He is revealed as an arrogant, demanding, ambitious and often conceited individual, all too ready to ask for unusual favours.'

Guilding's publication on the garden, written some years after Anderson died, is full of interesting observations and he mentions that books of great value, 'which had any reference to plants likely to be cultivated, were now sent out by His Majesty (George III), who was pleased to patronise the garden and felt much concern for its prosperity.' Guilding, in his description of the garden in its heyday, writes lyrically in detail of its charms – a few extracts paint the picture: 'The extent of the garden, which is of irregular figure, does not exceed 39 acres. The higher and hilly parts are a dense forest of useful Woods, Fruits and Palms; the bottom is the only part which has the least resemblance to the formal arrangement of an European garden. Here nature is unconfined and this beautiful wilderness is without doubt the most charming residence of Flora and all her domains. A noble avenue, interrupted only by a single towering palm *Areca catechu* runs from the house to the bottom, giving a view of the bay, the town and a group of smaller islands… and affords the sight of the bold blue outline of the noble mountain which terminates the landscape…

The ground seems overloaded with plants which have barely room enough for their development. The trunks of the older trees are everywhere covered with a thick drapery of Ferns, Mosses and Orchideous plants, which diffuse into the air the richest odours and almost conceal from sight the noble plant that upholds them.

But I should tire the reader by continuing to enumerate the vegetable wonders of this paradise. By the side of every rivulet rise large clusters of the Bamboo *Bambusa arundinacea*, nothing can exceed the beauty of this arborescent gramen, which rises to the height of 60 or 80 ft, waving its light and graceful foliage at every breath of the winds.'

Guilding was a great admirer of Anderson and describes the latter's zeal in collecting: 'all the most remarkable of the native plants, and in his excursions to other islands obtaining many curious species. In his travels over

White hibiscus, immigrant from Hawaii

our own mountains, in 1784, he discovered the crater of Morne Soufriere, which probably exceeds in magnitude and beauty that of any other volcano in the world.'

He also records: 'On the 8th September 1811, the virtuous Anderson was numbered with the dead. To this industrious and respectable botanist the garden owes its prosperity. His active labours, his intense assiduity could only be equalled by that urbanity and alacrity so conspicuous in his constant endeavours to oblige; and that zeal and pleasure which he always evinced in rendering the good intentions of His Majesty as beneficial as possible to the colonists at large. This truly good man and excellent Christian was not only the kindest master, but the moral and religious preceptor of his negroes. The following is the last verse in a long poem, written in Anderson's honour by a friend, who followed him to the grave'.

But now he's gone – life's fitful dream is o'er,-
O! frail and light illusion, swiftly fled –
Mourn then ye shades – ye rocks his fate deplore,
Weep Nature, weep – for Anderson is dead!

His friend William Lochhead succeeded him as Superintendent of the garden until he, too, died less than four years later.

Exploring round the beautiful gardens of St Vincent, after reading so much about them was a memorable experience. Curiously, very few of the colourful flowers decorating every part of the whole island such as hibiscus from Hawaii, allamanda from Brazil, ixora from the East Indies and many

Yonge Island, adjacent to St Vincent.

others from Mexico and South America are not indigenous to the island, but welcome immigrants. Here was the breadfruit sucker, the descendant of Bligh's introduction, and here too were plants of all the exotic spices you could think of, laid out in a spiral of terraces and well labelled. There were wonderful views in all directions, and at last a restful drink near the beach facing Yonge Island, named after Dr George Yonge who started the gardens all those years ago.

I could imagine the decorative, native Vincentian Parrot (*Amazona guildingii*) named after Guilding, locally known as 'Jacquot', described by Columbus as 'darkening the sky', flying noisily through the trees, but sadly this colourful character is only to be admired in a series of aviary cages where a breeding programme is underway to protect him from the threatened extinction.

Amazona Guildingii – The St Vincent Parrot,
now only visible in the Island wildlife aviary, successfully breeding in captivity.

CHAPTER 2

The Botanic Gardens, Jamaica

It is not generally known that Sir Hans Sloane was responsible for one of our most agreeable global addictions, but the story of his inspired brainchild, described in *Voyages of Discovery* by Dr Tony Rice, must be included in this account. He found *Therobromo cacao* or chocolate growing in Jamaica, but it originates from Central and South America.

He was a notable early visitor to Jamaica as a young Irish-born physician setting out on a long distinguished medical career in late 17thC London. In 1687 Hans Sloane was 27 years old and firmly ensconced in the capital among such revolutionary thinkers as John Rae (1627-1705), the father of British natural history, and the philosopher John Locke (1632-1704). Sloane was elected a Fellow of the Royal Society in 1685, by then it had the world's most respected scientific membership. His love of botany had been fostered by the Society of Apothecaries at the Chelsea Physic Garden, where he had been able to study 'simples', the drug plants from which most medicines were obtained.

But there were surely many more to be discovered in the New World, so when the Duke of Albermarle was appointed Governor of Jamaica and offered the young doctor the position of physician to his family he was delighted to accept. He sailed in the Duke's yacht – accompanied by two merchant vessels and an escorting naval ship – from Portsmouth in September 1687, stopping for 10 days at Barbados, and arriving at Port Royal, Jamaica in December of that year.

During the voyage Sloane kept a meticulous journal, recording all manner of observations on the daily shipboard routine, on natural phenomena, and on the birds, fishes and invertebrates encountered on the way. He continued his writing during the fifteen months ashore, making notes on all sorts of topics including weather, earthquakes, the island's topography, the behaviour of the local inhabitants – mostly escaped African slaves.

On his way he collected many human artefacts, animals and particularly plants, which whenever possible he pressed and dried for return to England. Many of his samples, especially fruits, could not be preserved adequately so he employed a local artist, the Rev Garret Moore, to travel with him and illustrate them while they were still in a fresh state, including the many fishes, birds and insects that they encountered. Some 700 species of plants eventually accompanied Sloane back to England.

Among them was chocolate, which Sloane had found was taken widely in Jamaica for its medicinal properties, but which was 'nauseous and hard of digestion, from its great oiliness'. Sloane discovered it was much more palatable when mixed with milk and his patented recipe brought him a con-

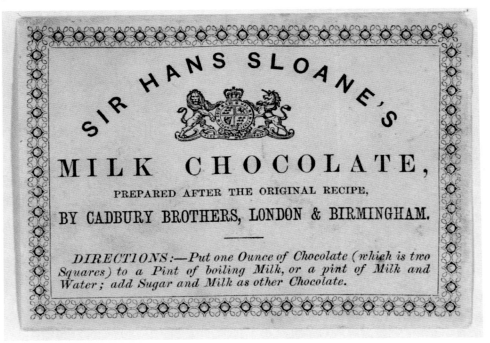

An original Cadbury chocolate wrapper from the 19thC crediting Sir Hans Sloane with the recipe for milk chocolate. Sloane brought to England the beans from the cacao tree from Jamaica, where he observed that the Indians made a chocolate drink from the beans, which they took 'neat'. The Spaniards, however - who could drink chocolate as much as five or six times a day – liked to mix theirs with savoury spices.

siderable income during his lifetime. In the 19thC, long after Sloane's death, the recipe was taken over by Cadbury, a name now almost synonymous with milk chocolate all over the world.

Sloane's official duties were of course to care for the health of the Duke, but despite his ministrations the Duke died in 1688, so the stay in Jamaica was cut short when the Duchess decided to return home – his last duty to his employer being to embalm him for the return journey.

This voyage must have been much enlivened by Sloane's choice of creatures to accompany him which included an iguana, a crocodile and a seven foot long snake.

Sadly none of these survived – the iguana inadvertently jumped overboard and was drowned, the crocodile died of natural causes, while the snake, which Sloane had had 'tam'd by an Indian, whom it would follow as a Dog would its Master' escaped one day from the large jar in which it lived, and was shot by one of the Duchess's alarmed domestic servants.

Once back in England, Sloane returned to private medicine in fashionable Bloomsbury, married an heiress and became rich and famous; he continued with his collections, wrote a full account of his Jamaican experiences called *Natural History of Jamaica* and was elected President of the Royal Society in 1727. He died at the age of 93 in 1753.

Rivalling the St Vincent Botanic Garden in the West Indies was the originally private garden of Hinton East, the Receiver General of Jamaica, who had successfully acclimatised mango, yam, jack tree, date palm and all sorts of useful and ornamental plants. A Bill supported by East in the Jamaica House of Assembly led to the establishment of a 'Tropical Garden' at Bath in 1779. East had been corresponding with Sir Joseph Banks in London as early as 1784, sending seeds to him and the Royal Gardens at Kew. He was one of the first who questioned Banks about the value of the breadfruit as an alternative food to bananas. Everyone now turned to Sir Joseph, whose 'knowledge, philanthropy and influence are superior to all others.' The garden at Bath was found to be subject to flooding, so was replaced by the Castleton Gardens in 1779. Nearby are the Cinchona Botanic Gardens established in 1868; as the Hill Gardens they were originally a dependency of the Castleton Botanic Garden and especially laid out in order to grow quinine trees, *Cinchona ssp*, brought from the highlands of Peru.

The Royal Botanic Garden, Hope, is probably the best known of the botanical gardens in Jamaica. It covers about three hundred and fifty acres and occupies one of Jamaica's historic places, the ancient Hope estate, once one of the most prosperous sugar estates in the West Indies. The gardens proper were established about one hundred years ago and cover about two thirds of the former estate; they are not the oldest botanical gardens in Jamaica, there had been a 'Spring Garden' at Gordon Town going back to 1770 and the first Government botanical garden, Enfield, adjacent to it was one of the places where Captain Bligh's breadfruit plants were grown, and where James Wiles of the second voyage was in charge.

Castleton was founded in 1862, and Nathaniel Wilson, the first Superintendent, was a very energetic and efficient man, greatly assisted by both William and Joseph Hooker. When the International Dendrology Society visited a few years ago Dr Heine, one of its most renowned members wrote that: 'The long standing Kew connection is still perceptible by a discriminating visitor – the mid-Victorian layout, the vistas, the formal pond with a highly original trefoil ground plan, impeccably kept lawns, hedges and trellises, as well as tastefully arranged mixed borders and flowerbeds. All this reveals the great English horticultural traditions of the heyday of the British Empire, when Kew was the very centre of systematic botany and the focal point of economic botany and horticulture of the Commonwealth.' He goes on: 'The Jamaicans obviously realise what a priceless heritage they have in these gardens, the upkeep of which is truly remarkable.'

Wilson was succeeded by his head gardener, originally from Kew, and then by Benjamin Fawcett, author of *'Flora of Jamaica (1910-1936)'*. Heine continues to describe in detail a uniquely huge fern, *Angiopteris evecta,* some splendid examples of palms, Betel Nut, Asiatic Sugar, Fishtail, Ostrich Feather and many others, followed by mouthwatering examples of huge and rare old trees from all over the world. These all decorate the magnificent site which offers a panoramic view over the whole of the eastern part of Jamaica.

The most valuable timber tree here, which is universally known, is of course the West Indian Mahogany, *Swietenia mahogoni,* a close relative of the West Indian Cedar, and belonging to the same family, *Meliaceae.*

The name 'Mahogany' originated on the island of Jamaica after the English occupation in 1655 says F Bruce Lamb (no relation to the author) in his *Mahogany of Tropical America)* and has been traced to the Nigerian name for African mahogany – '*Oganwo*' – members of the Yoruba tribe, brought from Nigeria to Jamaica as slaves. The latter would logically have used the expression *M'Oganwo* for a Jamaican tree so nearly identical to the tree known by this name in the forests of their homeland in West Africa. The word Mahogany was in common usage by 1700, and Catesby, with his excellent illustration in his book *Natural History of Carolina, Florida and the Bahama Islands*, was responsible for bringing it to the attention of botanists, pointing out the desirable characteristics of the wood, and establishing beyond doubt the relationship between the name, the tree and the wood. Linnaeus named the tree *Cedrela mahogoni* in 1759, but the genus was changed to *Swietenia* for the famous Dutch naturalist-physician Baron LB Swieten, retaining the specific name *mahogoni* used by Linnaeus, which soon became the accepted trade name in Europe.

The earliest imports of mahogany into England were probably from the cargoes of the numerous Spanish prize ships, captured by British privateers in the sixteenth century, which began to be shipped directly when Jamaica was

Catesby's Illustration of 'The Mahogony Tree' from his Natural History of Carolina, Florida and the Bahama Islands 1754.

taken by the British from Spain. British shipbuilders were quick to recognise the characteristic which made mahogany so suitable for naval construction; the superior qualities of the wood were frequently noted when ships were in dry dock for repairs; the mahogany planks and beams showed very little deterioration, whereas other woods, especially English oak, would be so decayed as to require replacement. Mahogany timbers were often removed from broken up ships and built into new ships or sold at high prices to cabinet makers. The most famous man-of-war to be captured from the Spanish fleet by Lord Rodney in 1780 was renamed *The Gibraltar*. When broken up after many years of distinguished service – she was one of the oldest ships in the Fleet – her mahogany timbers were still sound. This much prized timber was then distributed round the Fleet, and before long every important ship in the Royal Navy had a 'Gibraltar table'.

Mahogany's golden age in the mid 18th to 19th centuries was responsible for the master craftsmen's renown, when they found the large size of the planks allowed a greater flexibility in designing furniture; the richness and warmth of the reddish brown wood was easily worked and could be delicately carved, and the West Indian mahogany was found to be especially valuable for veneers and inlays and used with great effect.

By the middle of the 18th C, Jamaican mahogany was becoming scarce along the coasts and larger streams and was only available in the high and inaccessible hills. The logging season began in the dry months and consisted of felling and rolling the logs by hand into a river and rafting them to the coast. As the trees near the streams were cut down, logging moved back and ox teams were introduced for hauling. Due to the excessive heat in the dry season, all hauling was done at night with pine torches lighting the way and oxen pulling creaking log carts with their vast tree cargo down the jungle trails to a stream.

In the early days a logger relied solely on the skill and knowledge of his mahogany hunter, who would locate and mark the individual trees to be cut, although he also had to plan the trails to be opened up to drag each log out, but by about 1925, light airplanes were used in the preliminary location of the trees. It was usually in March that the mahogany leaves turned reddish brown, and the crown could be more easily distinguished from the air. It was still the job of the hunter to locate and select the actual trees to be cut, eliminating any defective trees before the expense of road building, felling and hauling were undertaken. Trees between 28 inches and sometimes as large as twelve feet in

Honduras Mahogany showing buttresses.

diameter were chosen. The highly skilled operation of felling began in the latter part of the rainy season and was done chiefly by axe, with the men working singly or in pairs on a pole scaffolding tied with vines, the latter constructed round the base of the tree, so that the cut could be made just above the buttressed roots which were often ten to fifteen feet high.

It was vitally important that the timber was ready by the time the roads had dried out enough to hold the hauling equipment, but the weather controlled the whole operation. The dry season could be extremely early or late with intermittent rain; logs were hauled to the collecting site on the edge of the stream, ready to be floated to the nearest tributary, there to be made into rafts – ten or twelve logs to a crib, ten or twelve cribs to a raft, for onward floating to the coast, with a power launch to tow them. Selection of any site was a gamble, as many of the streams failed to fill sufficiently to float the logs, or the rivers might rise to as much as forty feet and return to normal again in 48 hours. Estimates by experienced loggers indicate that only about fifty per cent of mahogany logs cut were finally loaded on to ships: losses in the woods, in dry streams, scattering in river margin forests or swamp by violent floods, or any other likely disasters accounted for the loss of the rest.

It was not only the huge quantities of mahogany timber exported from the West Indian islands and Central America that have depleted the vast forests of this beautiful and indispensable tree. Throughout most of this tropical country administration of public land was lax; there was certainly legislation protecting the forest resources and recommending measures for renewal of forests depleted by exploitation, but there was no trained administrative organisation to carry out this intent, and the legislation itself was often inadequate.

Primitive people in Latin America have destroyed as much mahogany as has commercial logging; large areas of this luxuriant hard wood producing forest have been destroyed in Central America by felling and burning in preparation for banana plantations. Indeed, in one such area – the forests of the lower Aguan River valley in Honduras – an important source of mahogany was cleared and large quantities used for lumber, railroad ties, and boiler fuel. Most of the land proved unsuitable for permanent banana culture and was abandoned after a few years. It is now covered with useless rubbish and will require over a hundred years to evolve naturally into forests capable of producing valuable saw timber.

Caroline de Horsey, the Admiral's wife who regales us later with her

Clearing mahogany down the rapids

impressions of Mauritius (see Chapter 5), paints an interesting picture of some of the joys and sorrows of Jamaica when she and her husband were appointed there – he in Command of the great flagship HMS *Aboukir*, and living at Admiralty House in 1865 for a three year stay. She tells us that: 'The entrance from seaward into the harbour of Port Royal is protected by cays and coral reefs, apparently not long risen above the surface, as little soil has collected upon them and one is nearly awash. It is a lovely sight' she says, 'on nearing these cays to watch the water gradually shoal. Little by little the limpid depths grow clearer and greener, till a fairy forest of living breathing coral appears as if but an inch or two below the surface; you cannot believe that six feet of water rolls over it. Sea-urchins, sea-anemones, star-fish and other fleshy zoophytes enjoy themselves in their own flabby way, expanding and collapsing with the gently heaving water, but retiring and lying flat on the bottom, shapeless jellies at the slightest hint of capture. Nothing more lovely can be conceived than the corals as seen from a boat. Large flat masses of the shape of a toadstool; great white branches like a deer's antlers, tipped with blue, red and violet rear themselves towards the surface in fragile loveliness, delicate filmy seaweed of every tint forms a soft carpet…'. In the garden she finds 'the wonderful growth of bamboo, one morning a great fat greenish grey shoot, exactly like giant asparagus, would appear just breaking through the friable reddish earth; next day it was twelve inches high, the day after over two feet, one could really see it grow till a fine feathery wand, tender and drooping shot up into the sky, strengthening with age'.

They found Admiralty House 'very large, cool, airy and pleasant, literally bowered on coconut palms, scarlet cordia, grape and almond trees, while the Bougainvillea and a gigantic lilac creeper stretched their arms and tendrils over the trellis covered walls. Figs, oleanders, pomegranates, delicate plumbagos, blue and scarlet cast a refreshing shade upon the creeping grass.'

'Our first miseries', she relates, 'were certainly owing to mosquitoes…never in any other place, have I seen anything like the vast army which drifted through the house towards sundown, each singing its own particular note and giving the idea of a multitude of bands advancing from a long distance.'

Caroline continues: 'About the middle of our time in Jamaica, the sides of the roads were observed to be covered with the yellow sickly-smelling blossoms of 'kill buckra', or yellow fever flower. Every waste space, previously quite arid, bloomed like a yellow carpet. A faint sickening odour wafted with the first breath of land wind, stole over Port Royal. The same smell was reported to have preceeded a former yellow fever epidemic. The men-of-war in harbour were moved to the outer buoys, where a fresher current of air was obtainable, and every sanitary precaution was adopted. But all was in vain. The first man, a stoker of the steam launch was seized – and this meant to die in three or four days time. Each man looked his comrade in the face, and wondered which of them would go next. The good deputy inspector at the hospital – who, if hourly heroism could win the Victoria Cross, earned his a hundred times over – stood by the bedside of the dying, some in violent fever held down by black nurses, some in deadly stertorous coma, and wrung his hands in despair at being unable to do anything to save them.'

This terrible epidemic raged on; five out of the seven of the galley crew died who had lived at Admiralty House, but worse was to come: after the death of so many it was not considered desirable for the family to remain near the Dockyard, so a house, 'Claremont', in the Port Royal mountains was taken for them. Caroline tells us that 'A short but sharp attack of yellow fever prostrated me the day after our arrival in the hills. Ill as I was, the extraordinary beauty of the view from this place struck me with admiration. Cotton trees of immense height cast a splendid shade all the blazing afternoon. Above you, at Claremont are the 'everlasting hills', mounting peak by peak into the air; below a winding bridle road leading to the gardens, the foaming Hope river lying like a silver streak at the bottom of the valley.'

Later, she describes her visits to the palisades or burying places where lovely young palms, scarlet cordia and mimosa wave about among the low graves of the many young Englishmen, many of them favourite friends, 'who have found here their long home. I very often went there, after a little child of our own rested among the whispering branches of the palms, which nodded and swayed among the tombs, and it may console many, whose dear ones lie here in their last sleep to know that their resting place is cared for and even pretty'.

Sobered, but inspired, by Caroline's lyrical descriptions, I can now describe how I was lucky enough to be able to join the International Dendrology Society expedition to see what remained of these beautiful, huge old mahogany trees, beginning in Belize, which used to be British Honduras. We had the pleasure of flying over 110 miles inland, west of Belize City to Gallon Jug, and travelling onward by bus to Chan Chich River Lodge.

Mahogany log, ready for clearing

Logging had last taken place in this area in 1977, when the trees cut were then about 2 m in girth at 2m high and about 80ft tall. Seeing a mahogany tree of that height lying on the ground gave one some idea of the difficulty of moving such a log to the sea. Flying low over the many mahogany trails, through the green forest and jungle, conjured up a picture of the old days when the seasonal logging industry was in full flow. Chan Chich Lodge is surrounded by an ancient Mayan city, and there were many temples and burial mounds – some with painted friezes still intact – reminders of the advanced civilization which disappeared so suddenly, for reasons not entirely understood.

There were magical jungle sounds, night and day, enough to satisfy a naturalist's dream, although mostly coming from nocturnal creatures. One could see and hear interesting birds such as Crested Guan, Great Curassow and Oscellated Turkey, or species such as spider and howler monkeys – not my favourites – though the prize of the shy creatures such as jaguar, tapir or peccary did not reveal themselves to me.

— Chapter 3 —

Singapore Botanic Garden

My opportunity to investigate this botanic garden came when, still under the aegis of the Royal Navy, we were lucky enough to spend three years in Singapore. Encumbered with three small offspring I travelled out in one of Her Majesty's troopships, a privilege until then confined to soldiers. Going through the Red Sea in August with a following wind, my misguided young insisted on having porridge for breakfast every day, with the result that they all came out in spots and I had the mortification of delivering on to the quayside in Singapore harbour three purple-painted children (gentian-violet being the sovereign remedy, cure-all, administered by military doctors of the day) to their father and a baby-amah he had thoughtfully brought to meet me. I remember saying: 'Take them all away. I never want to see any of them again'.

Malaya was a heavenly place to be; not only is it blissfully hot all the year

Home grown bananas in our Singapore garden.

Our *kabun* – Malayan gardener.

round but we lived in an eccentric house which had rattan blinds instead of walls, and delightfully old-fashioned ceiling fans instead of contemporary air conditioning, which is always too cold for me. The Chinese servants took the strain on all domestic fronts and one enjoyed the sort of colonial life that can only be read about now. In our garden we grew bananas, papaya (once I discovered that they had to be husband and wife), deliciously scented gardenias and employed a very small gardener – a 'kabun' who cut the grass sitting on his hunkers and wielding a miniature sickle. It didn't take me long to start finding out about the spectacular botanic garden.

While the British and French were fighting over the West Indies, The East India Company was embattled in argument with the Dutch and the French over trade in the East Indies. South-East Asia had been home for the company using Bantam, Batavia or Benkulen as a base under a Governor or Lieutenant Governor. Then Penang was discovered to have a useful harbour for the Royal Navy, and negotiations with the Sultan of Kedah who owned it resulted in its being ceded to the British in 1786. Thus the company gained a foothold in South-east Asia. They then renamed it Prince of Wales Island, and it was there that Thomas Stamford Raffles – a young and ambitious employee – took up his first overseas post. His mastery over the Malay language made him indispensable to the British Government, and he was later appointed translator to the Government of India. In 1808 Raffles realised that Penang would never fulfil the role envisaged for it, nor serve his purpose as a springboard to glory. Lord Minto, the new Governor-General, encouraged Raffles to invade Java, and the latter later recounted: 'from this moment, all my views, all my plans and all my mind was devoted to create such an interest towards Java as should lead to its annexation to our Eastern Empire'.

The actual invasion took place in 1811. Raffles had prepared the ground, chosen the invasion route and thoroughly mastered the political situation. He was made the Governor of what he now called 'this other India,' and was shortly after promoted to Governor of Sumatra as well. Raffles often disobeyed orders or wilfully misunderstood them, and when Java and Malacca were both handed back to the Dutch after peace had broken out, Raffles' hopes were dashed. Nothing daunted, his next idea was to seize, occupy and promote a new British settlement, and then argue about the rights of the matter later. Having done his homework, it was his inspired action to choose an island hard against the shore of Johore, covered like all the rest with dense jungle, and inhabited only by a few Malay fishermen and of no commercial consequence whatever. It was called Singapora. In a letter to Sir Joseph Banks dated 4 March 1819 he says: 'the Dutch were rapidly resuming control over the whole of the Archipelago, until I had the good fortune to check them by the establishment of the British Station at Singapore. At this they are furious; if the authorities at home interfere to define the rights of our respective authorities we shall have nothing but quarrels.'

On January 28th 1819 Raffle's little fleet had anchored at the mouth of the Singapore river. He was welcomed by the local chief into his rattan house and served with rambutan and other local fruit. Having discovered that the rightful ruler was the Sultan of Johore, Raffles came to an accommodation with him and the Sultan agreed to authorize a British factory; Raffles immediately disembarked his troops and on the following day he and the Sultan presided at a ceremonial signing, complete with a red carpet laid across the sand, a guard of honour and numerous artillery salutes. Within a matter of weeks over 2,000 Malays and Chinese had decamped from Malacca to set up shop in Singapore. By the summer, when the news of the acquisition reached London, the population had exceeded 5,000. Raffles wrote: 'Our object is not territory but trade, a great commercial emporium and fulcrum where we may extend our influence politically as circumstances may after require….one free port in these seas may eventually destroy the spell of Dutch monopoly – and what Malta is in the West, that may Singapore become in the East.'

The discoveries of these unknown islands gave Raffles wonderful opportunities to investigate the local flora and fauna; he was a serious naturalist, employing an expert Chinese draughtsman from Macau who made careful copies of the more perishable fruits and flowers, many of which he pressed between the thick pages of a book. With the construction of Raffles' bungalow an experimental garden was laid out on the slopes of Government Hill, and toward the close of 1819 he sent a gardener to plant cloves and nutmeg trees. These 125 trees, 1,000 seeds of nutmeg and 450 clove plants formed the foundation of Singapore Botanic Garden and the flourishing spice plantations dominated the island landscape for the next 35 years.

Under the influence of Kew Gardens' Director, Sir Joseph Banks, and the scientific circle of The Royal Society, Raffles had decided to apply himself directly to the study of natural history and actively sought out those who might further this interest. Up until the time of his death in 1820 Banks advised him, and Raffles sent him botanical and zoological specimens – much to the displeasure of the East India Company at the spending of company money in this manner.

It was the friendship between Raffles and Dr Nathaniel Wallich however that sealed the fate of the first botanic gardens in Singapore. This widely respected Danish surgeon and naturalist, who was then serving as Superintendent of the Royal Gardens at Calcutta, visited Singapore in October and November 1822 and stayed longer than he intended, trying to recover his health. Raffles came to depend upon Wallich's sound advice on many affairs and together they devised a much grander scheme for the spice plot. With Raffles' support, Wallich wrote a glowing report (November 1822) destined to sway the seat of Government toward the quick establishment of a botanic and experimental garden on the island. He describes Singapore as being:

'the most favourable for indigenous as well as foreign vegetation and forming part of the richest archipelago in the world – its soil yielding to none in fertility, its climate not exceeded by any in uniformity, mildness and salubrity. It abounds in an endless variety of plants equally interesting to the botanist, the agriculturist and the gardener, with unrivalled facilities and opportunities of disseminating these treasures and exchanging them for others.'

Wallich continued to elaborate on the island's rare plants, unknown to European collectors; the primeval forests 'that would surely yield timber fit for ship and house, and the great success already proven in the cultivation of clove, nutmeg, pepper, coffee and tea.'

The proposed 19 hectare site would take in the current Government garden and form an oblong tract. An ornamental park with shrubs and trees would be laid out, and the services of ten labourers and an overseer would be covered by $60, plus the splendid donation of $1,000 by its munificent founder and first patron, Stamford Raffles. Permission from the supreme authority at Bengal was slow in coming, but as revealed through the letters between Wallich and Raffles, in spite of considerable opposition from Raffles' enemies – those who wished to undermine his administration – Raffles forged ahead, cutting walks and constructing fencing to protect the young trees, as he was determined 'to lay out both the Garden and the Hill before I quit the place'.

The close friendship carried on through this correspondence also shows the difficulties Raffles suffered with many problems besides his own ill health – he was prone to unspeakable migraine headache attacks; the letters refer to the loss of all his natural history records and specimens, which went up in flames in the carrier ship *Fame*, to the illness of many of his close associates and friends, and finally to the death of his beloved child Flora as well.

At the end of Raffles' last term of residence the garden was reduced to medical support for the settlement. To maintain the roads, railings, 6 metre terraces, some 200 nutmeg trees in the nursery and the sadly barren clove trees required expenditure that the East India Company would not cover, and in June 1829 the first Botanic Garden, Singapore was discontinued and subsequently parcelled out – to the Armenians for a church, for a school and for the construction of a hospital – the site which today takes in the National Museum and the National Library.

In 1836 interest revived in the abandoned gardens, and the Governor, several planters and local officials formed an Agri-Horticultural Society – although ten years later this effort failed and the land was handed back to the Government.

Somehow Raffles' dream lived on and in 1859 another group of public-spirited citizens revived the Society and exchanged the dismal garden remains on Fort Canning for a more promising 23 hectare tract at Tanglin, which was becoming a more fashionable district for country houses. A note in *The Straits Times* of 12 November of that year announces: 'Some of our enterprising citizens have resolved to establish a Floricultural and Horticultural Society, which will receive our hearty concurrence and support. This will be the third attempt to organise a really useful association and we hope it will succeed.' The land in question belonged to Hoo Ah Kay, better known by his trade name 'Whampoa', an influential businessman, staunch supporter of the colony and a key figure in the new society. The southern portion of this land, shaped like a tilting bottle, had been described as 'a haunt of tigers' but four hectares of it persist to this day.

With 77 subscribers and a capital of $1,900 the ambitious garden plan began with a bandstand, surrounded by promenades and carefully arranged ring roads with connecting paths. The main gate and its roads came next, followed by a strip of land excavated to make the lake in 1866.

After one or two more financial hiccups and the addition of a zoo to make it more popular, it had developed from Raffles' experimental spice plot to a delightfully landscaped ornamental garden and pleasure park, but was now in great need of a qualified Superintendent with a strong background in botany. On Sir Joseph Hooker's recommendation, Henry James Murton was appointed as the first of many Kew-trained men who devoted years of professional and personal service to the gardens.

Murton was a young man, but a skilled and avid horticulturist, and some of his reports reveal a certain disapproval of what he found. 'It is my unpleasant duty', he says 'to report many serious infringements of the Rules (of which he encloses a copy), not only by natives but by Europeans. The latter on more than one occasion have been detected cutting flowers by moonlight'. He urges that the practise of supplying 700 baskets of flowers to subscribers be modified 'as the gardens can never present a gay appearance under existing circumstances.' One can tell from these reports that Murton was a somewhat harassed administrator, who would have preferred pure research to clean-up work on the gardens' grounds. Nevertheless, it is to Murton's credit that the character of the gardens was changed from merely recreational to a place of study and serious scientific experimentation.

Murton set up the system of plant exchange with other botanic institutions worldwide, and travelled extensively in the Malay Peninsula, thereby adding a great many new and exotic species to the collections. He introduced a Herbarium and investigated the potential of many plants which established the Economic Gardens in 1879. This was the 41 hectare site north of the Botanic Gardens which became the experimental station for cultivation of a wide variety of crops including the famous *Hevea brasiliensis*, better known as 'rubber'.

'Mad Ridley' or 'Rubber Ridley' was another inspired choice of Sir Joseph Hooker to succeed him; he came in 1888 from the botany staff of London's Natural History Museum as Director of the Singapore Botanic Garden, and for the next 23 years this enormously dynamic man was responsible not only for the garden's outstanding international reputation but for the foundation of Malaya's prospering rubber industry. He lived to be 102.

Henry Nicholas Ridley (1855-1956) was the second son of a Norfolk clergyman and from his mother inherited a great love of natural history; perhaps it had something to do with his being the great-great grandson of the Marquis of Bute, who had been the friend and garden adviser of Princess Augusta, mother of George III. After being educated at Haileybury, Ridley went to Oxford and studied anatomy, physiology, chemistry, physics,

"Mad" or "Rubber" Ridley – the remarkable pioneer of rubber plantations and who lived to the age of 102.

entomology and geology; although it seems that at this period his main interests were in zoology and geology. He was duly awarded the Burdett-Coutts Scholarship in geology and spent the next two years studying fossils. On the lookout for a paid post, he deliberately covered a wide range of subjects and his first job was at the botanical department of the British Museum where he stayed for eight years publishing a number of papers on both zoological and botanical subjects. He was then sent to Brazil where he collected animals, plants and minerals.

His appointment as Superintendent of the Botanic Gardens in Singapore was a dream come true, and his achievements were sensational; not only was he able to regenerate the garden adding greatly to its fame, but managed to create the rubber industry at the critical moment when it became a world requirement. He also made many explorations into the Malay Peninsula itself, often to previously unknown parts, collecting living plants for the garden and dried for the herbarium, amassing information and specimens upon which his five-volume work, *Flora of the Malay Peninsula,* was based. He visited northwards to southernmost Siam and Burma and southward to Malaya, Sumatra, Borneo, Java and Sarawak. Further afield he visited Christmas and the Keeling Islands, eventually going as far as Egypt, India and Jamaica. Wherever he went he gathered plants and constantly sent living material to Kew, enriching their collections. But his notebooks, written in his neat educated hand and in fine detail of all that he found of interest, are immensely valuable, illuminated by his very catholic tastes.

Ridley had always been fascinated by the problems of seed dispersal; his zoological studies had enabled him to do experiments studying the seed and fruit dissemination by birds and animals. He tried to determine the period of time that elapsed between the feeding of a bird and the evacuation of the seed so he could work out what different kinds of birds were effective agents for dispersal. He also paid attention to the seed contents of the droppings of animals and their habits of evacuation. In this context, he observed for example, that the Malayan rhinoceros, *R. sumatrensis,* frequently followed a regular route, taking a month or more of travel, when defecation would take place regularly at special spots upon this route. Ridley noted, however, that when a hut had been placed over one of these spots, the rhinoceros went through it 'like a living tank, but left his visiting card as usual'. Ridley's second magnus opus which was dedicated to this subject, *Dispersal of Plants throughout the World* was published in 1930.

Some of his notes on his arrival in Singapore in 1888 are revealing: 'The care and development of a Botanic Garden in the Tropics is the most delightful form of employment there can be. There is an ever absorbing interest in introducing new and ornamental or useful plants from other parts of the world and bringing down plants from the forests, cultivating them and sending them to different parts of the world, and there is an aesthetic pleasure in landscape gardening which is most enjoyable. Added to these it is open air work and far more healthy and lifegiving than office work of any kind.' He describes his daily routine: beginning work at daybreak – at 6am he would organise the coolies to their tasks and return to his office and work on the correspondence from 8am till 11. While the coolies were off duty between 11 and 1pm, he would have half an hour for lunch and spend time doing some plant drawing. At 1 o'clock 'I went over the whole garden inspecting the work till 4 when I usually returned for tea and played lawn tennis or drove out till 6 when it was dark. After dinner I wrote papers on botany or agricultural work for our monthly Bulletin till 11 or 12. Saturday afternoons and very wet days were spent in the Herbarium.'

Besides the botanic garden, Ridley had to manage the garden of Government House, 'a thankless job as the Governor usually grumbled and wanted to be supplied with English vegetables to save cost of purchase, and he insisted on having a fresh buttonhole of English violets every day. The plants are quite unsuited for the climate but by growing 84 pots of them we managed to do it.' He also had to inspect the coconut plantations all over the island to see that the half caste inspectors were doing their job, and spend time supervising the forests of the colony and the gardens of Penang and Malacca.

He opens another window into his personality when he tells us that before he left England he had been warned that there was 'a most objectionable body called The Gardens' Committee, appointed by Government and supposed to advise and control the Head of the Gardens. It comprised lawyers, merchants, officials and others, none of whom knew anything of horticulture, botany or the use of a botanic garden. 'They had wasted much of the proceeds on futile experiments and had worried and bullied my predecessor, a very nervous man. I suggested that the committee should be abolished but was told this could not be done; but I was appointed Chairman which my predecessor never had been. I found them conceited, ignorant obstructionists. Nothing was to be done without their permission and a quorum frequently did not attend the monthly meetings for months. No progress could be made which did not suit my ideas.'

At last they played into his hands: while Ridley was away on an expedition, the members went privately to the Governor and complained that Ridley refused to obey the Committee. The Governor sent for Ridley and together they drew up a form of Vote of Confidence which Ridley was to get them to sign at a specially called meeting. He goes on: 'at this meeting I began by saying that the (unnamed) members had been to the Governor behind my back making certain statements about me; up jumped the two culprits shouting 'I never said anything of the sort!'. I proved them wrong and drove them frantic with rage. It was a most amusing scene, I could hardly control my laughter, and my assistant, acting as secretary was in hardly suppressed giggles. Then I presented them with the vote of confidence which they were only too glad to sign and escape from the scene.'

Ridley had tea with the Governor that evening and presented him with the paper. He laughed at Ridley's account and 'declared he would dearly have liked to be in the back room and heard the fun.' Ridley had no more trouble with them, called the meeting once a month for the next twenty years and they never attended again! Ridley goes on : 'Now at last I was able to carry out my schemes for making the Garden one of the finest in the world, and a few years later it was pronounced by travelling horticulturists to be 'only surpassed by Kew in beauty and richness'.

He was particularly proud of his cannas which he says were magnificent; he had dug out a bed to the depth of two feet and filled it with manure, 'I got some to grow to a height of fifteen feet forming a brilliant crimson mass which could be seen for more than a mile.' His enthusiasm is infectious: 'on moonlight nights we got the Regimental Band to give performances, the bandstand and roads leading up to it being lit with Chinese lanterns; the heavy dew falls like rain from the forest trees, the shadows are of the deepest Prussian blue, while the dripping leaves shine like silver, the contrast of these with the pale blue sky overhead has the most beautiful effect.'

In another of his notebooks he describes how he was camping in the lowland forest of Johore: 'you could not put down the point of a stick without touching the fresh tracks of tiger, wild ox, elephant, rhinoceros, wild pig, deer or tapir; the more timid animals, deer and tapir, and even the elephant, move inaudibly as do their hunters, the tiger and the panther.' One evening he was strolling in the woods, and as he had heard there was a tiger's nest in the neighbourhood had taken his gun, but left it at a tree by the roadside outside the forest.

'Stooping to collect a moss on the ground I could just hear the pads of a tiger coming towards me; I rose up quietly and the faint feet stopped about a dozen yards away; the bushes were too thick for me to see the tiger. I retreated to the path as quietly as I could, but couldn't help making a rustling on the leaves and sticks and waited with my gun behind the tree to see the animal, but in vain. At last it got too dark and I went home. Immediately I retired, it crossed the road, went to the police station and ate the dog!'

A little known animal which much intrigued Ridley was the tapir. He tells of its being 'one of the most interesting animals of our forest as well as being the oldest type of mammal as it dates from the Micean period;' he goes on: ' it seems remarkable that the defenceless animal should still exist in

Tapir (*Tapir indicus*) – one of the world's oldest species of mammal dating from the Miocene period. Ridley, on looking out of his window, confused the white rear quarters for a large granite rock – it was infact his pet tapir called Eva!

countries where tigers and black panthers are common. Its only defence appears to be its cryptic colouring, being very deep purplish brown and white, and its quick hearing, so it can run off fast at the slightest noise. When it frequently enters the ponds and lakes it appears to walk on the bottom under water and not make any attempt to swim.' He tells of how he kept a pet one, Eva, for many years and how her camouflage was so amazing that he was often completely taken in. 'One evening in the dusk I looked out of my window and saw on the grass plot what appeared to be one of the large granite boulders and could not think how it got there; I went down to it and found it was Eva reposing on the plot, the grey white rump exactly resembling a round granite boulder…It was very tame and would romp with the dogs; if I left it in a room with a chair near a table it would climb on the chair and get onto the table often with disastrous results to the table.'

Wild exaggerated stories are told and retold about the origin of plantation rubber, but according to WJ Baukwill in *The History of Natural Rubber Production,* the credit for the conception of bringing the rubber tree from the New World to the Old must go to four gifted men – Clements Markham of the India Office; Joseph Hooker Director of Kew; Henry Wickham, planter, rubber trader and naturalist; and Henry Ridley, protégé of Hooker and Superintendent of the Garden.

Markham was the son of a vicar who was also Canon of Windsor, a post which required him to spend two months at the castle, where he was expected to dine with the King and Queen every Sunday. His great-grandfather, William Markham, had been Archbishop of York. After Westminster School, he joined the Navy spending eight years mostly in the Pacific, enabling him to visit such countries as Peru, Brazil, and Mexico. He then spent a year in Peru studying and writing several books about the Inca archaeological remains, and, on leaving the Navy, joined the Civil Service serving in the India Office.

From the India Office he provided the political initiative, his grand design being the development of profitable crops in India and Ceylon, and was sent back to Peru to collect species of the Cinchona tree (quinine) whose bark was valuable in treating malaria. Apparently Markham was never over burdened with botanical knowledge, but his ability in Spanish and his experience in Peru enabled him to persuade the Under-Secretary of State for India that he was well qualified to lead the expedition.

In 1872 he commissioned James Collins, an early proponent of the acclimatization of the different species of *Hevea* (rubber), to report on the rubber yielding plants of the world. The following year, working with Collins and Hooker of Kew, Markham arranged the purchase of 2,000 *Hevea brasiliensis* seeds, most of which failed. Despite this setback, Markham commissioned two further collections, one in 1874 when he offered Henry Wickham ten pounds for a thousand seeds. In 1875 Wickham received a letter from Markham, through Hooker, offering 'ten pounds per thousand seeds, for as many as he could collect'. The other order made by Markham was from Robert Cross (Kew gardener), who brought 1,000 plants from the Lower Amazon region.

A highly colourful story has persisted – in fact a book has been based on it, *The Thief at the end of the World* by Joe Jackson, published in 2008 – purports that Wickham actually smuggled out his precious *Hevea* seeds.

Jackson writes: 'Henry's theft was no different than that by scores of others before him, and yet in a fundamental way it was. He did not steal one seed or even a hundred, he stole 70,000. Thirty four years after Henry's theft, the British rubber, grown in the Far East from Henry's seeds would flood the market, collapsing the Amazonian economy in a single year and placing in the hands of a single power a major world resource.'

Yet according to John Loadman, who wrote *Tears of the Tree*, published in 2005, although the Brazilians described Wickham's action as 'despicable' and branded him a thief for carrying out an 'exploit hardly defensible in international law', it wasn't until 1884 that the Amazonas levied a massive export duty on rubber seeds, and in 1918 banned it completely. But in 1876 there were no restrictions in place. Loadman adds: ' It was that year that Wickham's extraction of 70,000 rubber seeds from Amazonia and their transportation to Kew, via Liverpool took place, but the complexities of the story are many and remain unresolved to this day.'

However, according to Baukwill, the export was officially authorized, as was later confirmed by the Brazilian Government. (This is according to W Wicherley (1968a), one time Head of Botany at the Rubber Research Institute of Malaysia).

The final unravelled mystery is with the 22 *Hevea* plants (not specified as either Wickham or Cross) which were sent from Kew, first to Ceylon and then to Singapore where they were raised and distributed in Malaya. They were thought to be the prime source of the '1,000 tappable trees' found by Ridley in 1888. But Ridley was of the firm opinion that these seedlings appeared different from the original (Wickham) seedlings and in a letter he says, 'I conclude therefore that the 22 plants which were sent to Singapore from which almost all the cultivated plantations derived are from Cross, not Wickham.'

When Ridley arrived in Singapore in November 1888 he had been instructed by Sir Joseph Hooker of Kew to investigate the state of affairs in the Singapore economic garden, where he found the rubber plantation almost hidden by the dense secondary forest, which had grown up during the year's interregnum between gardeners. Once he had felled and eradicated the scrub he could tell at once there was a future for the rubber plant. Based on considerable research in commercial possibilities, his suggestion to the local Government to plant rubber on a large scale met with stubborn opposition. The only commercial crop grown in Singapore was coffee: Ridley says 'the planters would not talk or think of anything else – nothing whatever was known about tapping, manufacturing, growing etc of rubber trees and all this had to be worked out.'

Henry N Ridley's (1855-1956) 'herring bone' method of tapping rubber trees, devised by himself and unchanged to this day, made possible the commercial production of rubber.

Undaunted and determined, Ridley pursued his course and eventually drew international attention to the gardens by writing a prodigious number of publications about his investigations into rubber. Armed with pockets full of seed and promoting his faith in the venture he urged everyone to give the crop a trial. There was a method in his madness – a method he devised himself of tapping the rubber trees, called the 'herring bone', which remains fundamentally unchanged to this day.

Conducting experiments on the gardens' healthy rubber trees, he discovered that by excising and paring the bark, the initial cut to the tree could be reopened at regular intervals, yielding more and better latex without permanent harm to the tree. Then he demonstrated ways of preparing sheets of coagulated latex for the market and convinced a few reluctant planters to speculate on this most practical crop.

Some of his notes at the time are remarkably interesting: 'Our difficulty at first was to find out exactly what the manufacturers wanted so as to make the rubber in the form and condition required. The different firms wanted it for different purposes and what suits one did not suit another. We sent a lot once to an Austrian firm, who wrote back to say it was no use to them, but about the time we got the letter we also got a telegram saying that it only required a slight modification for their vulcanising and it was the finest rubber they had ever got and a request for more.

To one firm we sent a very light smoked box, they said it was inferior and had no scent. We sent them another lot of the same only smoking the box till it smelt like a kipper and packing the rubber in it, they reported it excellent. They had only judged by the smell of the box when opened. One plantation had especially fine water and had been known for producing the finest tapioca in the east; when they took up rubber, their rubber was exquisitely clear and became much in demand for use as picture varnish - the rubber had to be quite clear and colourless.'

Among the first planters to take up Ridley's campaign was a tapioca planter in Malacca, Tan Chay Yan, who gave 16 hectares of his estate to the planting of rubber seeds supplied by Ridley from the Singapore Botanic Gardens in 1896. By 1901 Tan had devoted some 1,200 hectares to rubber, earning him the distinction of being the first practical rubber planter in Malaya.

The many obstinate planters who had refused even to try the rubber seed were devastated at this sensitive moment by the collapse of the coffee industry, caused by Brazilian competition and growing disease. In desperation they turned to rubber just in time for the growing demand from the motor car industry for tyres, whose rapid growth was accelerated by Henry Ford's mass production lines.

Ridley's perceptive vision proved right – rubber was ideal for Malaya; it was hardy, quick to give returns for a nominal investment and not fussy about where it was planted. Even better, it seemed to grow anywhere, both on overworked land and waste ground. Ridley turned the forest clearings and any land available to rubber, so that now the gardens were the major source of seed supply, when the rubber rush began at the turn of the century. Records show that by 1917 the gardens had distributed 7 million seeds and Ridley boasted of requests for as many as a million seeds per day.

Ridley was elected to the Fellowship of The Royal Society in 1907, four years before he retired from the Directorship of the Singapore Botanic Gardens. It was obvious that on his retirement he should choose to live at Kew, where he could continue his passionate interests. Here he completed the fifth volume of his magnus opus, *The Flora of the Malay Peninsular*, and finished writing his other important book on Plant Dispersal.

He was made a Fellow of the Linnean Society, attending their meetings, and from his wide experience adding much interest and information. He was also elected a member of the Linnean Society Dining Club where his powers of conversation and vivid reminiscences often enlivened the proceedings, and was awarded the Linnean Society's Gold Medal in 1950.

Until he was ninety-six Ridley visited the Kew Herbarium almost daily, and kept records of the bird life in the gardens, assiduously making notes and drawings of the magnolias that fruited there.

Just one more remarkable event in his life cannot go unrecorded: his busy and successful occupations do not seem to have allowed him the opportunity to get married, but just in time he obviously thought it the moment to put this right, and at the ripe old age of eighty-two he upped and married Lilian Doran; it is recorded that almost entirely due to her very devoted care he survived to reach and celebrate - as was his great hope – the centenary of his birthday. What a man.

Chapter 4

The Botanic Garden, Java

When Raffles invaded Java in 1811 and became its Governor, he had immediately attempted to lay out the Palace grounds as an English style landscaped garden, and after Java was ceded back to the Dutch in 1817 this was the foundation for the Botanic Garden which has flourished there ever since.

Sir Stamford Raffles once described his work as a naturalist and his passion for botany and gardens as 'that beautiful science', although his love of animals was almost greater. There are several revealing stories about his home life as Governor of Java and Sumatra and the many pet animals he kept, some

Sir Stamford Raffles had a pet Malaysian Sun Bear which often sat at his table
with his family, and enjoyed champagne and mangoes.

of which were brought up with his children in the nursery – indeed, a particular Malayan Sun Bear was often allowed to sit at his table, where it showed a strong penchant for champagne and mangoes, and one account accuses him of giving more attention to his pets than to his children.

Many animals were presented to him by the local rulers – the Sultan of Aceh gave him an elephant, several orang-utans came from the Sultan of Sambas in West Borneo, and Raffles even kept two tigers at his home in Java. His letters contain a lot of references to the animals, and it was his intense interest in them and in zoology in general that led him to found the Zoological Society of London with its menagerie in Regent's Park after he returned to London in 1824.

Raffles attraction to natural history is thought to have been inspired by his meeting with Dr Thomas Horsfield, the American naturalist whom he met in Java when he was appointed Governor, but he was deeply involved in serious study of botany and zoology long before that. The happiest time of his life was after the curtailment of his political activities, as he wrote to a friend in 1820: 'I have thrown politics far away and since I must have nothing to do with men, have taken to the wilder but less sophisticated animals of our woods' – he was at last able to enjoy the necessary leisure for natural history research.

Raffles wrote to Banks in August 1818 to introduce 'to your personal acquaintance, my valuable friend Dr Horsfield who has taken his passage for England, and is now on the eve of embarking.' He continues: 'To you who can so well appreciate his merits and discoveries, it would be presumptuous in me to offer my opinions on his valuable collections; they are immense and I have no doubt, will be found to contain ample materials for publishing the natural history of Java including quadrupeds, birds, insects and the geology of the island. From the extensive collections of drawings and manuscripts which he has shown me, and which have been collected during his residence of sixteen years in Java, it would appear that he has the materials for the following publications'. He then suggests a formidable list of diaries, essays, a herbarium of 2,000 specimens, maps, journals, sketches and other items.

Raffles goes on to describe Dr Horsfield's private character 'which is most estimable, he is universally respected, his modesty is conspicuous and his expectations moderate.'

We owe it to Raffles that Horsfield assigned all his unique collections to the East India Company and that he eventually took them to the company's museum in London.

When Raffles was in London later, he at last met and made friends with Sir Joseph Banks who wrote : 'We are all here delighted with the acquaintance of Governor Raffles; he is certainly among the best informed of men and possesses a larger stock of useful talent than any other individual of my acquaintance'.

With Banks' support, Raffles persuaded the East India Company to agree to his friend, the British naval surgeon Dr Joseph Arnold, accompanying him to Sumatra as a naturalist, and during the long voyage he and Lady Raffles gained much from Arnold's scientific instruction while reading various works on natural history.

Soon after arriving on the island Raffles proposed an excursion along the coast to Manna and thence through the romantic forests of Passumah. Here, on the Manna river, Arnold, in the company of Raffles, had the great excitement of finding a gigantic flower, whose name will be forever entwined with his in the scientific world. After two days journey in land, he discovered

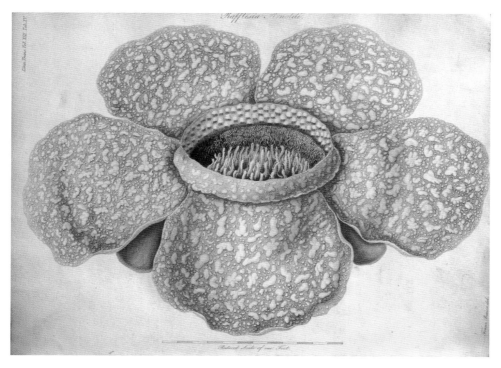

Rafflesia arnoldii, sometimes described as 'that five-petalled red and mottled, malodorous wonder'.

it by the river, growing close to the ground and without leaves, a flower of the most brilliant colours, measuring three feet across, weighing about fifteen pounds and which was totally unknown to naturalists. (It has also been described as 'that five-petalled red and mottled, malodorous wonder').

The Linnean Society afterwards proposed to call this new genus *Rafflesia*, in honour of Sir Stamford Raffles, and the species *Arnoldi* in memory of the actual discoverer. Raffles thus had the good fortune to have his name associated with a prodigy of nature that was to astonish the scientific world. Arnold's career as a naturalist in Sumatra was brief as he died of fever only four months after arriving on the island. Raffles wrote to his friends informing them of this sad event: 'He had endeared himself to Lady Raffles and myself by his most amiable disposition and unassuming manners. He formed part of our family and I regret his loss as that of a sincere friend'.

When the Dutch returned to Java in 1817, Caspar Carl Reinwardt – a German Professor who had worked in Amsterdam and afterwards in Leyden – was appointed Director in agricultural business, arts and sciences on Java and neighbouring islands. He was interested in gathering together all the plants used locally for domestic and medical purposes into the Buitenzorg Botanic Garden (as it was then called) and worked there until 1822, during which time he introduced about 900 living plants.

At the same time we find James Hooper, an Englishman, employed in a Dutch establishment as head gardener from 1817-1830, a clever young man who had worked at Kew for six years. We learn this from Dr Melchior Treub, (Director of Bogor – its new name from 1880), who wrote to Dr Thistleton-Dyer (Director of Kew) quoting from a letter written by Reinwardt (1817) to the Colonial Government: 'There is now a rare as well as favourable opportunity to get a very able and specially trained man for the service of a botanical garden. It is a man named James Hooper, who, by special recommendation of Sir Joseph Banks, joined the recent British Embassy to China. He stayed here to try to get a position. There is not only that recommendation, but Mr Abel, the naturalist to the Embassy and the Ambassador Lord Amherst himself gave me the best testimony as to Hooper's ability in cultivation and propagating plants. Lastly Hooper has had a service of six years in one of the most renowned and richest gardens of Europe – the Royal Gardens at Kew where he has had charge of the general cultivation of plants so I may suppose him to be quite the right man for the work I intend to charge him with.'

This proposition of Reinwardt's being accepted, James Hooper was appointed by the Colonial Government as 'hortulanus' of the new Botanical Garden at Bogor at a salary of 150 guilders monthly with the free use of a government house. He remained head gardener until 1830 when he left Java on leave in order to restore his health, but unluckily died on board the vessel without ever reaching home.

Treub continues: 'Our first head gardener, who stayed here twelve years, having been trained at Kew, will show you that Bogor has from the beginning been greatly indebted to Kew, 'that most renowned of European gardens'.

The Botanic Garden of Java has another claim to fame through a connection with a rather obscure Englishman, Charles Ledger (1818-1905). This is all to do with the quinine bark and the deadly disease, malaria, which still kills over a million people a year and is endemic in Africa, Asia and South America. One of the most common themes in the stories of our dedicated young botanists, so many of them trained and appointed from Kew, was the terrible waste of their valuable young lives when they caught and often died of fevers, prevalent in the unhealthy climates of south east Asia.

The story of Cinchona *ledgeriana* begins in the 17th C in South America. No-one has ever been able to agree about who first discovered the bark in treating fevers. A surgeon from Scotland who visited Ecuador in the 18th C tells us that the qualities and use of the Quina Bark were known to the Indians long before the arrival of any Spaniard; Indians were renowned as natural observers and talented botanists, with a wide knowledge of medicinal plants.

In 1653, a Jesuit priest wrote a description of the Fever Tree in which he says: 'In the district of Loja, diocese of Quito, grows a certain kind of large tree, which has bark like the cinnamon, a little more coarse and very bitter, which ground to powder is given to those who have a fever and with only this remedy it leaves them'. The Jesuits valued this tree so greatly that they taught the Indians how to cut off the bark in vertical strips, so as not to kill the tree, and to plant five new trees in the form of a cross for every one cut down.

However Von Humboldt, a scientist and naturalist exploring South America around 1800 says: 'In the deep and hot valleys of the mountains in Catomago, agues are extremely common, but the natives there, as well as at Loxa, of whatever caste they be, would die rather than have recourse to Cinchona Bark, which together with opiates they place in the class of poisons inciting mortification. The Indians treat their fevers with lemonade, with the oleaginous rind of the small green wild lemon with infusion of *Scoparia dulcis* and with strong coffee'.

The reputation of Jesuit Bark in dealing with malaria grew throughout the 17th and 18th centuries and it became obvious that the scarce resources of the tree would never sustain the ravages made upon it. Dutch and English botanists were the first to attempt to bring its cultivation from the New World to the Old. The Dutch chose Java as a likely location, and the English started plantations in India. Then in 1852 the Dutch sent JC Hasskarl, Superintendent of the Bogor Botanic Garden in Java, on a humanitarian venture to South America to collect seed and plants of the cinchona. Hasskarl made a perilous journey through the mountains of Peru and Bolivia, collecting thousands of specimens which he took to Java, but which were unfortunately of a variety with a very low percentage of quinine. Thus Java gradually became stocked with the cinchona trees between 1854 and 1864, but most of which proved worthless.

The English appointed Clements R Markham, who once more convinced his Government that he was the man to lead the English attempt. He was neither a botanist nor a horticulturist, but proposed to take some proper specialists with him, departing in 1859. In 1880 he published his '*Peruvian Bark*' stating that 'his introduction of Peruvian Bark trees into British India and Ceylon is now an assured success'. Alas, twenty years later more than a million of his trees were cut down because they were again of the wrong variety.

Now we can return to our Englishman, Charles Ledger, who was largely oblivious of these events, although he had lived for years in Peru and Bolivia – the region that always produced the best barks – and had not only traded in them but knew where the best quinine yielding trees were to be found. Travelling as always with his faithful guide, Manuel Incra Mamani, who could spot the true *Cinchona calisaya* (its bark was of exceptional richness) by looking at the forest canopy and by its foliage – when everyone else found the varieties indistinguishable – they had come upon an unknown grove of more than fifty trees in full flower – lilac scented and with rich red foliage – in a remote part of Bolivia.

Ledger paid Mamani to return to collect seed at the appropriate time. The first year no seeds were to be found; for the next four years the blossom was frosted; but in 1865 and after walking a thousand miles, he managed to collect 14 pounds of seed of this unique variety. Much of this story has been published recently by Fiammetta Rocco in her book *The Miraculous Fever Tree.*

Charles Ledger sent the seed to his brother George in London with instructions to sell it to the British Government for their plantations in India. The latter went straight to Kew, but Sir William Hooker – the main force behind the British cinchona initiative – had just died, and nobody else had the slightest idea of the ultimate value of this seed. The result was that the British Government turned it down. George then offered it to the Dutch Government for their plantations in Java, who bought one pound of the seed for 100 guilders, with a promise of further payment if the seed germinated. George now hawked the rest of the seed round London, and by chance it ended up with the British as he had wanted. But by now the seed was no longer viable, and it failed to germinate. Norman Taylor in his *Cinchona in Java,* published in 1945, says: 'no misfortune in the whole history of cinchona culture in India was so disastrous to the British; the country has the highest incidence of malaria in the world, and ever since the Ledger fiasco, in turning down his seed, the government has been obliged to grow the inferior varieties sent there by Markham, wasting thousands of pounds cultivating the wrong tree.'

The arrival of the single remaining pound of Ledger seed in Java in 1865 should have been a dramatic event, but no-one suspected that it would mean the end of all the Dutch failures, of which they were acutely aware. Hasskarl had been succeeded by KW van Gorkom, who employed a young chemist JCB Moens. About twenty thousand of the seeds in the precious one pound had germinated, and the following year twelve thousand seedlings were set out in the nursery bed, but it was not until 1872 that Moens removed a few pieces of bark from the saplings to test for their quinine content, expecting no better than 3% quinine, (which had hitherto been considered good quality) and was astonished to find a content of as much as 14%; after which, botanists studying Ledger's seeds, came to the conclusion that they were a previously unknown kind of cinchona and named it *Cinchona ledgeriana* in his honour.

There were still mighty problems: something like two million mature cinchona trees, some with a quinine content as low as 0.65%, were growing in adjacent plantations and these would be certain to pollute the *C. ledgeriana*. The cinchona is particularly prone to hybridise, being heterostylus – that is, having styles of three lengths, a device of nature to prevent self pollination, which in practice makes it almost impossible to keep the species pure. Van Gorkom undertook the enormous labour of deflowering the thousands of trees surrounding the main Ledger plantation.

There were other snags which required technical experiment before the ideal solution was discovered, all of which took time-consuming research and a great deal of money. The Netherland Indies Government, in charge of the whole performance, spent a fortune with no thought of profit in order to benefit the malaria-stricken populations of the world. Since 1945, cinchona culture has been in the hands of more than a hundred private planters, who are superbly organised and keep supplies of quinine going. Up in the hills of Java, and even at that date were still some of those magical trees from Charles Ledger's original seed.

The Dutch East Indies declared war on Japan in 1941, and the next year the Japanese marched into Bogor and took over the directorship of both the garden and the herbarium. Japanese botanists did try to protect the garden from their soldiers who were intent on cutting and using the trees from the garden for timber, during the invasion.

The Dutch took over again after the war until Indonesia achieved full independence. The garden suffered greatly for many years, but became a scientific establishment in the 1970s. At the same time the beautiful orchid house was restored, and collecting trips were made around the archipelago to increase the varieties it contained.

— CHAPTER 5 —

The Pamplemousses Botanic Garden, Mauritius

As your plane circles the island of Mauritius you have the delightful illusion that you are about to land on a brilliant green Doyenne de Comice pear surrounded by white lace. The chartreuse effect is caused by the fields of sugarcane, exports of which form the island's main economy – with the lacy effect caused by the peripheral coral reef. The long ago extinct volcanoes peak in the distance beyond the harbour of Port Louis lying in the north west.

This jewel lies just within the Tropic of Capricorn, about 900 km east of Madagascar in the Indian Ocean and is subject to very violent hurricanes. Its isolation led to unique fauna and flora, including giant tortoises and large flightless birds, and of course, the dodo – there were no mammals except for a fruit-eating bat. It is only recently that we hear that the remains of giant eggs have been found in Madagascar, the nearest neighbour, belonging to what is known as the Elephant Bird, or *Aepyornis,* whose fossil bones have lately been discovered.

We know little about the dodo, except that it lived as an original inhabitant on the Ile de France – as the island was then called – and that it is now extinct. But, according to the legend beside its portrait in the British Museum (Natural History), in 1638 a captive dodo was to be seen in London, and its apparent appetite for eating small pebbles 'excited no small curiosity among the local citizens.' Nobody knows how many other flightless birds and interesting, unique creatures flourished undisturbed among the valuable ebony forests, but the dread day in 1598 when the Dutch took possession of the island, naming it after Prince Maurice of Nassau, must have tolled their death knell.

The main attraction to the Dutch was the timber and marvellous stands of mature ebony, which they exported to the Cape of Good Hope and for their homeland. Ebony was being cut down at such a rate that concern was expressed even then in the 17thC. But rats escaped from the ships and destroyed many native vulnerable creatures, and when about forty years later, permanent inhabitants arrived bringing with them goats, pigs and dogs – the animals all became feral and finished the destruction, causing the island to undergo major ecological change.

In 1710 the Dutch abandoned the island leaving behind a few slaves, and several years later the French East India Company laid formal claim to Mauritius, occupying the well-watered flat plain to the north of the island, where it is thought they found trees bearing fruit like an orange or grapefruit, probably brought from Java by the Dutch. The fruit had a bitter-sweet taste, and was called 'bambolmas' in Tamil - hence 'pamplemousse', the French for grapefruit. The main harbour, Port Louis, was named as a tribute to King Louis XV, and the French built the Catholic Church of St Francis there in 1756, the oldest in the island.

An early Governor of the Ile de France (as the French called it) Bertrand-Francois Mahé, Comte de la Bourdonnais, acquired land in 1735, built a house and laid out a garden which he called Mon Plaisir. He grew subsistence crops such as manioc, which he brought from Brazil and from which tapioca is derived; it soon became a staple of the slave population. He also grew maize, potatoes, rice, cotton and indigo. When his wife and son both died he sold Mon Plaisir to the Compagnie des Indes, who transferred it to the French Crown in 1764. The French first planted mulberry trees over most of the estate, hoping to build up a silk worm industry. Subsequently the mulberries were replaced by a plantation of 'bois noir' (*Albizia lebbeck*), the charcoal of which could be used in the manufacture of gunpowder. The French had taken possession of the island as a naval base and the administration itself was geared towards taking adequate precautions against the possibility of the island being involved in a war.

The garden became entirely neglected until the French India Company commissioned an eminent horticulturist and botanist, M Fusee Aublet, to install a central pharmacy and botanic garden. Aublet was, however, a man of suspicious and morose disposition, who made himself thoroughly unpopular from the first. His character and prejudices appear in the preface to his book,

History of the Plants of French Guiana, and in his subsequent *Notes on the Plants of Ile de France*: 'It was considered odd at the Ile de France that I should have been sent there for no fault. I was asked if I had come for a change of air. Immediately I became suspect and was supposed to be condemning others, while only occupied in fulfilling my professional duties.' Soon after his arrival (August 1753), M Aublet took up his residence in Mon Plaisir and he describes how he collected all the rare and useful or curious plants he could find, planted useful trees, rounded up all the cattle belonging to the company and had them coralled, thus increasing their numbers to the company's advantage.

He adds : 'In the midst of these occupations, the gift of a so-called nutmeg tree and of nutmegs by M le Poivre caused me much annoyance, as I neither could nor would recognise this tree or its fruit for the true nutmeg of commerce. I reported to the company to this effect and thus made many personal enemies, who took their revenge by slandering me'.

Aublet persisted in his refusal to recognise the nutmeg tree or to plant them until formally ordered to do so by the Consul Superieur. The nutmegs died, however, and Aublet was suspected of foul play. It was even whispered that he had watered them with boiling water.

The M le Poivre referred to was the most important inhabitant of Ile de France at the time, a well travelled naturalist, whose overriding ambition was to establish a rival spice industry to the Dutch, after acquiring knowledge of spice tree culture on landing in Java and learning of the value of the trade monopoly. In 1766 he was appointed *Commissaire* of the Ile de France and bought the house and garden of Mon Plaisir as his residence.

He wrote: 'I have bought 'on credit' from the company a simple garden, ready-made and well watered, with the sole view of having somewhere ready and secure to put next March the plants that M l'Abbe Galloys will be sending me from China…I have bought the necessary slaves to cultivate the garden. I am having the land prepared specifically for this purpose, above all for the rare plants that I hope to obtain for this island, as well as for all the useful plants that I plan to gather from the different corners of Asia. I thought that the only way to succeed in this plan was to cultivate them at my expense, in my own way, under my eyes and on my own land, where I should be able to admit only those people that I wanted'.

It hardly sounds as if these two could get on. It is worthy of note that although both the Governor and Poivre were opposed to slavery in principle, it did not stop their employing them in practice.

In June 1770 two ships arrived in Port Louis harbour carrying the precious spices, a large number of nutmeg seeds and seedlings and a smaller quantity of clove seedlings. Poivre kept the plants under his direct control and it was from then that the serious history of Pamplemousses began as a botanic garden.

The Royal Palm is perhaps the most magnificent of all the palm trees, and when planted regularly their smooth tall trunks lend themselves to giving avenues of majestic grandeur

Although Poivre had spent a fortune on improvements and new installations at Mon Plaisir, he handed over the property to the Government on his departure in October 1772 for the same amount as he had spent on its purchase, and refused to accept a larger sum. He is remembered by Poivre Avenue either side of which the stately pillar-like Royal Palms are found.

Before his departure Poivre recommended as his successor his pupil and friend Jean Nicolas de Cère, who had for some time efficiently collaborated with Poivre in the work of the garden. Cère was a Major of Infantry; he had started his career in the Navy and after two campaigns settled in the Ile de France where he had inherited considerable property from his father. Soon after his arrival he met Poivre who was much taken with this serious and high minded young man, who showed such a pronounced taste for botany. Thus, the foundation for a lifelong friendship and co-operation was laid. Cère did not hesitate to emulate his friend and master in sacrificing his private fortune to carry out important improvements in the garden.

The growth and flowering of the first spice plants of the gardens were followed in France with great attention, and when the first nutmeg fruit was picked in December 1778 it was solemnly despatched to the King. Cère distributed seedlings of the spices to the inhabitants of the islands, a venture so successful that one private citizen reaped a harvest of 28,000 cloves a few years later, and another grew a plantation of 8,000 clove shrubs. Cère also sent cases of his plants to the French Colonies of America. A visiting traveller recorded his impressions of Mon Plaisir as one of the marvels of the world.

Sir Joseph Banks was much interested in 'our politic neighbours the French'. In a letter to Sir George Yonge FRS (who was involved with Banks in setting up the St Vincent Botanic Garden) written on 15 May 1787, he says: 'they have preceded us several years in the execution of similar projects, and from the results of their experiments we learn with certainty that His Majesty's (King George III) ideas will, if carried into full execution, be attended with the most ample success. M Poivre sent two expeditions each consisting of two vessels in search of the nobler species, and obtained by each a number of plants of nutmegs and cloves.

Banks continues: 'At present we learn that they have so large a quantity of both clove and nutmeg trees actually planted out that, from the state of them and their period of growth they have no doubt of being able, before the end of the present century, to supply as large a quantity of these spices as the whole consumption of Europe can demand. Nor have they stopped here.' And he goes on to tell of 'the nutmegs and cloves flourishing in their West India Islands which are fully equal to those of the Dutch, in every quality applicable either to the purpose of food, medicine or perfume.'

'With such an example before us, it is clearly demonstrable that nothing but activity is wanting to carry his Majesty's commands into execution on our part, and that a large portion of that virtue will be necessary to enable us to retrieve the advantage which our active neighbours have obtained over us in point of time. We may all remember, however in our united efforts to serve this interesting cause, which is so eminently honoured with his Majesty's protection, that we have nobler prospects in view than the mere attempt of filching from another country its commercial advantages.'

Among the fruits that Sir Joseph wanted sent to the West Indies was *Mangifera Indica* – mango. His interesting instructions were: 'As those which have been imported into the West Indies are of a very inferior sort, the best kinds would be a most acceptable addition. At Goa it has been the ancient custom, and it has been practised with success at Madras, to perform upon the trees the operation of circumcision, which is done by passing a branch through a box or basket filled with rich soil, and cutting off the bark quite round the part which rests in the middle of the box, which must be firmly fixed in its place. This operation should commence with the rainy season and, we are told, that before the end of it, some of the branches, for it does not constantly succeed, will have formed roots sufficient to maintain themselves. These branches being sawed off become trees which, we are certain will produce fruit of exactly the same flavour and quality as those produced by the mother tree.'

One of Sir Joseph's protégés was Matthew Flinders (1774-1814), a young man from Lincolnshire, Banks' home county – where Banks was something of a native cult hero. From an early age, Flinders longed to be a sailor explorer, and with Banks' help became a seaman, learning his seamanship, navigation and marine exploration with Captain Bligh, who had in turn learned from Captain Cook. He was to sail with Bligh on his second and successful breadfruit expedition in HMS *Providence*. Even this must have been quite a dramatic experience, following the notorious voyage of HMS *Bounty,* but he can hardly have expected his next appointment to end with the nightmare of being imprisoned as a spy on the Ile de France for nearly six years. This is how it happened.

Joseph Banks had been in constant touch with John King, Under Secretary at the Home Office, on the subject of Australian exploration. He longed to solve the great puzzle of the continental outline, having himself been in HMS *Endeavour* when they discovered the east coast of Australia (New South Wales as they first called it). Was it possible that a strait passed from north to south, which divided the land mass in two? In May 1798 he wrote regretting that in spite of possessing the country for over ten years, nothing has been found to recompense the mother country for her investment. He adds: 'it is impossible to conceive that such a body of land, as large as all Europe, should not produce some raw material of importance to a manufacturing country such as England.'

Spurred on by the knowledge that the French had sailed a well-equipped expedition in the *Geographe* and the *Naturaliste,* under the command of Captain Nicolas Baudin, to explore the southern coast of Australia in 1800, a three-masted vessel of 344 tons was at last approved by the Admiralty as a discovery ship to be called HMS *Investigator,* and Banks was asked to make the preparations. Matthew Flinders was appointed to command.

In addition to her crew of picked men (when Flinders needed another 11 men, he had the choice of 250 volunteers to select from); a civilian complement including a naturalist, a botanical artist and a gardener were also appointed and Flinders young cousin, John Franklin of future fame, went with them as midshipman. Robert Brown was chosen by Banks as naturalist, a post that Brown accepted with alacrity, the offer was beyond his wildest dreams.

Brown was a schoolboy botanist, trained as a doctor at Edinburgh University and with a considerable knowledge of British flora after years of study at the Banksian and Linnean Society's herbarium, where he was elected Associate member. At 28 he was an intuitive choice to sail with the equally enthusiastic 27 year old Flinders. Ferdinand Bauer from Austria was appointed botanical artist, one of the greatest of all time; his brother Franz, employed by Banks, painted at the Royal Botanical Gardens at Kew for over 50 years. Peter Good went as gardener, and when he died of dysentery at the end of the arduous circumnavigation of Australia, in 1803 Brown wrote: 'I shall often lament the loss of Peter Good, who was not only an experienced cultivator, but an acute observer and an indefatigable collector'. Flinders in his turn considered it fortunate for science that two such men as Mr Brown and Mr Bauer had been selected, 'their application is beyond what I have been accustomed to.'

They sailed from England in July 1801, with Flinders' last message to Sir Joseph, recording: 'received provisions, lashed and ready for sea'. It was soon apparent that the ship may have been ready but was quite inadequate for such a voyage – before they even left the channel she was taking in water as much as 5" on some tacks; these rotten old hulks were the best the Admiralty could provide for exploration, Britain needed all her sound ships to protect the seas and fight the French.

They reached the Cape where some repairs were made, and sighted Port Leewin SW Australia in December, then making the survey along the great Australian Bight, the entire south coast of Australia, to meet the French in Encounter Bay (later Adelaide). Baudin had started out with 22 botanists, zoologists, painters, draughtsmen and gardeners, but by now had only one botanist in action, depleted as they were by scurvy.

Investigator reached Port Jackson (Sydney) in May 1802, without having discovered any of the navigable rivers up which they had hoped to explore the interior, and found no evidence of the river which it had been thought might bisect the continent, flowing from Carpentaria Bay. Brown wrote to Banks: 'our excursions have nowhere extended more than a few miles from the shore, the interior of New Holland is therefore as completely unknown as ever.'

Just a year later they arrived in Port Jackson again, having completely circumnavigated the whole continent 'northabout'. Before leaving Carpentaria Bay westward, Flinders beached and inspected *Investigator* and found hardly a sound timber in her, but, determined to complete his mission, he waited for better weather and nursed her back to Port Jackson where she was condemned as unseaworthy.

It is not possible to over emphasise the personal courage and dedication of these intrepid and able young men, their professionalism surveying and charting of every inch of the coast line and their skill in seamanship – pitted not only against the elements, but the very real danger of their own ship foundering.

So it was that Flinders found himself on the other side of the world and without a ship. His adventures, desperately trying to hitchhike back to England, would make almost another book and are in fact described in several. It was his desperate attempt to sail back to England in the tiny, unsuitably small *Cumberland* – Hobson's choice – from which he landed in Mauritius, not knowing that England was now once more at war with France, that caused him to be taken prisoner, suspected of being a spy, and kept for over six years, which adds a little to this account of the island.

When Banks heard of his plight, he wrote to Robert Brown, still stranded in New South Wales. 'Poor Flinders is a prisoner, and I fear not very well treated. He put in the little Cumberland into L'Ile de France for water, provisions and some repairs, wholly ignorant of the war. The Governor, unwilling I suppose to believe that any person would venture upon so long a voyage in so small a vessel (29 tons) accused him of being a spy, and maltreated him. His letters sent by stealth to the Admiralty state all this but conclude in saying that he was, when he wrote them, rather better treated. All means possible here have been taken to promote his release which, as the French are great favorers of science, and as the ship had a passport, will I hope in time be effected.'

Flinders' bad luck was to be unfairly imprisoned, but as it turned out there are few more beautiful islands in the world in which to be incarcerated, and while continually trying to persuade the rather difficult Governor, General de Caen, to release him, his place of seclusion was changed to what became known as the Garden Prison. This was a great improvement on the previous rather insalubrious captivity and to his surprise he found that as time went by, he became much in demand socially on this small island, and everybody wanted to meet him.

Although Flinders' fame is for his explorations, his skill as navigator and cartographer and his experiments on magnetism in ships (as a result of which no ship would put to sea without a Flinder's Bar), his formalistic skills live on. From day one of his landing on the island he kept a remarkable journal, which after seven years of his captivity consisted of 235 pages. It is edited by his great nephew and shows him to be a perspicacious witness of every element of life in the early days of the 19thC. He suffered greatly from peaks and troughs of hope and despair, fearing in his most melancholy moments that he would never get away. In deep gloom he filled his time having lessons in French and giving lessons in astronomy, navigation and maths to the sons of his friends and worked endlessly on his charts and maps relating to his circumnavigation of Australia. He also learned to play the flute.

Flinders observed everything that went on in the island, the crops of cotton, coffee, sugarcane and products of the beautiful gardens so often wrecked by the massive hurricanes that swept through them. He recorded some observations on birds of the island, martins that he never saw by day, and then noticed one evening by some tall bamboos, between 2,000 and 10,000 of them. He also studied the geology of the island and measured the fall of the four cascades on the river Tamarin (today a source of hydroelectric power) – up to 200 feet into deep pools, and spent a lot of time reading, particularly Grant's history of the Ile de France, which he endeavoured to translate into French.

His friends did all they could to divert him from his depression, for example taking him shooting – there were a few spotted partridges, some deer and wild hogs – and he went fishing for mullet, carp and some huge eels. They also took him to the theatre where he noticed the audience consisted of some very pretty young women: 'the older ladies were generally rather fat, but with dress equally gay and bosoms equally bare with the younger.' Flinders considered that, 'an equal number of women so undressed would cause an uproar in an English theatre, and that man of the world as he certainly was, the modest would be offended, prudes would break their fans, the aged would cry shame and the libertines would exult and clap while the old lechers would apply their opera glasses!'

An original document, found among his papers as late as 1971 in the National Maritime Museum at Greenwich, is a delightful little *jeu d'esprit*, written by him about his beloved and faithful ship's cat – *Trim*.

A drawing of Flinders' faithful ship's cat – Trim.

Trim accompanied him in four of his ships, taking part in all his adventures and imprisoned with him as he recounts. This feline friend was born on board, and sometimes when playing with his brothers and sisters on deck by moonlight, 'the energy and elasticity of his movements carried him so far beyond his mark that he fell overboard; but this was far from being a misfortune for he learnt to swim and have no fear of the water and when a rope was thrown to him, he took hold of it like a man and ran up it like a cat'. Flinders describes him as one of the finest animals he ever saw with a long large and bushy tail, long and graceful whiskers: 'his robe was clear jet black, with the exception of his four feet which seemed to have been dipped in snow and his underlip which rivalled them in whiteness – he also had a large white star on his breast.' Trim was excessively vain about his snow white feet, and would often place himself on the quarter deck spreading out his two white paws in the posture of *lion couchant*, where the officers could not fail to admire him; he was also interested in nautical astronomy and experimental philosophy, but above all in practical seamanship; 'he knew what good discipline required and in taking in a reef, never presumed to go aloft until the order was issued, but at the words 'away up aloft' up he jumped along with the seamen and 'none could reach the top before, nor so soon as he did.'

Trim was admitted to the table and always the first ready for dinner; commonly seated a quarter of an hour before any other person, 'his voice was not heard until everybody else was served, then he put in his request by a little gently caressing mew, for a little, little bit from the plate of each; and it was to no purpose to refuse it, for Trim was enterprising in time of need. Without the greatest attention to each morsel, in the person he had petitioned in vain, he would whip it off the fork with his paw on its passage to the mouth with such dexterity that it rather excited admiration than anger.'

Their last voyage together coincided with a time when Flinders was especially anxious to get home, not only to get another ship and return to Australia to finish his mission but also to see his much loved wife Ann, his childhood sweetheart. They had married just before he left England on this voyage, which it was his life's passion to carry out, and if the truth were known he had intended to take Ann with him. Luckily or unluckily for them both, this was discovered and he had to make the painful decision to leave her behind or give up his command. It was to be nearly ten years before he returned.

When Flinders and his officers, accompanied by Trim, were moved to the Garden Prison, Flinders wrote: 'a French lady offered to be Trim's security, in order to have him for her little daughter; and the fear of some clandestine proceedings on the part of the soldiers of the guard induced me to comply, on finding it would give no umbrage to His Excellency the French governor and captain general. A fortnight had scarcely passed when the public gazette of the island announced that he was nowhere to be found and offered a reward of ten Spanish dollars to 'anyone who would conduct him back to his afflicted little mistress.'

Flinders writes: 'My sorrow may be better conceived than described; I would have given 50 dollars to have had my friend and companion restored to me. All research and offers of recompense were in vain, poor Trim was effectively lost; and it is but too probable that this excellent unsuspecting animal was stewed and eaten by some hungry black slave, in whose eyes all his merits could not balance against the avidity excited by his sleek body and fine furred skin'.

He adds: 'Thus perished my faithful intelligent Trim! The sporting affectionate and useful companion of my voyages during four years. Never, my Trim, 'to take thee all in all, shall I see thy like again, and this shall be thy epitaph.' This little book, published in Australia in 1984 is profusely illustrated by Annette Macarthur-Onslow, a direct descendant of the Macarthur family whom we come to later.

When Charles Darwin paused at Mauritius, on his way home in HMS *Beagle*, he gives us a perceptive opinion of his view of the island describing it as follows on April 29th 1836: 'in the morning we passed round the northern end of Mauritius. From this point of view the aspect of the island equalled the expectations raised by the well known descriptions of its beautiful scenery. The sloping plain of the Pamplemousses, interspersed with houses and coloured by the large fields of sugarcane of a bright green composed the foreground; the brilliancy of the green was the more remarkable because it is a colour which is generally conspicuous only from a very short distance. Towards the centre of the island groups of wooded mountains rose out of this highly-cultivated plain; their summits as so commonly happens with ancient volcanic rocks being jagged into the sharpest points. Masses of white clouds were collected around these pinnacles, as if for the sake of pleasing the stranger's eye. The whole island, with its sloping border and central mountains, was adorned with an air of perfect elegance; the scenery, if I may use such an expression, appeared to the sight harmonious.

I spent the greater part of the next day in walking about the town and visiting different people. The town is of considerable size and said to contain 20,000 inhabitants; the streets are very clean and regular. Although the island has been for so many years under the English Government, the general character of the place is quite French; Englishmen speak to their servants in that language and the shops are all French; indeed I should think Calais or Boulogne was much more Anglicised. There is a very pretty little theatre in which operas are excellently performed. We were also surprised at seeing large booksellers' shops with well-stored shelves.

The various races of men walking in the streets afford the most interesting spectacle in Port Louis. Convicts from India are banished here for life; at present there are about 800 and they are employed in various public works. Before seeing these people I had no idea that the inhabitants of India were such noble looking figures. Their skin is extremely dark and many of the older men had large moustaches and beards of snow-white colour; this together with the fire of their expression gave them quite an imposing aspect. The greater number had been banished for murder and the worst crimes; others for causes which can scarcely be considered as moral faults, such as for not obeying, from superstitious motives the English laws. These men are generally quiet and well conducted, from their outward conduct, their cleanliness and faithful observance of their strange religious rites, it was impossible to look at them with the same eyes as on our wretched convicts in New South Wales.

Captain Lloyd took us to the Rivière Noire, which is several miles to the southward, that I might examine some rocks of elevated coral. We passed through pleasant gardens, and fine fields of sugarcane, growing among huge blocks of lava. The roads were bordered by hedges of mimosa and near many of the houses there were avenues of the mango. Captain Lloyd possessed an elephant, and he sent it half-way with us, that we might enjoy a ride in true Indian fashion. The circumstance which surprised me most was its quiet noiseless step. The elephant is the only one at present on the island, but it is said others will be sent for.'

Another graphic description of an experience in the region in 1861 is written by Caroline de Horsey when on a cruise with her husband, Admiral Reginald de Horsey, in HMS *Mozambique*. This was probably the last time that a commanding officer in the Royal Navy was accompanied on such a voyage by his wife.

'Much of my time', she says, 'when I happened not to be ill, was passed on the bridge watching the enormous size of the waves and the pretty sea birds that hovered round us.' On course from the Cape, 'weather approaching to a hurricane burst upon us. The sun went down like a ball of sulphur-coloured fire, night closing in upon a sky as black as ink; barometer fast falling. By nine pm everything was furled, save the fore and main topsails, treble reefed and at last lowered on the cap. I went on deck about midnight and a grand scene it was. The inky sky, the foaming roaring sea, all lit up with almost a continual sheet of lightning, showing the little rag of sail and the outline of masts and rigging as clear as the day. Had I been by myself standing on the wet deck, surrounded by the wind's fierce howling, I should have been almost dead with fright; but I had a fearless heart and strong arm by my side, so I looked on till shivering with cold, I went to bed. Let no one imagine to sleep however. Everything in the ship must have fetched away, owing to our violent pitching and rolling, even the pivot gun overhead, and principally the first lieutenant, who was supposed to have pitched into his water jug, from which perilous position he was rescued by the sentry, legs uppermost. At least it sounded like this and my pretty rose water jug, that has gone half round the world in safety, took its last cruise that night, flying out of its place and lying in splinters under the bed. Then the table took charge and smashed the bulkhead. It was a night long to be remembered.'

She continues: 'When nearing Mauritius, I was up before daylight to see the mountain tops lift out of the sea, gilded by the beams of the rising sun. The mountainsides run down steep into the sea, with gorges and valleys bright with light green patches of sugarcane. A remarkable set of hillocks called 'The Cat and Kittens' shows out plainly, a reef projects for some distance past a curious mountain called the Pouce or thumb which it exactly resembles. Our moorings were off Cooper's Island, close to the shore and very convenient for landing. No sooner were we safely moored than numberless boats surrounded us, full of hospitable friends anxious that we and the officers should stay with them. I certainly give the palm to Mauritius over all the countries of the world I have visited for kindliest hospitality.

What a babble of sounds met my ears! Chinamen, Lascars, and coolies were vociferating, bellowing and quarrelling with Mauritians, English and

Dutchmen, at the same time ceaselessly running along with a curious shamble, bearing huge bags of sugar on their backs to the ships alongside. Chartering a carriage, a lean Hindoo took possession of us and proceeded to drive in a truly remarkable manner; he gesticulated, screamed, flung the reins at the horses' heads, caught them again very cleverly and finally set off with a wild whoop, quite regardless of the legs and shins of the passers-by. On our way to Reduit, the Governor's country house, we had to get out several times, the horses refusing to go on, threatening to jib and bolt down the long hill back into Port Louis. The driver adjured, threatened and coaxed in turns as if they were reasoning creatures. 'Scelerat, vaurien, vieux brigand' were the mildest terms of reproach heaped on the poor beasts.

Night here was like fairyland, a grand moon sailing high in the sky showed all nature, glorified and lit up by its pure beams. Night, too, drew out the scent of flowers, and we wandered through a leafy labyrinth, the air heavy and laden with the scent of vanilla, whose large succulent fleshy leaves climbed and clung to the larger trees, and hung over the path, its heavy pods drooping and opening as they ripened. The crop must be a profitable one as they charge a shilling in Port Louis for each fine pod.

The botanical gardens at Pamplemousses are well worth a visit, were it only to see the Madagascar lace fern, and to drink of the pure water spurting out of the traveller's tree, on an incision being made.

Caroline goes on to describe a gun salute in her honour: 'They stood on tiptoe about three feet from the gun, and having clapped the lighted brand on the touch hole, took to their heels and fled. Sailing out of Port Louis with but the whisper of the breath of wind, we glided under a crowd of canvas, straight as an arrow into the outer harbour, where a breeze caught us, which we carried all the way to the Seychelles, making a splendid straight run of five days.'

She now comes to their arrival: 'we went into the harbour of Port Victoria, Mahé, under sail, an intricate and risky passage with coral reefs on each hand, so that having cleared one, we stood directly for the other, and as we approached that altered course instantly for the next. Having wriggled in this way into the confined little harbour, we let go in a space about twice the length of the ship, where people usually hesitate even to steam in without a pilot.'

Here they found Bishop Mackenzie, 'bishop of the tribes', who had accompanied Livingstone on the Zambezi, 'who had a simple hearted idea that he must accustom himself to nautical evolutions as part of his mission of

usefulness, used to practise going aloft, and on one occasion went on to the topsail yard with the men, blowing fresh, and furled the sail. It must have been a sight, his tall, gaunt frame with black gaiters and cassock disporting on the yard.'

They stayed in the civil commissioner's bungalow, 'charmingly perched on a small height above the town, surrounded and clothed with bowers of vanilla, lanes of cinnamon, betel nut and nutmeg, interspersed with palms and mandarin oranges, a winding path shaded with fruit trees, which drooped over our heads entreating to be picked, leading to the highest spot on the island, Signal Hill, about one thousand one hundred feet.

Everything seemed to flourish here as in Paradise, without the sweat of the brow. A zigzag path took us to the other side of the island where jackfruit, mango and orange grow wild by the wayside and passed one ravine quite carpeted with pineapples. We dined on rich turtle soup, fin of turtle with palm salad – the last a cruel luxury, for it is the crown of the young coconut, and is of course the death of the tree.'

Another day: 'In the evening we ran over to Curieuse Bay in the galley, the island being appropriated alone to lepers. We were met by the Superintendent who took one of our party to visit the poor wretches officially. There are but ten now alive who have the whole beautiful island to themselves. Each one kept his or her coffin in his or her hut. It would seem like an unnecessary aggravation of their distress but it is their own desire, in consequence of one of them having once died too poor to purchase a coffin. One was thankful to shake the dust off one's feet on leaving this lovely island – far too beautiful and fertile a spot to be 'a place of skulls', shunned by the whole world.'

Vanilla planifolia, a useful as well as beautiful orchid.
Each fine pod cost a shilling at Port Louis, Mauritius, in 1860.

It had been in 1810 that the Ile de France passed from the French to the British and was renamed Mauritius. Peter Poivre had left the island, his spices had not been a success. The garden remained in French hands until Dr William Burke, Government Chief Medical Officer, was brought in as Superintendent. When he not surprisingly laid emphasis on medical plants and introduced various species used in traditional medicine, sadly the garden began to decline.

Codiaeum pictum, reproduction of a 19th C engraving,
based on a drawing by William Jackson Hooker, 1831.

Responsibility for the Garden became divided between Superintendent and Director, and Charles Telfair, a surgeon and experienced naturalist, was appointed to the former post, while the London minister responsible sent out John Newman as Director. The latter seems to have been a disaster, obtaining a concession of part of the land in order to form an experimental garden, after which he diverted some of the irrigation to his own land, exploiting the available labour to his own profit and growing vegetables and pineapples.

Newman died in 1848, and as a temporary measure, an eminent botanist of Czech origin, Dr Wenceslas Bojer – who had known Mauritius since 1821 – was appointed acting Director. He was a founder member of what became the Royal Society of Arts and Sciences and in 1837 published *Hortus Mauritianus*, a catalogue of over 2,000 plants found in Mauritius.

Charles Telfair, however was very busy about the garden and was responsible for sending crotons, *Codiaeum,* shrubs with leaves striped yellow, green and brown, to Sir William Hooker – up to then Professor of Botany at Glasgow. Crotons came originally from the Moluccas, and were studied by the Dutch botanists in the 17th C and named by Linnaeus. Telfair writes an interesting letter from Mauritius in July 1829 to Charles Fraser of the Sydney Botanic Garden: 'Mrs Telfair has sent to Mrs Darling' (the Governor's wife) 'a case of plants from our garden selected by Professor Bojer. I hope they may arrive safe. I sent you some seeds of our beautiful dahlias, which will I hope prosper with you as I know them to be fertile and will keep in a dry state for a considerable time; they are seeds of some that I raised from seed sent to me from England. I send you a good quantity that you may give them an extensive trial by distributing them among your flowering friends. The New Holland chestnut *Castanosperman australe* seeds you sent me are now beautiful plants four feet high. The gigantic lily, *Doryanthes excelsa,* our excellent friend Cunningham sent me seven or eight years ago are in high health and one of them has flowered to the great admiration and astonishment of all. The flowering stalk is at least 23 feet long, it has been in full bloom these three months past, giving most magnificent scarlet flowers coming out in a succession of flowerets. I hope most sincerely it may give seed, for it has never yet given any offshoots from the root, and I fear we may lose it unless it seeds. Pray try to send me some more.'

Things went downhill in Pamplemousses after this, and a visitor to the garden in 1838 reported that trees were dying of old age, avenues were blocked, and whole areas abandoned. No-one seemed to be working there. Bojer described the garden as being 'in a state of wilderness, overgrown with useless plants, weeds and destructive creepers'. But by this time the Secretary of State for the Colonies, Earl Grey, had taken up the case in London, and exercising his powers of appointment and patronage appointed his own head gardener – James Duncan – to be the next Director of the Royal Botanic Garden, in Mauritius. In the summer of 1849 James Duncan and his family set sail for the island.

It seems that James Duncan, who was in his late forties, was not entirely happy about his new appointment. Mauritius was known to be very expensive, and the fact that he was told that his salary, £250 pa, was liable to be reduced by up to 10% could not have been very encouraging – it is also amazing that he was supposed to pay his own fare. Earl Grey wrote to Sir William Hooker at Kew, saying that he had instructed Duncan to call upon him in case Sir William had any plants he wished Duncan to take to Mauritius. Hooker had some doubts about the appointment as well; it had been his practice to hand-pick the Superintendents of Botanic Gardens round the world, and he always chose a man with a scientific or botanic background, something which Duncan did not have; Earl Grey wrote to Sir William again explaining that with the salary offered – £250 pa – in such an expensive colony 'it would be quite impossible to expect any gentleman of scientific education to accept and hold the appointment, also that the services of such a gentleman are not in fact required. What is wanted, as I learn from persons well acquainted with the island is a good practical cultivator, there being in the Committee by which the garden is superintended two or three gentlemen of much scientific knowledge' (no doubt referring to Dr Bojer), 'whatever is wanted in this respect.'

Duncan himself also wrote to Hooker thanking him for the interest he had taken in the appointment, but told him that he had learned that his passage money was not going to be paid in Britain, and could Hooker help by sending letters to officials in Mauritius on his behalf? Duncan added: 'After I reach the island and get a little settled I hope to have the pleasure of occasionally writing to you'. Duncan sailed with his family and two glazed Wardian cases (cases invented by Nathaniel Ward in 1831, especially for plant travel) holding ten varieties of rose and a dozen vines, both white and black, including chasselas, muscat and frontignan. The journey in a sailing ship took five months and when ten years later James corresponded with Kew about a proposed assistant, he strongly recommended that the new man should travel on a steamer and not on a sailing boat: 'On board these steamers there is plenty of good provisions, medical attendance, etc and these things at sea are of very great importance to health and comfort.'

It was almost a year before James Duncan wrote a full report to Earl Grey on what he found in the Botanic Gardens on his arrival at the end of December 1849. But before this he wrote a rather desperate letter to the Colonial Secretary: 'I respectfully beg to represent to you that the tools belonging to the Garden are becoming much worn. Some of them are almost useless. I therefore beg that those articles which are worthy of it may be repaired and new ones supplied in their place…I herewith enclose a list…'

Among other requirements he mentions garden pots and frames for propagation, large stone hammers, 6 watering pots needing new bottoms, 100 garden pots, 20 hoes, 12 bill hooks, sickles, scythes, saws, and pruning knives. The estimate for his modest requirements came to £43 11s 10d. He was to be allowed to spend £15!

His detailed report of the state of the garden to Earl Grey left nothing out, nor did his description of the 50 acres of land and water, some of it overflowed by a stream: 'a great part of it is as complete a jungle as could be found in any native forest'. This must have been a shock to Duncan, and he describes how he began by opening some walks where nutmeg and cloves and other fruits had been planted, but where the native self-sown plants had been allowed 'to overtop and all but destroy them'. There had been a public road which ran alongside the garden but when the bridge – part of the road – was carried away by a flood, the road was diverted through the garden; the bridge had never been rebuilt 'so the road divides the garden in two, a great inconvenience, were the garden to be again put in proper order.'

There were no boundaries to the garden, not even a gate at the entrance; the walks could not be used in wet weather since they had never been stoned or gravelled, and no plant had ever been named or numbered.

He goes on to say how useful a promenade would be for the public, who were very fond of planting and ornamenting their places if they could get plants – 'they long for the Garden to be put in order again.' He was upset to find that: 'The worst abuses of the Garden are from some evilly disposed people who have free access to the garden from all parts and at all times. If I plant a new or choice plant in a few days it is cut to pieces, so it is quite disheartening to attempt doing anything at present ; I have a small spot of ground near my house, where I am obliged to keep all my choice little plants'.

One notes that his first action, when conditions allowed, was to surround the garden with an impenetrable hedge of Madagascar plum, *Flacourtia Ramontchi.* There was no nursery on the island, so the inhabitants came to the garden to get plants or seeds. Duncan continues: 'I have distributed upwards of 1,000 plants per month ever since I came here, besides cases that have been sent full of plants to Calcutta, Bombay, The Cape, Port Natal, Hobart Town and Sydney, as vessels sail from this port to nearly every part of the world with sugar, this would be an excellent central depot for plants as they could be afterwards sent to any Colony – all tropical plants would grow well here, in this Garden.'

He makes very reasonable suggestions as to the number of workmen he would require, and as the prison is only two miles from the garden 'a great number of the Malabar prisoners could be used for cutting down trees and trenching the ground – their labour would be at no additional expense – at present I believe they hardly know how to employ them.' He adds: 'Should the above suggestions be approved and carried out, which could be done at a small expense, this Garden, instead of being a disgrace to the Crown and the Colony would soon be a credit to both.'

Transport was another urgent requirement: two mules and a cart should be allowed for the use of the Garden, at present if I have to send away a case of plants, if I cannot borrow a mule and cart I must pay 7/6d out of my own pocket to hire one and take it to town. At present everything from the Garden must be carried on men's heads, which is a great waste of time and labour'.

He also requests a proper assistant to help him with his many duties, propagating, sorting and packing plants, dealing with correspondence 'is more than I can well accomplish (a number of people are always asking me to go and see their places and give them my advice, but I have little time and no conveyance allowed me.)'

Duncan then writes a letter to Sir William Hooker in a less formal tone: 'I make no doubt but you will have been expecting to hear from me some little time back but really ever since I came here I have had but little time and moreover I felt so disgusted with the Garden that I did not know what to think

or say about it. I am sure you have no idea of the wretched state it is in' …
(and he goes into the same details). He asks Sir William to use his influence
with Earl Grey to recommend the garden being restored to its original state of
beauty and usefulness, and to get the restoration put on a different footing
altogether: 'The expense of doing so would not be great and many of the
inhabitants are very anxious it should be done.'

He describes the plants he is sending to Sir William in a box about three
feet long on board the *Lord Haddo*, in the care of Captain Smith, a friend of
his. This contains 'a bottle of preserved nutmegs, a scape in fruit, and also one
in flower of the *Sagus Ruffia*, a fruit with the seeds of *Lecythis Minor*, a seedpod
of *Beaumontia Grandiflora*, a Spath with the flower not opened and one in
fruit of *Euterpe oleracea* and a white Ants nest, all of which I hope will be useful
for your Museum. Also a lot of seeds perhaps you will find something
interesting among them. As other things are to be got I will send you more.'
He regrets that he has not yet managed to get the 'double cocoa-nuts' for
rearing for him – this must be the *Coco-de-mer* from the Seychelles. He also
regrets that most of the plants sent out by Sir William with him have died,
owing to the length of the voyage and the difficulties on arrival, but hopes 'to
be better prepared when you send again, which I hope you will often do. I will
return your case full sometime during the summer, by that time I hope to have
had time to visit the hills and get some of the curious plants'.

Duncan is most anxious that Sir William might help him to improve his
relations with Mr Bojer, whom he says could be most helpful to him by being
more communicative, as there are many plants with which he is unacquainted, and Mr Bojer, who has only visited the garden once since Duncan arrived,
refused to make a tour of it with him – 'he is very distant and seems to be a
very selfish man.' Duncan believes that Bojer had intended to buy the garden
if, as he hoped, it came up for sale, and then open a hotel and make a sort of
tea garden. He adds: 'I would be glad if Mr Bojer would help me for a while
as he would enable me to do my duty much better. If not I will send you some
dried specimens among the plants I am unacquainted with…and if you have
any books that you can spare that will assist me pray send them'.

He finishes by describing the Malabar Indians, 19 of whom are his allowance
of labour for 50 acres of garden. 'They are a very lazy set of men and very awkward;
many of them never worked until they were brought here; they require to be
constantly watched otherwise they will do nothing, they are also terrible thieves.'

A year later poor James is driven to have another go at the Colonial Secretary. He writes that he is most surprised at the opinion expressed in the Finance Committee's report that they do not consider the use of the botanical garden to the colony commensurate with the expense of its maintenance, and suggesting that an enquiry be made into the best means of making it more useful. He wonders whether the gentlemen composing the Committee are aware of the extent to which the botanical garden is useful as a nursery for raising young plants for the colony, and he informs them that during the last twelve months over 16,000 plants have been issued from the garden to the inhabitants of the colony as well as a large quantity of seeds. A number of plants and seeds have also been exchanged with other colonies. 'James continues: 'considering the garden only in the light of a nursery for distributing plants and seed it must be allowed to have been of very great service. As well as this it spreads a taste for cultivating plants and fruits which must add to the comforts and enjoyments and what is as of much importance is the morals of inhabitants generally, and I therefore beg to differ from the gentlemen composing the Committee when they say that its utility to the Colony is not commensurate with the expense of its maintenance'.

This is his moment and he seizes it, by saying how much he could do if he had more men and a travelling allowance for keeping a horse; that the garden should be properly fenced with a gate at the entrance and a lodge for a gatekeeper to live in; that the public road should be turned back to its former route and the bridge rebuilt; and that the canal – which always overflows into the garden when it floods after heavy rains – should be cleared and enlarged, and that some other ponds also require cleaning out. He also recommends that 'a large portion of the garden should be cleared of the useless bushes growing on it, the ground trenched and replanted with a fresh collection of plants, a portion might be planted out with flowering plants with which the visitors are acquiring a great taste; the walks could be gravelled with broken stones which could be broken on the spot by the prisoners, almost free of expense'. And he hasn't finished yet, he thinks that: 'no person should be allowed to enter or depart from the enclosed area but by one entrance and that the attention of the police might be called to this, especially on Sundays. A carpenter is much needed for making and repairing plant cases, a few new cases would cost as much as a carpenter's pay for the year; the timber could be used from old boxes and the plentiful supply of useless trees; the carpenter could also keep up the buildings, sheds etc and sharpen the labourers tools.' And lastly he adds that: 'All the plants could be numbered and a catalogue compiled.'

He finishes his broadside by saying that if the above suggestions were carried out, they would add very much to the usefulness as well as the beauty of the garden and the additional expense would be trifling – just the gatekeeper and the carpenter and the regular assistance of a band of prisoners: 'In a few years the garden would not only be as now a place of recreation and a nursery for the inhabitants of the colony, but become better known and appreciated abroad and tend considerably to enrich the vegetable resources of this beautiful and fertile island.'

James Duncan certainly made an impact this time – members of the Finance Committee made an early visit to the garden (no doubt driven by the vision of its success raising the moral tone of the island), and reported that the site had much improved under James Duncan's charge, while recommending nearly all the requests made, though the bridge restoration costing £200 was too much for them at that stage.

Duncan's next letter to Sir William is more cheerful; he explains that when he first landed, the garden was very unpopular with the public who felt it was so badly kept it was not worth coming to see, so by supplying their wants of plants and trees he could somewhat redeem its good name. 'I am now beginning to feel my way a little here, when I first arrived a great number of plants were strangers to me and I did not understand the language commonly spoken here, a sort of broken French called Creole; now I can jabber away a good deal'.

The Council then voted six more Malabars for the garden and a band of prisoners to get the area enclosed, with a gate to be built and a porter to take charge of it. Things were certainly looking up. As Duncan sends some rare plants to Hooker, he adds: 'You will perhaps laugh at my pots but necessity they say is the mother of invention – when I came here I had not got a single garden pot nor would the Government give me any for a long time so I set to work and made bamboo pots, and they are much better than small clay pots for hot climates as they do not absorb the heat so much'.

It was not only to Kew that James was sending plants, he despatched a case of seeds to Calcutta, and 20 specimens to Sydney – which returned 24 including palms, ferns, cycads and orchids, as well as Australian trees such as the Norfolk Island pine and the Moreton Bay chestnut. There were also plant exchanges with Ferdinand von Mueller – whom we come to later – of the Melbourne Botanic Garden.

Things were going much better for the next few years, though the death of his younger son of fever at eighteen years was a terrible blow.

James Duncan spent fifteen years completely rebuilding the Royal Botanic Gardens in Mauritius from the destitute remains he found and described in his letters home to its wonderful revival. It is an astonishing achievement for an untravelled and unsophisticated Victorian gardener from Scotland who found himself transplanted to and responsible for creating a beautiful tropical garden for future generations.

Robert Duncan's excellent account of his ancestor's career (*James Duncan and the Garden of Mauritius*) tells the whole story, and quotes from the American Consul Nicolas Pike's description of the garden, written about four years after James Duncan retired, and during the five years that he lived on the island. Pike calls it 'the favourite resort of the citizens of Port Louis'.

He writes of how he enters by the newly installed iron gates – the result of Duncan's frequent requests – and 'as far as the eye can see, a long straight avenue extends, thickly lined on each side by the Mauritius Palm, and towering above them to a great height the slender stems of the areca nut palm, with its small tuft of feathery leaves forming its crown. In the far distance in the centre of the avenue is an obelisk erected to the memory of those who have introduced into Mauritius either useful plants or animals; round this monument are some fine specimens of a rare and beautiful palm the *Latania aurea* of Rodrigues, from which the natives of that island build their houses with the outer slabs of its trunk, making the rafters of its leaf stalks which sometimes attain the length of six to ten feet and thatch them with its leaves.

From the obelisk we pass over a little bridge, spanning a clear stream, so densely shaded by the Travellers Tree and others that it is impervious to the sun at noonday, and gives a better idea of tropical scenery than any other part of the garden. Here and there are clumps of feathery bamboo, which partly conceal little pavilions with seats and tables, where you may breakfast or dine quite undisturbed by passers-by.' He goes on to describe a small lake, 'full of blue and white lotus plants, and close by a larger lake with islands and bridges; there are interesting walks shaded by such trees as the *Lecythis minor* with large fruits and the Illipie tree whose fruits yield oil used for lamps and also the Teak tree. In the shade of these trees flower beds are planted with begonias, fuchsias, gloxinias and many others and everywhere are seats for visitors to rest and admire the spectacular views of the mountains beyond.'

Pike is clearly enraptured by the wonderful variety not only of tropical flowers but also of some honeysuckle and roses here and there which remind him of home. 'Round the Garden Director's house is a verandah completely hidden by bougainvillea, the scarlet ipomoeia and monster passion flowers; nearby this lush exhibition lies the Fernery, which contains many hundreds of ferns and orchids, situated on a rocky bank with a sparkling stream at its foot. Here also is the famous Coco-de-Mer from the Seychelles with its amazing twin nuts.'

James Duncan was not a botanist and seems not to have had the advice and assistance he sought from M Bojer; the catalogue he made of the plants in the garden reflect his horticultural rather than scientific background. His descendant and biographer writes : 'Duncan was undoubtedly at the receiving end of academic snobbery, as demonstrated by his entry in the historical intro-duction to the *Flora* written by the arch-Kewite and Hooker lackey JG Baker which consists of a meagre five lines – a reference to his catalogue and the single sentence 'Duncan was the predecessor of Mr Horne'. By contrast the Bohemian Bojer, a *bone fide* botanist, gets 28 lines in the same work.' It is of note that 'the Hooker lackey', Mr Baker, wrote the *Flora of Mauritius and the Seychelles* (referred to) without once visiting those same islands.

John Horne was another hand-picked botanist sent out from Kew in 1861, attached to the department of Works and Forests, and appointed as assistant to Duncan, eventually becoming Director of the Garden, when the latter retired in 1864. Horne was a keen plant hunter, and went off to the Seychelles Islands spending three months there investigating the flora. He writes enthusiastically to Hooker in November 1874: 'All these islands I travelled over, and searched carefully and minutely, visiting every locality where a new or rare plant might be found, never allowing my thoughts to deceive me. I can assure you I worked very hard knocking up the men that were with me as guides several times but enjoyed my work very much, and considerably improved my health notwithstanding fatigues and frequent wettings.'

He collected about three hundred species, some of which he had seen before on a previous tour, although most of them were new to him and he promised to send them off to Kew by the next mail, hoping that they would be interesting geographically.

Horne is surprised to note that the Seychelles flora have more affinities to those of Madagascar, East Africa, South India, the Malay Islands and Polynesia than to those of Mauritius or Bourbon and that he has yet to discover a genus, or even a species, which is only found in the Seychelles and the last two named places. He thinks the geological formations of the islands may have something to do with the distribution of plants, the Seychelles being granitic.

Here I break off briefly, reminded of my own visit to the Seychelles in 2004; the huge boulders of pink granite lay decorously about the islands and the beaches. On Praslin grows the most famous unique plant, the Coco-de-Mer – a huge tourist attraction for its extraordinary, double seeds; these can weigh up to 20 kg and are the world's largest and heaviest. The leaves also hold the record and can be 10m long x 4.5 m wide, while the flowers are the biggest of any palm.

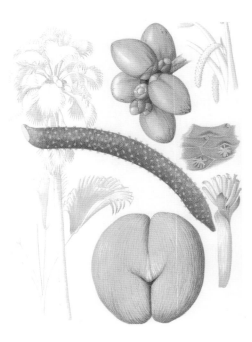

The Coco-de-Mer – its huge double seeds can weigh up to 20kg. Now a famous Seychelles tourist attraction and indigenous to the Vallée de Mai which, in 1881, General Gordon of Khartoum described its background as the original Garden of Eden.

The Coco-de-Mer leaves hold the record and can be up to 10m long x 4.5m wide.

To walk through the Vallée de Mai, the conservation area specially reserved for these palms on the island of Praslin, is an experience not to be missed – though it is advisable to keep an eye open for any of the seeds ripe enough to fall, as, from a height of 34m, its tallest, you could have a nasty bump.

I was visiting the Seychelles in the most comfortable means of transport, which is of course a ship. I had found a small French cruise ship, which provided for my every indulgence, called *Le Ponant,* a three-masted sailing vessel exploring all the islands for a week – but so long a flight for so short a cruise seemed absurd, so I decided to do the whole voyage twice. This gave me the chance of spending more time sitting on deck and luxuriating in that pleasure, if I decided an island did not rate a second visit – very large tortoises for instance need only be admired once.

Aride was my favourite island (now administered by the Royal Society for Nature Conservation) where an Englishman, Christopher Cadbury (son of the chocolate family), bought the island in 1973 and completely cleared it of predators, so the birds – about ten species of seabirds – can nest in total safety under the roots of trees, which appears to be their choice. Seabirds sometimes lay their eggs on a rather twiglike branch, where they balance, sitting on the eggs, and hatching out the nestlings at great peril. One walks round this exotic island where flocks of elegant frigate birds, the lesser and greater frigates, glide on the thermals or attack returning sea birds; these are then forced to

Among the many sea birds that nest safely on the ground in Aride are shearwaters, sooty terns and puffins.

regurgitate their catch, which the acrobatic frigates swoop to retrieve. The latter only roost on Aride – choosing a nearby island, Aldabra, for their exclusive breeding ground.

One of the reasons for choosing this cruise was the huge attraction of the visit to Aride, where Wright's Gardenia, now only found on this island, is to be seen. I had great difficulty in finding out about Edward Percival Wright, Professor of Botany in Dublin, who visited the island and first found the gardenia in 1867. Horne found it in Praslin in 1871 and in Mahé 1874, but it seems the dreaded scale insect has reduced its habitat to Aride. I had been looking forward to tracking it down from the beginning of the cruise, and the Seychelloise naturalist, Gemma, who came with us, told me that its rather pernickety habit was only to flower precisely ten days after rain. Gemma signalled ahead to see if our visit was likely to coincide with its delicate require-ments - there had been rain, and a local inspection having taken place, one flower had come out and was reported visible on a bush halfway up the mountain, Gros la Tête.

One or two more passengers were now interested in Wright's Gardenia so we set off for what was supposed to be about a twenty minute climb. However after about half an hour of very slippery boulders, covered in dead leaves, I enquired if we were half way. Another half hour of arduous climb later – and there it was. I note in my diary when I returned: 'Well I have seen it, so honour

'Worthy of an arduous climb' – the endangered Wright's gardenia which was once fairly common in the Seychelles but now only found on the island of Aride.

is satisfied. There was just this one rather sad little flower, white, as expected but seemed to have very faint pink markings; after a massive climb up, which took over an hour, it was worse going down – even with Gemma's help. How I didn't break both ankles I will never know.' (I had just got over breaking one, so was rather aware of the peril.)

Wright describes his gardenia in a privately printed letter addressed to the President of the University Board (Transactions of the Royal Irish Academy XX1V (1871). After his botanical description, mostly in Latin, he translates the plant as: 'A low tree or shrub three to seven feet high, the flowers, five petalled, white, sprinkled with brownish black. This species, which I believe to be undescribed grows in some quantities on Ile Aride. This is one of the smallest islands of the group and is situated to the north-east of Praslin. The island is little more than a collection of large granite rocks. On the side opposite Praslin there is a level portion of very rich ground, which is cultivated, but otherwise the island is altogether in possession of countless myriads of birds and has a desolate and arid look. The Gardenia grows in hollow places between granite boulders. It was in full flower in the month of October, but the fruit in all stages hung at the same time from the branches.'

Horne's next adventure was in 1877 when he accepted an invitation from Sir Arthur Gordon, then Governor of Fiji, to visit those islands, which had become a Crown Colony in 1874; he spent a year's leave exploring the archipelago, which comprises about 840 islands of which only 100 are inhabited. He had been asked to study in particular the varieties of sugarcane, the staple product, and in 1880 published his account of *A Year in Fiji or An Inquiry into the Botanical, Agricultural and Economical Resources of the Colony.*

A few extracts may be of interest. Travelling by canoe up the river Rewa he says: 'I was delightfully surprised with the fertility of the land, the size of the river, the fine scenery and the luxuriance of the cultivated sugarcanes.' He gleaned useful information respecting the peculiarities of each of the twenty different kinds he found, samples of which he sent to Mauritius in 16 Wardian cases. On the banks of this river and its affluent streams, including the deltas formed by its several mouths, 'there are about 400 square miles of land unrivalled in quality especially well adapted for growing cane, most of it belonging to settlers, some of whom cultivate sugarcanes, but others do not because they cannot get their canes crushed, the sugar mills being either insufficient or too far away.' Horne found that the want of a mill or the means to purchase one was a common hindrance to cultivation.

Horne also describes the situation as regards labourers: 'These are mostly obtained from the New Hebrides, Solomon Islands etc and are engaged for three years; they prefer payment in kind to money as they do not understand its value.' He says they are strong hardy labourers, 'but utter savages when they land in Fiji; they have to be taught everything and require a good deal of breaking in before they are useful. They are extremely lazy and the expense of overseeing them is very great, besides their work is generally badly done. Their only reasons for expatriating themselves for a few years are scarcity of food, quarrels, cruel inter-tribal wars, and above all a desire to obtain fire-arms. To obtain cheap and good labourers, the Government of Fiji have arranged with the Government of India to get coolies from there, so with India to draw upon no planter who possesses means, need, in Fiji, fear the want of labourers to cultivate his fields.'

John Horne strongly recommended that: 'In a new colony like Fiji a Botanic Garden would be of the greatest importance and utility, independently of the knowledge of botany as a science, and the taste for plant culture which it would foster and diffuse in the colony and would be highly popular with the settlers. He adds that: 'reliable practical information on tropical cultivation is much needed in Fiji, most of the settlers know next to nothing about the husbandry of sugarcane, coffee, tea, cinchona and other products of the tropics'.

He also found that 'the forest of Fiji contained many valuable timber trees' and recommends that in addition, the soil and climate would greatly favour the growth and bring to perfection the salvian products of other tropical countries, such as teak, ebony, sal, mahogany etc and suggests that growing them in a semi-wild state would be 'highly remunerative'.

Covering the unwooded areas with timber would benefit the state of the soil as the dense mists and heavy showers seldom descend to these low-lying plains and valleys. This work was approved, and by 1905 a large number of exotic trees were already established.

The Suva Botanical Gardens, as they are called, occupies the site of the original Fijian town of Suva. In 1919 the Curator of the Museum stated that: 'Twenty five years ago the moat and rampart were practically intact, but there are now no traces of them left, nothing to tell the visitor that this was once a busy fortified town, nor that in 1843 it was burned, and was the scene of one of the fiercest and bloodiest fights in Fijian history. Founded in 1820 by a powerful chief with nearly a thousand warriors, it was attacked and burned in 1843 and many of its inhabitants were killed and eaten.'

John Horne is best known for his work, *A Year in Fiji,* just described but this volume also contained valuable Appendices which comprise the author's recommendations as to India rubber, sandalwood and general forest matters, with a list of the species known to occur on the islands – many new species with mere names – which were in part taken up by later writers. The total number of specimens sent by Mr Horne to the Royal Botanic Gardens Kew, between 1865 and 1883, amounted to nearly 3,000. On retiring from the Colonial Service he settled in Jersey, where he died in 1905.

CHAPTER 6

The Peradeniya Botanic Garden, Ceylon

Henry Cave, writing in the late 1800s, describes arriving at first light in Colombo Harbour, Ceylon, or Sri Lanka as it is now called. This vividly recalled my last visit, made to the island on our journey home to England after three years in the service of the Royal Navy in Singapore. He writes: 'We look ahead and behold the mountain zone 'where the tea comes from', rising in one mighty upheaval from the plains of Ceylon, capped in the centre by the venerable peak, named after our first parent (Adam's Peak). The mists are as yet lying in the valleys, and the cool blue tones above them give us the true contour of those fertile mountains upon which millions of tea bushes are flourishing. Here we get the best idea of the formation of those highlands, whose deep ravines and grassy plains, dense forests and open valleys, gentle streams and roaring cataracts, which we shall see in the full detail of close inspection'. This gives one a good idea of what to expect in this beautiful island of contrasting countryside.

Travelling once more in one of Her Majesty's trooper ships, we (myself, husband and three children between the ages of six and two) had decided to break the journey in Ceylon, renting a house up in the hills of Diayatalawa for a month, and then catching the next trooper home. It was going to be Christmas on board for the second half of the journey, and the Army – who used to run troopships – were extremely generous in their provisions, which included festivities, turkey, decorations, and even presents. Returning to a wintry England, no Chinese servants, thick clothes and the kitchen sink – it was good to luxuriate in a final free holiday.

There have been gardens in Ceylon since 1371 under the rule of the early Kings of Kandi, the greater part of the land being a royal 'demesne'. However in the 17th C, The Dutch were the first to make a botanic garden in Ceylon, which they chose to create in Slave Island, Colombo; this took its name from the Dutch East India Company slaves who lived and worked there. This was the idea of Paul Hermann, Chief Medical Officer in the company's service in Ceylon from 1672-1677, who became interested in botanical research in the island, collecting plants in the Maritime Province, and making notes on their uses. When he left Ceylon, Hermann became Professor of Botany at Leyden, Holland, and published some drawings and descriptions of Ceylonese plants.

In 1745 Hermann's Ceylon Herbarium came into the hands of Linnaeus, who examined and described all the specimens which had survived, and in 1747 published an account of them under the title *Flora Zeylanica*. In this work, the plants are arranged according to the system of classification which Linnaeus had recently proposed. Thus Ceylon has the honour of possessing one of the earliest Floras based on the Linnean system, and written by the great man himself.

Ceylon came into British hands in 1796, but it was not until 1810 that Sir Joseph Banks, President of the Royal Society, suggested and drew up plans for a proper botanical garden in Ceylon, named Kew, and also on Slave Island. Banks wrote to William Kerr (one of his faithful plant collectors based in Canton, China) to inform him that the King (George III) had agreed to the founding of a botanical garden in Ceylon, and that he had been appointed Superintendent there in recognition of his diligence at Canton and the many valuable plant additions to Kew he had provided. This was to be rewarded by a liberal salary and a retirement pension that Banks had secured for him from the King, during the last months of Banks' and the King's working association, which deteriorated with the King's illness.

The site on Slave Island was soon discovered to be liable to floods, so in 1813 the garden was moved to Kalutara for the reception of economic plants which could be cultivated there on a larger scale than on Slave Island. Among Kerr's duties he was instructed to 'make discoveries in Botany and form a Herbarium of dried plants for the future use of the establishment'. Kerr died in 1814, but lived long enough to move the garden again and establish it at Peradeniya, Kandi.

Mr Alexander Moon – 'a smart young man trained at Kew' – was selected by Sir Joseph Banks to succeed him, and entered on his new career at the very good salary of £512 per annum. On his journey out to Ceylon in HMS *Minden* he was landed at Gibraltar, while the battleship attended to some action against the pirates of Algeria. Moon took the opportunity to collect plants and seed in southern Spain and Spanish Morocco, sending them off to Banks before rejoining the *Minden* for Ceylon.

This 'indefatigable personage', as he was described, was responsible for the first planning out of the garden and the making of roads within it. For the next eight years he managed to range widely over the island, and his last letter to Banks (received just before Banks died) listed 373 kinds of seed for Kew and some fifty skins of birds and mammals for the British Museum. He made vast collections of specimens for his herbarium, and eventually *Moon's Catalogue of the Indigenous and Exotic Plants growing in Ceylon* was published in 1824, and included botanical and native names of 1,127 plants which he found in the island.

Moon was told that he should give attention to 'the growth of coffee which His Excellency, the Governor has particularly at heart to see established throughout the island'. Some areas of the garden were planted with coffee and considerable plantations were established within its vicinity.

After Moon's death from fever in 1825, a succession of more or less unqualified persons followed him and for nearly twenty years the garden made no progress, being used chiefly for growing coffee, jack fruit and coconuts for sale by the Government, while botanical science was completely neglected. There was however a long line of eminent amateur botanists who had studied the Ceylon flora and contributed considerably to the collections, before, during and after this flat period. Moon's vast herbarium – requiring ten carts to carry it – was now removed to the care of Dr Wight, botanist at Madras in India. Dr Wight had been asked by the then Governor of Ceylon to revise Moon's collections and make a catalogue of them – to which he readily agreed, and began by arranging the plants in natural orders, but was horrified to find that few of them were even labelled, and his task was to 'glue down and arrange between two and three thousand species now occupying loose sheets in the collection'.

In August 1844 Dr George Gardner, Surgeon, FLS, was selected by Sir William Hooker, by then Director of The Royal Botanic Gardens, Kew, and appointed Superintendent of the Royal Botanic Garden, Peradeniya, Kandy. He had been a travelling botanist in Brazil and Mauritius, his passion being to collect and describe native plants. Gardner now threw himself energetically into the work of investigating the Ceylon flora.

Meanwhile, Captain JG Champion of the 95th Regiment (one of the eminent amateur botanists of great ability who was in Ceylon from 1838 to 1847) wrote to the Colonial Secretary regarding the herbarium and recorded that he had sent to Dr Wight 'between 6 and 700 of the Flora of the interior and Galle, numbered to correspond with my own collection, many valuable plants which I hope may prove entirely new.' Champion received a letter from Sir William Hooker in which he says: 'Mr Gardner's arrival would in a measure have been an answer to your principal query, viz. respecting the names of General Walker's Ceylon Plants (General/Colonel and Mrs GW Walker were foremost of the amateur botanists) for the proposed Catalogue; Mr Gardner himself took out a full set of these plants with him, and great as the difficulty is in making a list of plants where so many are new or rare, depend upon it they can be done nowhere so well as by a botanist such as Gardner *in the Country*. Indeed my most urgent advice would be that no Catalogue be prepared till Mr Gardner is conscious that such a thing can be done in a way that would not discredit the authors and the Garden.'

On taking up his appointment in August 1844, Gardner wrote a report to the Governor: 'In doing myself the honour to lay before his Excellency the Governor a statement of the condition in which I found the Royal Botanic Garden at Peradeniya, on my taking over the charge of it on May last'. He begins with what he considers will be his duty, the improvements he means to make and the aim and object of a Colonial Botanic Garden:

'Besides the staple articles cultivated at present for commercial purposes such as coffee, sugar, cinnamon, cotton there are many other productions peculiar to tropical Countries which might be cultivated on a large scale in the island, not only with profit to the Agriculturist, but as a source of increase to the public revenue. A Colonial Botanic Garden should be allowed the means of introducing from other Countries the best qualities of fruits, vegetables and other useful productions, and be a nursery for their propagation, their amelioration and their diffusion throughout the Colony. As the *dulce* ought always to go hand in hand with the *utile,* the production of ornamental Exotic Herbaceous plants, shrubs and trees and their dispersion among the Colonists has always been considered among the great objects of such a Garden as the one at Peradeniya. Nothing contributes more to the health of those who are obliged to reside in towns than the existence of public *promenades à cheval* as well as *au pied*.

These are most important matters, which relate to the benefit of the Colony itself, but the Mother Country has claims on her Colonial Botanic Gardens which do not seem to be understood here, and which can only be understood by those who have devoted their lives to scientific pursuit.'

He notes that: 'for the last three hundred years the great desire of their promoters has been to introduce into them as many as possible of the vegetable productions of other countries. Not for their beauty and utility alone, but to ascertain the various modifications of their structure and functions...all these investigations are fraught with much interest to a philosophic mind; it is only by multiplying researches that knowledge can be increased.'

He points out that almost all that has been discovered in England has been by private means, but 'that it is only an institution maintained at the public expense which is able to undertake in an efficient manner the investigation of such matters.'

But now: 'The Royal Botanic Garden at Kew, which for the last twenty years (since Banks and the King died in 1820) have been a disgrace to the nation, have lately been put under the direction of Sir WJ Hooker, one of the most accomplished Botanists of Europe; and all who have the pleasure of knowing him feel satisfied that if much be required of him much will be accomplished by his great talents and unwearied industry.'

Gardner was surprised to find that of all the British possessions in India the vegetation of Ceylon is the least known to the botanists of Europe 'and most of what is known is the result of the investigations of a lady – the accomplished and indefatigable Mrs Col. Walker.' He thinks the reason for this is the liberality of the East India Company, who have supported numerous collectors and draughtsmen, under the direction of the Superintendents: 'always well educated medical men, passionately devoted to the furtherance of their science.' He wishes to carry out scientific experiments on the environment, and congratulates Mr Moon for his judgment in choosing the site and his taste in laying out the grounds. His further intention is to make experiments in the use of manures, particularly guano which has lately been found to be successful in Great Britain – 'half a ton of guano would go a great length.'

Now he comes to the state of the Garden: 'On my arrival at Peradeniya I found nearly all the principal borders and other parts overrun with white-ant hills, most of them several feet in height, very offensive to the eye as well as injurious to the plants.' He employed a number of men to root them out and destroy any that reappeared. Many of the paths were overrun with weeds and needed to be cleared and relaid with gravel; the main one he intended to keep up was 'the great central one down to the river, and from thence up the stream to the upper part of the Garden, so that there may be a carriage drive round at least the greater half of the whole grounds.'

Gardner had been informed that a small but valuable collection of Ceylon plants, many of them from Nuwera Eilia and other elevated parts of the island, had been presented to the garden and he eventually found them in an old box half devoured by rats; no-one could be blamed for this misfortune, because there was no safe place connected to the garden where they could have been housed. Dr Gardner notes that he intends that 'before Dr Wight returns the Ceylon Herbarium from Madras that a proper building will be prepared for its reception. It is with sorrow I make the remark that the room which serves as an office for the Clerk, as well as for a place to keep specimens and seed is so damp naturally and so pervious to rain, that nothing can be kept dry in it.'

A valuable chemical apparatus had recently been added to the garden for the purpose of analysing soils, but only part of it could be unpacked there being nowhere else to put it, and quite a number of articles belonging to the garden were at present housed in part of the Superintendent's own residence. The few books, which had been collected by Moon – some of great value, had been allowed to become completely ruined. One of his main concerns was to have all the plants in the garden correctly labelled: 'The difficulty and labour of determining the name of a plant that one has not before seen is much greater than is generally supposed. As about 100,000 species of plants are now described in books, it requires, beyond the labour, a very extensive library; that which belongs to the garden is far too limited for such a purpose. I have however, brought out with me from England, at a very great personal expense my own Library, which is a very perfect working one, as well as an Herbarium of nearly 20,000 species of dried plants from all parts of the world; and with the use of these, I trust to be able to go on steadily with the work of determining not only the plants in the garden, but those of the island generally.'

Another important task Gardner sees ahead of him is to collect the interesting varieties of indigenous trees from the forests, where much of the country has been cleared for the spread of cultivation, and make an *arboretum* which would be left in grass.

Mr Gardner did not approve when he found on his arrival that 'a large portion of the Botanic Garden had been converted into a market garden, in which one third of the labourers allowed for the entire operations were daily occupied – 'indeed I may say that at that period nearly double the number mentioned were engaged in this department; as the drought was then excessive and the watercourse out of repair, ten men were constantly occupied in carrying water from the river; the greater part of which was used in the kitchen garden. I likewise found that another man with a bullock cart was daily sent to Kandy with vegetables etc for sale, the returns for which seldom exceeded a shilling or two, and not infrequently the paltry sum of ninepence. To this I have put a stop, as I consider it detrimental to the purpose for which the garden was originally intended, and certainly derogatory not only to the dignity of an institution maintained by the British Government but to science.'

In the nursery department he found plenty to do. There was a market for most of the useful plants and particularly for the nutmeg; of the few mature nutmeg trees growing there he could expect five or six hundreds seeds all of which were bespoke, but no small plants were to be found. Of the three clove trees he hoped for a yield of 2,000 plants; there were plenty of pepper trees. He had several large orders for coffee plants which could not be supplied, so 'he caused a nursery to be prepared into which about 50,000 seedlings have already been planted. He gives a long list of fruits – both indigenous and imported – also young trees which were to be propagated.

Gardner proposed to make a small nursery up in the hills of Nuwera Eilia where he could establish, propagate and naturalise plants from Europe in the quasi-European climate of the hills; this would also 'be useful as a depot for Hill plants of the country previous to their being sent back to Europe.' This became the famous and beautiful Hakgalla Garden, the seat of acclimatisation of plants from temperate lands outside the tropics and from the tropical heights of other countries. Here also the important work of extending and improving the various species of plants was carried out in order that the natural resources of the country might be utilised to the best advantage. In this place of practical science agricultural theories were translated into actual fact, and provided invaluable material for the enterprise and speculation of the colonist.

Showing a rather charming aspect of George Gardner's character, I include this note which he adds to his report: 'I cannot conclude this part of my report without taking notice of the very small salary allowance to the draughtsman – only £3 a month. His equal as botanical artist I am certain does not exist in India; he is a diligent and faithful servant to the institution for upwards of twenty years. I trust that measures will be taken to render his position more comfortable from a pecuniary point of view.'

George Gardner took very seriously the role of Peradeniya in enhancing the economic value of plants. The scientific era of the garden may be said to have begun with his fortunate appointment.

The story of coffee in Ceylon became quite another saga; it was probably introduced into the colony from Java by the Dutch, but Moon – on the instruction of the Governor in 1822 – had been responsible for promoting its growth.

From a despatch dated July 5 1848, Viscount Torrington writes from Queen's House, Colombo, to Earl Grey (Colonial Secretary). 'I have alluded to the ravages produced by rats (in the coffee plantations) and the still more formidable destruction caused by the invasion of the coffee bug. With regard to the latter I now send the reports made to me by Dr Gardner, from which your Lordship will perceive the extent of danger to be apprehended from this visitation and the mystery which still invests the causes of its coming.' He notes that the production of coffee in a single season, which should have been 2,000 cwt, fell suddenly to 700 cwt, caused in a few months by the deadly bug.

These disasters, however, were not the only causes of the decline. He continues: 'Eight or ten years ago when coffee planting had become a mania amongst the civil and military officers in Ceylon, and when capitalists from England and India were eagerly investing their funds in land for its cultivation.......the result was a more than oriental extravaganza in every item of expenditure, and a wild race of competition as to who would first have their estate in bearing, which raised the wages of labour and every article of expenditure to a pitch actually absurd; Superintendents were employed to oversee the work at excessive salaries – men who had never seen a tree planted or a crop of coffee prepared for market. Soldiers whose discharge was purchased from the ranks, also grossly overpaid were sent up to manage the plantations, while the proprietors were mortgaging every available security at 9 or 10 per cent, to support this extravagance, confidently expecting the first golden harvest.'

At this exact time England fell into a recession, coffee prices fell and the rats and bugs chose this dread moment to emerge and commence their field day.

It was in the year 1847 that the rats appeared suddenly – and for the first time amongst some of the highest and most productive plantations of coffee. No reasonable conjectures could satisfactorily account for their invasion, but the most probable was that the long continuance of the rains had rotted the nillo and other plants on which they used to feed. The proximity of the coffee plantations enabled them to pour out of the jungle in prodigious numbers to attack the coffee trees, gnawing off the fruit-bearing branches, though strangely not for the berries but for the pith of the plant which contains a small proportion of farina. Then, after the rats came the fatal coffee bug.

Dr Gardner says in his report that it would not be possible to understand the effects this insect produces without 'having a knowledge of its structure and functions'. He therefore intends to detail these, giving us a lively picture of the loathsome creature, which seems to be closely related to my old enemy, known to me as 'mealy bug', which attacks not only my camellias but especially my lapagerias in the greenhouse. Here is Dr Gardner's graphic description of this destructive brute – I relish his particularly unattractive but choice words, which simply egg on my murderous instincts.

Gardner starts: 'The young shoots and leaves of a coffee tree, infested for some time with the bug are covered with brownish coloured wart-like bodies – each of these warts or scales is a transformed female 'bug', containing a large number of eggs which are hatched within it. As they come out from their nest they run about all over the plant, looking very much like small wood-lice.

Soon after they hatch the males seek the underside of the leaves while the females prefer the young shoots as a place of abode. The underside of the leaf will then be found to be studded with minute, yellowish, white-coloured specks of an oblong form – these are the male larvae being transformed into pupae beneath their own skin; some of these will have the rudiments of a wing on each side attached to the lower part of the thorax; it has six legs, the four hind ones being directed backwards, and the two anterior ones forwards. When it has reached maturity it makes its way out of its pellucid case – the head is of globular form with two rather prominent black eyes in front and two long antennae, each with eleven joints, hairy throughout and with a tuft of a few longer hairs at their apices. The legs are also hairy. The female, as soon as she has fixed herself on a young shoot punctures the cuticle with a proboscis, which she has on her chest and by which she extracts the juices which nourish her. Until she has reached nearly her full size she still possesses the power of locomotion, and her six feet are easily distinguishable on the under surface of her corpulent body, but at no period of her existence has she wings.'

Dr Gardner goes on: 'it is about the period of her attaining her full size that impregnation takes place, after which the scale becomes somewhat more conical, assumes a darker colour, and at length, if permanently fixed to the surface of the plant by means of a cottony substance, interposes between it and the cuticle to which it adheres.' He adds, 'the scale when full grown exactly resembles in miniature the hat of a Cornish miner, there being a narrow rim at the base which gives increased surface for attachment. The number of eggs contained in one of these scales is enormous, amounting in one which I counted to no less than 691. The eggs are of an oblong shape, of a pale flesh colour and perfectly smooth; in some of the scales which I have examined the eggs had just been hatched, and when laid in the field of a microscope, exactly resembled those masses of life so often seen in dry old cheeses!'

He identifies the insect as belonging to the genus *Coccus* and thus a relation of that which produces the cochineal of commerce. 'So far as the only books within my reach enable me to judge, it seems to be the *Coccus asnidum* of Linnaeus, which he mentions as being common on evergreen trees in Asia, such as the camellia. It is the excretion from this scale insect which forms a black mould on the leaves and affects the nutrition by cutting off the sunlight'.

Dr Gardner continues: 'it was not until after two or three years that the pest has been on an estate that it shows itself to an alarming extent; a number of the berries fall off before reaching maturity – the whole plant begins to assume a deep black colour having the appearance of soot being thrown over it. This black is caused by the growth of a black parasite fungus on the young shoots and the upper side of the leaves, where it forms a thin fibrous coating. By this time two thirds of the crop will be lost. It was truly painful to find that trees, which in a healthy state would produce two to three pounds of coffee were either entirely destitute of berries or only producing a few shrivelled ones that will hardly repay the expense of collecting.'

Here I must quote from a paragraph in Mr W H Ukers' definitive book, *All About Coffee,* which tells us that chief among the enemies of the coffee tree are not only insects, rodents and fungi but 'elephants, buffalo and native cattle - all have a special liking for the tender leaves of the coffee plant.'

Research into methods of controlling the disease were investigated at the Experiment Station at Peradeniya, and every possible remedy was tried to eradicate the fatal bug: chloride of lime, lime-water, urine and manuring with guano were all suggested on one estate, while powdered lime, rich manuring with horse dung and rotten coffee-pulp and tobacco or sulphur fumigation were tried on another; cutting the trees down or close pruning them, sprinkling the trees over with a mixture of equal parts of saltpetre and quicklime, but all to no avail. It seemed that no remedy would ever be found that was sufficiently cheap and easy to apply for the large scale needed on the coffee estates. So the coffee industry of the colony collapsed completely to the ruin of most estates and financial embarrassment of the Government.

When George Gardner died suddenly in 1849 he was succeeded by Dr George Thwaites FRS CMG, carefully chosen once more by Sir William Hooker of Kew. Thwaites worked tirelessly for more than thirty years maintaining Peradeniya in a high state of efficiency, and made it famous as a scientific as well as a utilitarian institution. His great acquirements and steady devotion to science added a prestige to the gardens and gave them a worldwide reputation. He died in Kandy in 1882, never having left the island since he arrived in 1849.

The annihilation of the prosperous coffee enterprise of Ceylon was a devastating blow to the planters who had invested so much money (much of it borrowed) into their estates, which extended to about a quarter of a million acres. Henry Tremen was now sent out from Kew to replace Thwaites, who faced a considerable challenge. The original coffee introduced by the Dutch had come from Java, and the Peradeniya Garden had supplied the estates with seedlings of the Arabian variety; a new kind of coffee from Liberia was now trialled and some special seed was sent from Mauritius, and with Tremen's help the planters introduced new agricultural industries, making extensive trials with other products. Cacao was found to be quite successful, and the 300 acres growing there in 1878 was upped to 21,000 by 1900, an export worth about £300,000. Cinnamon, the oldest export and indigenous to the island, was now cultivated to the full extent of its profitable demand, while pepper, cardamoms, vanilla and coconuts were all grown to their maximum possibility.

A field of tea had been planted in Ceylon as early as 1842, but no real

Coconuts being harvested – the sap from the flower clusters was often used to produce palm
wine – also known as 'toddy'

attempt had been made to create a commercial success of it until now in the 1880s, when necessity gave the impetus. The planters were immensely brave, risking everything to rebuild their fortunes, having to turn away from a crop which had given them their livelihood for fifty years or so and stake everything on a plant that had barely proved itself.

In Henry Cave's *Golden Tips – Ceylon and its Great Tea Industry*, published in 1900, his contemporary description is full of interest. He tells us how when the planters first decided to grow coffee on the fertile hillsides of Ceylon, they needed coolies for the donkey work; the Singhalese had no desire to work on the estates in the mountain districts - hitherto uninhabited - they were quite satisfied with their lot, living in the plains – 'sufficient unto the day is the evil thereof' – being their philosophy. But living on the adjoining continent were millions of people, 'born to till the soil, whose earnings in their native land of Southern India amounted only to the miserable pittance of about three farthings a day, while in times of famine, which occurred then as now with lamentable frequency, wages disappeared altogether. Could not some of them be induced to emigrate to Ceylon? They had but to cross a few miles of sea and walk a hundred miles or so to reach a paradise where they might increase their earnings tenfold and return one day to become landowners and capitalists in their own country?' And so it came about that the planters in Ceylon became entirely dependent on immigrant Tamil labour. The absence of cart roads and railways at one time necessitated the transport of produce upon coolies' heads for great distances; the Tamil was quite prepared to take on this arduous work, 'but the more effeminate Singhalese is not prepared to earn his rice by so much sweat of the brow'.

Later the main transport would be undertaken by the humped bulls – 'a pair of such animals would draw more than a ton of tea up the steep incline, by the mere pressure of their humps against a huge crossbar, resting upon their necks and attached in the centre to the pole of the cart; in the days of coffee, before the railway was made, such a pair would take down to the port of Colombo a hundred and twenty bushels of coffee, with the necessary food for the journey, at the rate of twenty miles a day.'

A most remarkable man in the history of commercial Ceylon was a Major Skinner, who arrived in the island at the age of fourteen in 1814, at a time when the journey from Colombo to Kandy across swamps and jungle and ravines took six weeks. According to Henry Cave 'two years after his arrival young Skinner was entrusted by the Governor, Sir Edward Barnes with the most difficult part of the road which was soon to bring this hitherto almost inaccessible region within five days' march of Colombo. Becoming an officer of the Ceylon Rifles, Skinner soon applied military organisation to the work for which his abilities so obviously fitted him, by enlisting a pioneer force of about four thousand men, in order that he might have trained labourers on whom he could always rely. With an army of experienced workmen he spent nearly fifty years in the construction of roads and bridges, often undergoing the greatest privations during his surveys of trackless wilderness. The magnificent network of roads all over the country is his lasting memorial. Upon his arrival there were none and at his departure there were three thousand miles, mostly due to his genius, pluck, energy and self reliance. The superb railway line from Colombo to Kandy was opened in 1867.

When coffee failed and tea was considered a possible replacement, the Government sent a Commissioner to Assam to study its cultivation about which very little was known.

We now come to James Taylor's important part in the saga of tea, told by DM Forrest in his book called *A Hundred Years of Ceylon Tea 1867-1967*, published in 1967. James Taylor became a legend in his day; he was an enormous man, a giant with a long beard – he weighed two hundred and forty six pounds and one of his fingers was as thick as three bunched together, which was all he needed to knock a man down. When he died, twenty four men carried him into Kandy, over a distance of about eighteen miles – two gangs of twelve taking turns every four miles – they called him *'sami-dorai'* – the master who is God.

At the age of 16 in 1852, Taylor travelled from his home town Golconda in Kincardineshire, Scotland to Colombo, where he was appointed to be Assistant Superintendent on a coffee estate near Kandy called Loolecondera, at the annual salary of £100. This was a coffee estate in embryo; some clearance had already been done, cutting and burning the timber and ploughing up the ground, sometimes using elephants. His job was to be the building of roads on the estate, constructing thatched buildings, and getting the area ready for planting. A letter home describes his accommodation: 'Whenever the light is out a flock of rats from the jungle beside us come in, looking out for something to eat, and the wind blows a perfect hurricane in the bungalow sometimes so as to blow out the lamp.'

He was a natural technician, and whatever he was told to do he did thoroughly, learning as he went along, and with the help of 200 coolies the estate was prepared for planting within the year. Taylor's employer is quoted as saying of him that 'he is a man who, of all who I have known, is the most entirely devoted to his work. Self advancement has been I believe as nothing in his eyes. He has cared for his work and that only; here lies the root of the wonderful success attained and it was therefore, without hesitation that we entrusted the tea experiment to his care'.

It was in 1866 that James Taylor first planted tea seed on a commercial scale – 19 acres – raised from Assam seed in number 7 field on Loolecondera Estate, 'thus leading to the development of Ceylon's tea-producing industry', as states the bronze plaque in his memory .

To begin with, the manufacture of tea had been carried on in the corner of the old coffee store; the leaf was rolled on tables by hand, i.e. from wrists to elbow, while firing was accomplished by means of a pit filled with charcoal, over which the trays of rolled leaf were placed; as progress was made this arrangement was succeeded by a large factory, eventually at each estate, fitted with the latest-invented machinery driven by steam and water power.

Mr Morris, Assistant Director of Kew, who visited Ceylon several times in the 1870s, said of Taylor: 'In his plodding careful way he worked out *unaided* the details of tea manufacture' – in fact Taylor, himself, in his correspondence, tells us of several people who helped and advised him – he was always ready to learn, and when he was first experimenting (in his China phase) a North Indian planter, a Mr Noble, showed him how to pluck, wither and roll the little leaf, all by hand, and told him about fermenting and panning and all the rest of the process. Much later Taylor recounts how an Assam planter, a Mr Cameron, explained to him that he had not pruned sufficiently, so he did his entire acreage all over again. Taylor relates: 'Mr Cameron started finer plucking than I had been doing – I also took to weekly plucking and topped the sales list for a time; the finer plucking largely increased the selling price of the tea and still more largely the selling price per acre.' Taylor also recounts that up to the end of 1876 he sold all his tea in Ceylon 'for well over twice the price we could get for it in London and saved the expense of sending it home'. The Loolecondera mark first turned up in Mincing Lane in 1881.

When coffee was in serious decline it was James Taylor who was given the credit for the first planting of both cinchona and tea. Taylor, the master technician, was never satisfied with makeshift devices: he wanted to build a fully equipped tea house of his own design; he describes it as being fitted for an acreage of 50 or 100 acres of tea in full bearing; the most exciting thing of all was, of course its rolling machine, the first ever made in Ceylon. Taylor writes in a letter: 'I have a machine of my own invention being made in Kandy for rolling the tea which I think will be successful. If so we cannot help making a profit on tea if it grows of fair quality in this country. The picking or gathering the leaves and the rolling are the greatest expenses in the production; the rolling costs nearly as much as the gathering.'

It was from Mr Thwaites, Superintendent at the Peradeniya garden, that Taylor received the first tea seed in the early 1860s – and this would have been some of the Assam Indigenous seed descended from the Wallich importations of 1839/40. Thwaites is known to have given Taylor seeds of the China Bohea variety as well.

Some samples of Taylor's tea were sent to Calcutta, and in one report Taylor says with justified pride, 'all but two of these were described as being better than the Indian teas being sold there.' The ideal at which he was then aiming was the China flavour; tea that tasted like the China tea sold in the shops.

Henry Cave says: 'The success which attended every effort in changing the surface of the coffee land to that of tea must have been an immense relief to the enterprising proprietors, who were facing ruin with desperate courage. Nothing but the most plucky and determined resourcefulness, characteristic of the true Briton, prevented the whole planting community in the early eighties from abandoning their estates in despair.'

The courageous tea planters managed their whole new factory operation which was carried out with military precision: young seedlings of the tea plant *Camellia sinensis* were each allotted twelve square feet of surface soil, planted so that they could obtain the greatest exposure to the sun; if left to nature the plant would grow to about twenty feet, with a similar circumference, but the artifice of the planter keeps it down to about three feet by constant prunings; a two year old plant is ready for harvesting and is then subjected for a further two years to regular plucking every nine or ten days; fairly exhausted by then it is severely pruned to a small stump, but behaving as all camellias do it recovers and bursts forth with renewed vigour in time for further regular plucking.

The climate of Ceylon was particularly beneficial to the tea industry having no seasonal loss of rhythm; day after day, year after year the routine went on and it continued too, right round the clock, since the factory worked all night on the processing of the leaf which had been coming in throughout the previous day – a cycle of almost 24 hours. The comparison with the coffee industry was very marked with the harvesting being confined to only two or three months in the year, beginning in early November – it was all over by mid-January and sometimes it all had to be harvested within six weeks, the biggest problem being the constant necessity of how to keep the under-capitalised planter's head above water through the long months while he was waiting for the coffee beans to ripen.

What is also amazing is that when Forrest wrote his book in 1967, up to 70% of the tea bushes then being plucked had been planted by the pioneers before 1885 – venerable octogenarians.

Plucking was usually carried out by young women as it required nimble fingers and much dexterity. They filled and refilled the baskets, suspended by ropes from their heads, into which they threw the leaves over their shoulders; these baskets held about fourteen pounds weight when full and earned the girls about four pence a day. Cave says of them: 'They look very picturesque, with

Nimble fingered girls plucking the young shoots from the tea plants, filling the baskets by throwing the leaves over their shoulders.

their fine glossy hair and dreamy black eyes, their ears, necks, arms and ankles adorned with silver ornaments, their gay clothes of many colours falling in graceful folds while standing intent upon their work among the bushes.' Only the young and succulent leaves could be used in the manufacture and the younger the leaf the finer the quality of tea; for a specially delicate quality only the bud and two extreme leaves of each shoot would be taken. The male coolies did the pruning, a hard labour with constant stooping in a field of perhaps fifty acres – some two hundred thousand bushes would be dealt with.

To produce the finished article of tea for export, several technical processes were undergone in the factory, and as the industry developed these were all done by rolling machinery; this was how Ceylon tea was kept free

Map of Ceylon (Sri Lanka) showing tea growing areas.

Humped bulls carting Ceylon tea to the Matale Railway Station.

from the dirt which found its way into the teas of China, where the operations were performed by hand. The final process sieved the tea through four different meshes, 'the finest of these throws the pure Ceylon Golden tips, small quantities of which have been sold in London from £10 to £35 per pound.' Packing was done in purpose-built sheds; the tea tipped into lead-lined chests, all of which was done by machinery; a new trade was growing in packeted tea, and Henry Cave tells us that this was done 'by Singhalese girls, nicely clad and perfectly clean, who press the tea into the lead packet – not with their hands but with wooden pressure mallets', this was then soldered down and affixed with outer labels. Loads of tea were taken from the estate factories by the humped bulls to the newly finished railway which took the final product to be loaded on to ships in Colombo harbour.

Up in the hills of Ceylon, the bungalow that we rented while staying in Diyatalawa, was very different to our rattan house in Singapore. To begin with it had been built for prisoners of the Boer war many years ago and the plumbing was non-existent except for what was known as 'Dan, Dan, the lavatory man'. The kitchen was best not investigated, and I wished I had not done so.

One day we were invited to spend a day on a tea estate belonging to old friends. No-one had warned us about leeches, so walking through the paths which separated the serried ranks of tea plants I happened to look down at my feet to find them covered in blood. I tore off my shoes and socks and hurled them into the distance, which was not a sound move as I had to go and retrieve them. That night I found no trace of leeches in my shoes but many little puncture holes around my ankles. After our exploration we foregathered for a drink before lunch, and when I spotted a leech on my six year old's leg – our planter host casually attended to it with his lighted cigarette end.

It is interesting to read Henry Cave's description of the leech pest, which so many years later seems unchanged: 'If we wander indiscriminately among the tea plantations, thousands of eyes will be turned upon us from creatures having five pairs each: and they undoubtedly want our blood. In size they are about an inch in length and as fine as a common knitting needle, but capable of distension till they equal a quill in thickness and attain a length of nearly two inches. Their structure is so flexible that they can insinuate themselves through the meshes of the finest stocking and this is the favourite opportunity of the terrestrial ten-eyed leech of the Ceylon highlands; their size is so insignificant and the wound they make so skilfully punctured, that both are generally imperceptible, and the first intimation of their onslaught is the trickling of blood or the chill feeling of the leech.'

The wonderful variety of wild animals, besides cockroaches and leeches, which inhabit Ceylon tend to be nocturnal and inhabit the mountain summits. By day the elephant and the leopard remain hidden in the deepest recesses, and the best game hunting is for the elk, which swoops down at night in great numbers, destroying the bungalow gardens and eating the vegetables. These are difficult to hunt on account of the depth of the forest, also because of the interference of the leopards; when the dogs come upon these, they give tongue and chase them – receiving in return a pat on the head which puts a sudden end to their career.

It would have been wonderful to see the elephants in their native country from the railway, but the train was also nocturnal so I took the children to an elephant orphanage in Colombo. There these highly intelligent creatures performed a circular dance for us, and I learned that the senior lady elephant was in charge of distributing the sugarcane to all her juniors, in strict pecking order, one huge bundle for each family.

Thistleton-Dyer, Assistant Director of RBG Kew, and son-in-law of Sir William Hooker, sums up the state of Ceylon in 1880, at its most dire moment in the crippled state of its coffee industry: 'It is impossible not to feel the deepest sympathy with the planters in their present distress and disappointment. Kew has done everything that is possible to alleviate it. But, whatever be the result I do not doubt that one consequence will be to put botanical enterprise in Ceylon on a far sounder basis than heretofore. The cultivation of tea, cinchona, Liberian coffee and cacao will in a few years no longer leave the planters, if they are wise in disposing their investments in the soil, at the mercy of the failure of a particular kind of crop. Ceylon is admirably equipped with a chain of gardens, representing different zones of climate, which the island possesses. It is to us a place of peculiar interest and ought indeed to be regarded as the Kew of the East.'

— CHAPTER 7 —

The Royal Botanic Garden, Calcutta

The story behind this garden is linked to the simultaneous history of the ups and downs of Peradeniya Gardens, Ceylon. Sir Joseph Banks was involved with the emergence of both gardens and happily promoting and advising on the introduction and produce of tea.

Having just related the coffee and tea saga of Ceylon and left it in 1900, burgeoning with tens of thousands of acres of flourishing tea plants, it is interesting to relate the development of the equally successful tea industry in the Himalayas which took several different paths. For this we must first return to the 17th C when tea was just heard of in Europe. It all began with the most expensive green variety as a medicine or *digestif* in the 1660s, imported from China at about 60/- a lb and a great bound in demand came in 1720 with the import of a cheaper variety called Bohea. At that time tea was imported in tea chests – ready for the customer to buy; we had no idea how to grow the plant from which it came or how to process it. The 200,000 lbs imported in 1720 rose to 3 million by 1760, and 9 million by 1770.

The Royal Botanic Garden, Calcutta is situated on the west bank of the river Hooghli, a few miles from Calcutta. It was the idea of Colonel Robert Kyd of the Bengal Infantry, then Superintendent of the East India Company's dockyard and Secretary to the Military Board at Fort William, a keen horticul-turist, he wrote on the 1st June 1786 to the Governor of Bengal to suggest forming a botanic garden.

His concern was 'to benefit the people of India and to justify British rule; I know not of any other benefit we can claim the merit of affording them, while they still remain subject to the greatest of all calamities, that of desolation by famine and subsequent pestilence.' He points out that the botanic garden would not be 'for the purpose of collecting rare plants (though they also have their use) as things of mere curiosity or furnishing articles for the gratification of luxury, but for establishing a stock for disseminating such articles as the sago and date palm as may prove beneficial to the inhabitants as well as the natives of Great Britain, and which ultimately may tend to the extension of the national commerce and riches.'

Kyd himself was an ardent gardener, and at that time collected and grew in the compound of his country house, nearby at Sibpur, many foreign plants of economic and horticultural value. He used to acquire these plants from the captains of the company ships returning to Calcutta from voyages to the Far East. Hence his own experience had convinced him that some of the spices of the East Indies could grow in India. If he could achieve this, it would have the pleasing result of breaking the monopoly of the Dutch of the highly prized cinnamon and other valuable commodities.

The suggestion was warmly received by the East India Company, who referred it to Sir Joseph Banks, their unofficial adviser on all botanical matters. Banks gave strong support to Kyd's proposals for introducing the sago and date palm and was enthusiastic about the likely benefits.

He says, 'let all honour be given to Col Kyd, by whose means benefits of such importance will speedily be conferred on 20 millions of people in a manner which will secure them to their latest posterity, who will wonder their ancestors were able to exist without them, and revere the name of their British Conquerors to whom they will be indebted for the abolition of famine, the most severe scourge with which providence had afflicted them.'

Banks goes on to suggest that the British should use the productive potential of Bengal to export to China: 'why should we not then, if proper means are taken, discover the plants which produce the articles they want, and by means of the Garden, the cultivation is set on foot, why should we not, I say, be able to undersell the Chinese at their own market, and diminish at least if not annihilate, the immense debt of silver we are annually obliged to furnish from Europe.' (This was the currency of the day in our Chinese markets).

Kyd wanted to grow teak especially, as many of the East Indian Company ships came in for repairs. Cinnamon was also top of his list, because he had found it growing wild nearby and thought it might be the same very superior variety that was indigenous to and exported from Ceylon – at that date (until

1796) still in Dutch hands. Kyd was no botanist but he was very ambitious and keen to try all desirable economic plants of every country; he wrote to many parts of Asia and secured an amazing variety of species, such as Persian dates, Persian tobacco, Chinese tea, oranges, English apples, cherries, apricots and sandalwood from the Malabar coast. He also intended to try growing the much sought after spices: cardamom, cloves, black and white pepper and nutmeg, as well as cotton, tobacco, coffee, camphor, and tea. Sadly, many of these failed completely, but at least it was useful to know for the future what would not grow in the Calcutta Garden.

Kyd chose a large site for the garden, covering about 310 acres, next door to his country residence. He worked hard to establish it and was pleased to get a letter from the Court having 'noticed the zeal and ability of Col Kyd in promoting the study of Natural History and his laudable endeavours to advance the Cultivation of useful trees and plants in Bengal'. Banks, who was so influential in the East India Company's decision to approve the Garden, remained an active and involved supporter.

In spite of Kyd's concerns about famine relief he had no illusions about the difficulty of the task. He wrote to Banks in 1788 'that the natives are so strongly addicted to the customs of their ancestors, that they will not, without the utmost difficulty, even in the case of famine adopt any species of food that they are unaccustomed to.' There is no more mention of the sago and date palms, it must have become clear quite rapidly that they were not going to be the panaceas that Kyd and Banks had hoped. Nor was breadfruit a success; the only food crop which did thrive was sugarcane; considerable quantities of which were distributed, and also exported to England where disruption in the West Indies had caused shortages. But from the beginning Kyd was keen to establish a wide geographical network and to experiment with plants from all over India and East Asia. He had difficulty in collecting from China but was able to get plants from Penang and the East Indies and he was also asked to supply plants for Anderson in His Majesty's Botanic Garden at St Vincent. At first the main focus of this collecting was economic, and the aim was to transfer plants which were potential commercial crops, but gradually a scientific element came in.

When coffee failed in Ceylon and the desperate planters had to turn to alternative crops, tea turned out to be the most successful, but apart from actually finding out whether they could grow it there, as previously explained, they had no idea how to process it. The Chinese, from whom we in Europe had imported huge amounts of tea, were very secretive and never allowed 'foreign devils' to investigate the process or to explore their country. When Mr Devaynes of the East India Company consulted Sir Joseph Banks in 1788 about growing it in the new botanic garden in Calcutta, Banks replied as follows: 'In obedience to your wishes I readily undertake to give my opinion relative to the possibility of Tea becoming an object of cultivation and manufacture in the possessions of the East India Company, and the probable means of effecting that very desirable object.'

Banks had in his library four folio volumes of *Description de l'Empire de Chine* by Jean Baptiste du Halde (1674-1743), a French Jesuit and geographer, and an authority on most Chinese subjects including agriculture, trees and plants. From this source he says: 'It appears probable that all merchantable teas are grown between the 26th and 35th degree of latitude, able for the culture of black teas and between the 30th and 34th for green teas.' However, unknown to him at that time, it transpired that this was exactly where tea was found (by the Bruce brothers) growing indigenously in Assam a few years later.

Banks wrote to Mr Devaynes: 'The inhabitants of Canton are now in the habit of shipping themselves on board our Indiamen, whenever hands are wanted; we therefore safely conclude that their neighbours at Ho Nan may be induced by the offer of liberal terms to follow their example, and moreover to embark their tea shrubs and all their tools of culture and manufacture and migrate with them to Calcutta, where they will find the Botanic Gardens ready to receive them, twenty acres of which is already prepared, and lying very nearly under the same latitude as Canton could not fail to suit in every particular this infant adventure.'

He advises against allowing the business to be arranged by the supercargoes, (or 'foremen') locally, as they will 'have an interest in its failure', but that it should commence with the Court of Directors, here, with officers capable of executing commissions of every degree of delicacy, and conducted in secrecy. He offers any advice or assistance: 'I shall be at all times ready to come forward, convinced that the object is of real importance, not only to the Company but to the country at large.'

Whether they took all this advice is doubtful, as a letter from Colonel Kyd quotes the supercargoes in China who 'declare themselves unable to procure the draughtsmen wanted as such people can get a comfortable living at home and cannot be induced to migrate.'

In September 1789 Kyd wrote to complain of the slow progress the garden was making, that the tea plants which arrived were smothered by other plants, and of the inattention of the supercargoes when packing the tea plants; also that only the inferior sorts were sent – it all sounds very predictable. Nevertheless, it is a historic fact that in 1848, nearly 30 years after Banks had died, the East India Company sent Robert Fortune (1813-1880) to China on exactly the same mission: 'to obtain the finest variety of the tea plant, as well as native manufacturers and implements for the Government Tea plantations in the Himalayas.' His expedition is described shortly.

Kyd died in 1793, at the age of 47. By then the garden was firmly established, and thus it is his real memorial, and a monument was put up in the grounds to honour him. Kyd's death was the first crisis for the garden, but no-one now questioned whether the work should continue. The Council in Calcutta wrote that his death 'leaves the office of the Superintendent of your Botanical establishment which has proved of much general utility and is very deserving of encouragement, vacant.' The Bengal Government moved quickly to find a successor, and the obvious candidate was Dr William Roxburgh (1751-1815).

Banks had admired Kyd for his energy and commitment but was concerned at his lack of botanical knowledge. There is a change in the tone of Banks' quite lengthy correspondence with Roxburgh; here are two professionals talking to each other.

Roxburgh was not especially impressed by the garden, describing it as 'a good Indian orchard and nursery but of too large an extent'. However, by the end of 1793 he was distributing teak seed, Bengal hemp, Virginia tobacco, Caerulean indigo, and Arabian coffee, sending plants to England, St Helena, the West Indies and different parts of India.

In reply to a letter from Banks to the East India Company itself, they formally acknowledged for the first time in January 1807 that the garden had a scientific purpose; thus it moved steadily away from an acclimatisation site to being a recognised scientific institution during its first twenty years. The support of the EIC was partly because of the calibre of the people running it – Kyd had been an energetic and committed founder, and Roxburgh was the most distinguished botanist in India at the time.

Some of the early experiments, such as the attempted introduction of

English trees, now seem naïve, but the modern ideas of ecology and environment evolved from the efforts of people like Kyd and Roxburgh, and the latter passed on the knowledge that he gained for future generations by his articles and especially his *Flora Indica.*

Throughout the period the garden had the invaluable help of Sir Joseph Banks, whose plans had always been for a worldwide network of botanic gardens, exchanging crops to the benefit of all and particularly of the British Empire.

Roxburgh was an East India Company surgeon who had made his name as the Superintendent of a small botanic garden in Samalcot in the Madras Presidency. There he grew economic and medicinal plants, including coffee, cinnamon, nutmeg, arnotto, sappanwood, mulberry and pepper vines. He sent home to Banks a flood of botanical drawings by native artists, amounting to over 2,000, and Banks published a selection of these as *Plants of the Coromandel* (1795-1819). Roxburgh also sent to Kew great quantities of material – specimens, seeds and living plants. The catalogue he compiled of the plants in the Calcutta Garden listed no less than 3,249 species. Later, Hooker's *Flora of British India,* which comprised 35 volumes, was very largely based on Roxburgh's contributions.

When he inherited the garden there were 300 varieties of plant, and when he left 3,500. The exchange of plants and seed continued, and the importance of his scientific work was recognised in Britain: he received three gold medals from the Society of Arts for his research into fibres and other useful substances.

In 1809 when Roxburgh was nearly sixty, the company appointed a twenty-three year old Dane to help him, Nathaniel Wallich (1786-1854), who was born and educated in Copenhagen and came to India in 1807 as surgeon to the Dutch settlement at Serampore, which in 1808 was captured by British forces. Wallich was imprisoned but released to help Roxburgh. After three years together the younger man's health broke down and he went to Mauritius for recovery, and it was on his way back that he stayed in Singapore and advised Raffles. He then joined the East India Company as an army surgeon and was appointed Director of the Calcutta Garden when Roxburgh died, a position he held for the next thirty years.

Here Wallich was in his prime; the number of species was doubled and the garden was celebrated as the most beautiful in the East and renowned throughout Europe as, in Joseph Hooker's words when he visited on his way to Nepal, 'having contributed more useful and ornamental tropical plants to the public and private gardens of the world than any other establishment before or since.'

From the first Wallich had been interested in the possibility of obtaining plants from regions inaccessible to Europeans; he trained and sent two native gardeners to Nepal in 1817 – the year of his appointment and three years before he was able to visit the region himself. The British Resident in Kathmandu was an eager amateur botanist himself, and sent Wallich frequent consignments of seeds and specimens. Between January 1818 and March 1819 Wallich sent to England six consignments of Nepalese seeds, including those of *Rhododendron arboreum*, solicitously – and successfully packed in tins of brown sugar. In December 1819 he notified Sir Joseph Banks that he was sending (for Kew) two chests of live plants, a chest of bulbs and tubers, and a box of Nepal seeds on the *Rose* and *Minerva,* and similar consignments on each of the remaining nine ships of that season's fleet, besides packets for the

This 1825 watercolour captures the pandemonium caused amongst plantation workers as a wild elephant appears beyond a very large fig tree (*Ficus benjamina*)

Edinburgh Botanic Garden and various friends and a live musk deer.

Sadly, this wonderful time did not last; the Garden was destined to endure years of official neglect, difficulties and disasters. The Government cut its allowance and Wallich's salary and its further development became impossible.

Wallich's health necessitated another break with the climate, and while he was visiting the Cape, William Griffith (1810–1845) a brilliant young botanist who had entered the Company's service some three years before, officiated in his absence as Superintendent. In 1843 he submitted a comprehensive report on the condition of the garden, herbarium and library, in which he made many pertinent criticisms and suggestions, some of them reflecting unfavourably on Wallich's management; not very fair considering the financial restrictions Wallich had to endure. Griffith began his well meant but ill-judged scheme for reorganising the garden on strictly botanical-textbook lines, according to his own ideas and with characteristic energy, but when he was unexpectedly transferred to Malacca he left behind him devastating evidence of the destructive part of his plan, which involved the ruthless felling of the avenue of sago-palms and the groves of teak, mahogany, cinnamon and cloves to make way for open clay beds, disposed in concentric circles and baking into brick under the fierce heat of the Bengal sun. The fine Amherstia was nearly killed by the exposure of its roots to the heat. Griffith's intention was to put the place on what he thought a 'proper footing', but the havoc in the garden when Wallich returned in 1844 must have nearly broken his heart. He stayed on for three more years and retired, finally beaten by the climate and died in London seven years later.

It was during Wallich's reign over the garden at Calcutta in 1823 that a Major Robert Bruce discovered the tea plant growing indigenously in Assam; from an account written by William Griffith we learn that Bruce sent specimens of the plant to his brother, Mr CA Bruce, a midshipman serving in a ship of the East India Company, who forwarded them on to the Superintendent Wallich at the Calcutta Garden. Wallich did not agree that it was the tea plant from which the Chinese manufacture their tea, although he allowed that it was of the camellia family. In 1832 the Government ordered a report on the resources of Assam, and the existence of the tea plant was once more brought to the fore by CA Bruce. Its identity with the tea of commerce was still doubted by Wallich, but its existence was believed to prove that the latter would thrive in India and the Government began to bestir itself to introduce it.

Closing its eyes to the facts of the case, The East India Company for years refused to permit any interference with its monopoly of the China tea trade, and thus did all it could to discourage tea cultivation in India. However in 1833 the treaty with China expired and the Chinese refused to renew it; it was then that the Governor General Lord William Bentinck (1774-1839) appointed a committee to enquire into the possibility of introducing China tea plants into India. A Tea Committee consisting of Mr George James Gordon as Secretary, seven civilians, three Calcutta merchants, two native gentlemen and Dr Wallich of the Botanical Gardens was formed to further this object.

The Governor General, in spite of the shared scepticism of the committee members of the ultimate success of any attempt to cultivate tea in India, insisted with great courage and determination that they should proceed with the survey work in hand and that the proposition be given a trial; Mr Gordon was despatched to China for the purpose of studying cultivation and manufacturing methods and to secure seeds, plants and Chinese workmen – echoing Banks' plan, and for many years China tea seed was imported regularly into India for the cultivation of the tea shrub.

Then the tremendously important discovery was made that genuine tea trees were at that very time growing wild in the hills of Assam; the reports submitted had at last convinced the botanists (including Wallich), the Tea Committee and the Government of the identity of the Assam plant with that of China. (Incidentally, various other people have claimed to have first found the Assam tea plant, but in Wallich's report dated 1885, he states that 'it was Mr Bruce and his late brother Major Robert Bruce who originally brought the Assam tea to public notice many years ago, when no one had the slightest idea of its existence').

Dr Wallich and Dr Griffith – not the best of friends one imagines – were now sent to Assam in 1835 to investigate the question of tea cultivation, but although it was admitted that the Assam plant was undoubtedly a variety of the true tea plant of China, it was still thought to have degenerated by neglect of cultivation; Dr Griffith thought 'a wild plant is not likely to give as good produce as one that has been cultivated for centuries', and that the proper course would be to introduce the cultivated plant from that country; Dr

Wallich argued that since the native plants were actually tea there was no need to import, as 'there is no ground for supposing the various sorts of tea seeds brought from China will produce anything but the shrub in its natural (Indian) state.' They could not even agree on the best locality for experimental gardens. Dr Wallich favoured the Himalayas, but Dr Griffith preferred Upper Assam.

It was not until sometime later, when large tracts had been given up to the cultivation of the imported China tea, that the Assam planters became convinced of the great superiority of the indigenous variety in respect both of quality and output, and found that, for most soils, the best plant of all was the hybrid in which the indigenous element largely prevailed.

During the next few years the new industry made rapid strides and the conspicuous success of the Assam Company led to the most extravagant ideas regarding the prospects of the industry. Fresh gardens were opened in all directions and a period of wild excitement supervened. The mania extended even to Government officers, just as it had in Ceylon, several of whom threw up their appointments to engage in tea planting; land was taken up irrespective of its suitability or for the supply of labour available. The result was disaster, with some of them showing 'as much folly in their hurry to get out of tea as they had a few years before in their eagerness to undertake the speculation'.

When the cultivation of tea began in Assam nothing was known of the habits of the tea bush, and it was the British pioneer tea planters who eventually discovered how to grow tea from studying the indigenous plants in Assam. Before that, much time and money was wasted when they could not agree where to grow it, and chose – disastrously – the only place in Assam where it was impossible for it to thrive, being regularly drowned by the confluence of two huge rivers.

Having described the best practice of tea manufacture in the Ceylon chapter it is only necessary to say that, as in Ceylon, one of the greatest improvements in Assam was the introduction of machinery whereby the handling of the tea was reduced to the minimum.

It was in 1835 when Wallich first went to Assam to assess the prospects of the indigenous tea plant that he sent some seed, no doubt including some Assam indigenous to the Peradeniya Botanic garden in Ceylon and when George Thwaites FRS CMG was appointed Superintendent of that garden in

1849, Thwaites distributed some of it to James Taylor, whose contribution to Ceylon tea is described in the last chapter.

But in India, in spite of continual research and experiment, the debate went on for years as to which were superior, the China seed or that of Assam. While the argument raged, the East India Company finally decided in 1838 to send Robert Fortune (1813-1880) on the same mission originally suggested by Banks: 'to obtain the finest variety of the China tea plant, as well as native manufacturers and implements for the Government tea plantations in the Himalayas'.

Fortune carried out the most daring research in China, and this was nearly thirty years after the death of Banks. He was probably the only person who could have attempted such a mission: he had travelled in China before and written a book called *Three Years Wanderings in China* on his return, and knew better than anyone how dangerous it was to venture inland. Foreigners – known as 'foreign devils' or 'barbarians' – were not tolerated, and could easily be tortured or killed if caught beyond the limits allowed. He knew the Chinese character well, and although he has some harsh things to say about them, he understood and rather admired their crafty ways, making friends with the few he trusted and travelled with, but also making sure he was always a jump ahead. He says: 'From the highest Mandarin to the meanest beggar they are filled with the most conceited notions of their own importance and power and fancy that no people however civilised and no country however powerful are for one moment to be compared with them'. Furthermore he could make himself understood in many of the dialects, and knew enough of their ways to arrange his travel without raising suspicions.

The best teas grown in China came from the Hwuy-chow district, which is more than 200 miles inland from Shanghai; Fortune says: 'It is a sealed country to Europeans and if we except Jesuit missionaries no one has ever entered within the sacred precincts of Hwuy-chow'. He planned to penetrate the area himself and procure not only the true plants which produce the finest green teas of commerce, but also gain some information about the nature of the soil of the district and the best modes of cultivation. He had two Hwuy-chow men in his service at the time and could have arranged for agents to go and procure the tea plants, but, as he says: 'How could I be at all certain that the plants or seeds had been obtained in the districts in question? No dependence can be placed upon the veracity of the Chinese who will say anything that suits their purpose and rarely give themselves any trouble to ascertain whether the information they give be true or false…latterly I made a practise of disbelieving everything they told me until I had an opportunity of judging for myself.'

He enquired of Wang, one of the servants, whether it would be possible to get so far inland into the country, and the latter replied it would be easy to do so and offered to accompany him, only stipulating that he should adopt the dress of the country. Fortune says 'I knew that this was indispensible if I wished to accomplish the object in view and readily acceded to the terms.'

Fortune anticipated some difficulty in hiring a boat for his journey as some of the local boatmen had recently been severely punished by the Chinese authorities for taking three or four foreigners some distance inland to see the silk districts. However, on his instructions, Wang engaged a boat in his own name and arranged that two other people would accompany him. Wang now procured him a Chinese dress and had the pig-tail (which Fortune had worn on his previous inland travel with Wang, and which he said came to his ankles) 'nicely dressed by the barber'. Fortune did not enjoy having his head shaved. The two servants now started to quarrel about who should manage the arrangements for the journey, but, as with most problems with the Chinese, an extra dollar or 'squeeze' settled the problem. As Fortune conjectured: 'the journey was a long one, the way was unknown to me and I should have been placed in an awkward position if they decided to rob me and then run off, leaving me far inland,' so he retained them both.

The first part of the journey seems to have taken two or three weeks, mostly up canals and rivers by boat, but when crossing the hills he was carried by two coolies in a chair and they stayed overnight in local inns. At these inns he noted that nobody took the slightest notice of him, which led him to believe he made a pretty good Chinaman, but one problem arose on the first night when dinner was served at the inn, and he recollected that he was out of practice using chopsticks and was afraid of drawing attention to himself if he used them clumsily, so he decided in spite of his hunger, to make some excuse and leave the table. The arrangement for food when travelling by boat was quite simple: a passenger agreed for three meals a day at a certain fixed rate: conge in the morning, rice at midday and rice-conge in the evening. Anything else such as tea, fish, meat, or vegetables he had to provide and cook for himself. It would all be laid out and a bowl with chopsticks provided. He decided when he was hungry enough to eat the conge, uninviting as it was, he would disregard what the Chinese might think of his awkwardness with chopsticks. 'I got on very well and found that I had not forgotten the art of eating with these highly civilised instruments – it is easier to eat rice with them than anything else for the basin is brought to the mouth and its contents partly sucked and partly shovelled in!'

This reminded me very much of our Chinese cook, Sui, when we had lived in Singapore for three years while following Her Majesty's Fleet round the world: our cook and his wife Nan, and his two children, a boy and a girl, much the same age as ours but about six inches smaller – lived in quarters behind our rattan house, which was out at Loyang near Changi. I had thought, to begin with, that our children and theirs would not play together, but of course I was wrong, and in no time they were inventing obscure games which always seem to end up with the smallest little girl being tied up to a tree with many shrieks and yells. Sui and Nan worked for us for the three years we were there, but although we thought we knew and liked them, I never quite managed to penetrate the inscrutable façade and would not have been surprised to wake up with my throat cut! I came upon Sui one morning eating his breakfast and was astonished to find him squatting on his hunkers on top of his table, waited on by his wife, doing exactly what Fortune describes, with the bowl right up to his chin, shovelling the rice into his mouth with chopsticks.

There was no such thing as a cabin on Fortune's boat, and the first class passengers occupied side berths while their servants and coolies slept in the passage. A Chinese bed on board one of these boats was not very luxurious: it consisted of a mat to lie upon, a hard square pillow for the head and a coverlet stuffed with cotton as a protection from the cold. A surprise Fortune had not anticipated occurred after a journey lasting several weeks; when they arrived alongside and the floorboards under his bed were taken up to extract the cargo, there – immediately under where Fortune had been sleeping – were two enormous coffins, each containing the body of a Chinaman!

The slow progress up the River Yangtze suited Fortune very well; he was able to explore the botanical riches along the banks and nearby countryside while keeping an eye on the boat's progress from a hilltop. 'Every now and then' Fortune recounts 'we came to some rapids, which took us hours to get over, notwithstanding that fifteen men, with long ropes fastened to the mast of our boat were tracking along the shore and five or six more were poling with long bamboos; nothing shows so much as this the indefatigable perseverance of the Chinese, when looking upon a river such as this one would think it quite impossible to navigate.'

Here, I have to add my Chinese experience to Fortune's, when in 2003 I was planning to join the conference of the International Camellia Society at Shanghai. On my way out I was determined to sail down the Yangtze by river boat, just before the first flooding – in 2003 – preparatory to the huge dam being built. I was supposed to embark at Chongqing, but there was not enough water in the river, so I had to travel by bus to join her further down. Communications with my guide were minimal and when she left me, having pointed out my bus, I felt a little nervous. There I was in the middle of China, with no other European in sight. I had thought I had understood the arrangement, but after sitting in the partly-filled bus which showed no signs of moving, I felt the need of confirmation that it was the right one, so bravely got to my feet and asked loudly: 'Is there was anyone on board who speaks English?' A stunned silence greeted my words but to my great relief a young man got to his feet and greeted me politely in welcome American. Thankfully, it was the right bus.

These are the tracks which Robert Fortune's crew, on his tea collecting expedition in 1838, used to haul their boat up river against the flow – fifteen men with ropes tied to the mast. The author photographed these same tracks on her down river trip in 2003.

Sailing down the river was a much faster journey than going against the flow upstream as Fortune had been doing. I imagined Fortune's boat facing the rapids, with the trackers hauling away up river, and keeping their foothold on the narrow tracks with difficulty. I could see and photograph the clearly marked paths, cut out of the rock on the steep and almost sheer sides of the isthmus, through which the river ran.

The next part of Fortune's journey was overland, he was carried in a chair as more coolies carried the luggage, and halfway along the route a fight broke out between two sets of 'chairmen' which had to be settled by Fortune distributing a dollar or two. It was better to sort things out this way, as he says: 'If the row had resulted in a mob taking sides it might be revealed that a foreigner was in the heart of a city', and that would have compromised his position.

Fortune describes the wonderful vegetation and the interesting plants he collected, how he kept a low profile while progressing through the towns – not wishing to take any risks of discovery – until he at last arrived at the Hwuy-chow district, an extensive hilly and beautiful valley. Nearly all this lowland was

A more sedate age...a more sedate method of travelling. A mountain chair in 1844.

under tea cultivation where the soil was rich and fertile, and consequently the bushes grew most luxuriantly. Fortune says: 'I had never before seen the tea plant in such a flourishing condition, and this convinced me that soil had much to do with the superiority of the Hwuy-chow green teas.' They reached their destination – a house which belonged to Wang's father, just before dark, and for the first time he saw the far-famed Sung-lo-shan, the hill where the green tea plant is said to have been discovered and green tea first manufactured.

Old Mr Wang had been a prosperous farmer but was now in very reduced circumstances. 'He received us in the kindest manner and seemed to have a great affection for his son; his wife joined us and soon, chopsticks in hand we did ample justice to the fare put before us.'

Next morning the rain fell in torrents. Four families resided in the cottage in which he stayed, two upstairs and two below, each with a separate kitchen, but as there were no chimneys the smoke had to find its way out through windows, doors or the roof of the house. Fortune found the smoke intolerable, but there was no alternative except to go out in the heavy downpour. For three days it rained incessantly, but at last on the fourth day, the clouds cleared away and the sun came out 'and the whole face of nature wore a cheerful and smiling aspect'. Fortune from then on was out every day from early morning until evening busily employed collecting tea seeds, and obtaining information regarding the cultivation and manufacture of green tea.

The tea plant is propagated from seed in China which is why there was confusion when the Bruce brothers found it growing in Assam, and also possibly explains why Wallich could not immediately identify it as the true tea plant. As Fortune points out, when a plant is multiplied by seed: 'it is perfectly impossible that the produce can be identical in every respect with the parent', and there would also always be slight differences due to soil and climate.

Fortune had arrived at the end of October just when the seeds were ripe for picking, and made a fine collection of the seeds and young plants by the end of November when he was ready to start the long journey back to Shanghai. He made a diversion on arriving at Ning Po, visiting Silver Island, one of the Chusan archipelago, to collect more tea seeds from the centre of the island, where a very special variety of the tea shrub was grown extensively, and on arriving in Shanghai he began packing the plants and seeds in Ward cases for their onward journey to India.

These cases were the greatest boon to plant collectors, providing an almost foolproof way for plants to travel safely; they were miniature, portable greenhouses, invented by Nathaniel Ward in 1831 – the development from plant cabins built to Joseph Banks' own design on ships. You sowed your seed, placed your plants directly in the glazed case, watered them well and once closed it had to be kept in full daylight so photosynthesis could take place and the water vapour thus released would be recycled and the plants kept damp for months at a time.

Now that this collection of plants was well packed in the Ward cases, Fortune set about arranging its journey to Calcutta, and because there was no boat in Shanghai bound for Calcutta direct, he determined to take it to Hong Kong himself and then ship it on to India from there. He describes his journey in the ship which, as well as its usual cargo, was laden with game of all kinds, shooting being a favourite Chinese sport. His fellow travellers had spread their prey – pheasants, woodcock, hares, ducks, geese and teal – over every airy place on board, poop-rail, davits and boats, intending them for their friends in Hong Kong. This all went freight-free as there was a good understanding between the sender and the master of the vessel that should any of the game show signs of going bad, it should be eaten or thrown overboard. As Fortune says: 'we were lucky in having a medical man on board to give the verdict, and I can honestly say that no plump woodcock, wild duck or pheasant was ever condemned to be thrown overboard'. The tea plants having arrived at Hong Kong in good order, he immediately had them transferred to four different vessels, (in case of accident), onward bound for India, where they subsequently arrived in excellent condition.

Having dealt with the Hwuy-chow tea plants, his next object was to engage some first rate tea manufacturers for the Indian plantations, to procure a supply of the implements used in the best districts, and to get together another large collection of tea plants. These he intended to find up the river Min and in the Bohea hills. 'I did not like the idea of returning to Europe without being perfectly certain that I had introduced the tea plant from the best black-tea districts of China into the Government plantations in the North western Provinces of India'. He would start from Ning po where the people were not so prejudiced against foreigners as they were in the south.

Travelling on again, partly by boat and then by chair, Fortune arrived at the beautiful range of hills – the Bohea mountains and finally Woo-e-shan, considered by the Chinese to be one of the most wonderful as well as the most sacred spots in the empire. Its chief renown is derived from its many productions, those of tea being the most celebrated.

The Buddhist priests seemed always to choose the most beautiful spots for the creation of their temples and dwellings, and Fortune had chosen a temple for their night's rest, which was on the sloping side of a small valley where the high priest soon arrived and received them with great politeness, as

Tea plantations - View in the Green Tea District.

Sing-Hoo explained that they wanted food and lodging for a few nights. Fortune was greeted with a small quantity of Chinese tobacco rolled by the high priest and presented to him to fill his pipe; this and a cup of tea indicated a welcome. Fortune describes him as 'about sixty years of age, and appeared to be very intelligent; his countenance was such as one likes to look upon; meekness, honesty and truth were stamped unmistakenly upon it'. Cautious as ever, Fortune left the conversation to his servant who explained that his master came from a far country 'beyond the great wall'. Wine was served with dinner

The delightfully named 'Stream of Nine Windings and Strange Rocks' in the renowned tea region of the Woo-e-shan hills.

and the table was crowded with small basins, each containing a different article of food such as young bamboo shoots, cabbages of various kinds, turnips, peas, beans and a particularly delicious fungus 'of the mushroom tribe'. They pressed him to eat everything, and even went slightly too far, as Fortune explains, by 'plunging their own chopsticks into such delicate morsels as they thought I should prefer, saying 'eat this, eat this!' – we were the best of friends.'

Exploring further the next day they came to a solitary temple on the banks of a small river, known as the Stream of Nine Windings, after the circuitous turns it took among the hills of Woo-e-shan, where the finest souchongs (tea) and pekoes are produced. The river was very rapid and numerous pleasure boats seemed to fly past when going with the current, and on all sides the strangest rocks and hills were observed with curious marks on the perpendicular rocks, which seemed as if they were the impress of some gigantic hands.

Fortune now visited many of the tea farms and successfully procured four hundred young tea plants which were sent on to Shanghai to await his own return to the city, but by yet another route. On his arrival he found that, acting on his previous instructions, some excellent tea manufacturers and lead box makers had been engaged and everything had succeeded 'far beyond my most sanguine expectations.' A large assortment of implements for the manufacture of tea had also arrived; 'nothing therefore remained for me to do but pack up my plants and proceed on my voyage to India'.

Previously, before he had Ward cases, he had sent large quantities of tea seeds packed in loose canvas bags, while some were mixed with dry earth and put into boxes and others put into very small packages, but none of these methods had been satisfactory. As he says: 'Tea seeds retain their vitality for a very short period if they are out of the ground; the next year however I succeeded in finding a sure and certain method of transporting tea seeds and any other short lived seeds as well – it was simply to sow the seeds in Ward cases soon after they are gathered. The whole was now watered and fastened down with a few cross bars to keep it in place. The case was then screwed down in the usual way and made as tight as possible, and the tea seeds germinated during the voyage.' Dr Falconer, writing to him on receipt of this case, found the young tea plants were sprouting 'as thick as they could come up.' From then on, large quantities of tea seeds were planted in the cases of tea plants in between the plants – in all sixteen of the cases that he was personally escorting to Calcutta and then further to the Himalayas. By this means about twelve thousand plants were added to the plantations.

Fortune was quite shocked by the state of the Calcutta Garden when he arrived there, now under the superintendency of Dr Falconer: 'From the time of Dr Wallich's retirement until the appointment of Dr Falconer extensive alterations appear to have been made; it must be confessed however that some of these alterations have been most injurious to the Garden. We look in vain for the noble specimens of palm trees which must have been planted in the days of Roxburgh and Wallich, while in their place we find small 'botanical arrangements' which cannot be carried out and which are never likely to answer the purpose for which they were intended'. But he does approve of

The remarkable *Amherstia nobilis*, hand coloured lithograph by WH Fitch Botanical magazine 1849.

Falconer's alterations, now in progress, which appear to be the results of a well digested plan: a large Arboretum is to be established and Fortune particularly admires 'the remarkable *Amherstia nobilis* and the *Jonesia Asoca*, the former with its long racemes of scarlet flowers and the latter laden with fine orange blossoms.' Fortune continues his journey with his collections on the orders of the Indian Government, and as the river Hooghli was shallow at the time of year, the boat had to cross part of the huge Ganges river delta, mostly uninhabited except by the Bengal tiger who 'roams unmolested in his native wilds. Sometimes when native woodsmen come to cut wood they are carried off by this creature, in spite of being accompanied by a priest who is supposed to cast a spell upon tigers – but sadly he is frequently the first victim.' The boat took him as far as the fortress of Allahabad, after which they continued the journey by land. The Chinese and their effects, with the tea plants and implements for manufacture, filled nine wagons, but the tea plants were all found to be in a healthy state on arrival. No fewer than 12,838 were counted with many more germinating, and 'they seemed as green and vigorous as if they had been all the while growing on the Chinese hills.'

In Saharunpore Fortune received orders from the Governor-General of India to visit all the tea plantations in the districts of Gurhwal and Kumaon, and draw up a report upon their condition and future prospects. He was accompanied on this tour of inspection by Dr Jameson who was in charge of all Government tea plantations, and the first one they visited was Dehra Doon.

In 1998 I had visited Dehra Doon and its Forest Reserve Institute myself, while on a tour with the International Dendrology Society, and had driven up from Delhi on my way to Simla and then Nepal. I had felt obliged to visit Delhi because I was descended, through my father, from Hercules Skinner who married a Princess, of the fearsome and warlike Rajput tribe. James Skinner, his son – a Persian scholar and soldier of fortune – was born in 1778, and when his mother realised that, as a half- caste, her son could not join either his native or the English Army, she killed herself by cutting her throat in front of her seven year old son, James. He grew up and became a soldier in Madhaji Scindia's army, and became so successful and famous as a fighter and the founder of Skinner's Horse that he, with his 'Yellow Boys' (so named because of their yellow jackets), was invited to join the English forces under Lord Lake in 1803, who then made him a Lieutenant Colonel. His regiment eventually became the First Duke of York's Own Skinner's Horse. Skinner built the Church of St James in Delhi in fulfilment of a vow he made on the battlefield in 1800, and I had also made a vow that on visiting Delhi I would go and inspect this historic church.

On the drive up from Delhi I noted in my diary that the road consisted of miles and miles of hairpin bending, the driver managing with skill and determination to avoid head on crashes (with one exception, but luckily no fatalities) or sending us over the many precipices.

The Dehra Doon Forest Research Institute is a large and impressive establishment. The garden and arboreta cover 500 hectares; the main building having been completed in 1929 was arranged round courtyards and occupied over 2 hectares. The establishment was founded in 1906 and now acts as the main forestry institute, not only for India but also for other countries of south east Asia. Its activities cover research, scientific services, training and education and it has university status. Its facilities include the arboreta, a botanic garden, a herbarium and no less than seven museums devoted to separate aspects of forestry. Walking round the museums one appreciated the importance of trees to India: they are a major source of raw materials both to industry and village life and provide not only timber but also food for both humans and animals, and are the source of many medicines, chemicals and artefacts.

The botanic garden was a feast of trees and shrubs, the most exotic I can remember being the *Eucalyptus deglupta*, which I photographed – a native of Papua New Guinea with a smooth trunk, its bark vertically striped in red yellow and brown and one of the few of the species not native to Australia.

Fortune's investigations into the Chinese methods of growing and manufacturing the tea plant were fundamental to the Indian tea industry. As mentioned before, the British planters had no knowledge of the Chinese methods of growing or manufacturing it, while the Chinese had purposely kept this information secret, knowing very well that it was our intention to cut them out of the western market. When the idea of growing tea in India was first mooted it was Sir Joseph Banks idea, his 'infant adventure', to persuade some Chinese manufacturers to bring their expertise from Canton to India but Colonel Kyd's original attempt had not been successful. Perhaps this later trial, Mr Gordon's expedition, (the Secretary of the Tea Committee) was the best result until Fortune arrived on the scene. The workmen obtained by Gordon and the plants they brought were, in Fortune's opinion, far from first rate; 'indeed' he says, 'I doubt if any of them learned their trade in China. They

ought to be gradually got rid of and their places supplied by better men for it is a great pity to teach the natives an inferior method of manipulation. Considering that until lately we had little or no information as to how the tea plant was managed in China, the only wonder is that so few mistakes have been made.'

Fortune presses the point when he says that, 'as a result of his mission nearly twenty thousand plants from the best black and green tea countries of Central China have been introduced to the Himalayas. Six first rate manufacturers, two lead men and a large supply of implements from the celebrated Hwuy-chow districts were also brought and safely located on the Government plantations in the hills'.

What an extraordinary stroke of luck that Robert Fortune emerged at this precise moment for the whole India tea industry: not only had he been able to travel the length and breadth of China disguised as a Chinaman seeking the absolute requirements of the tea plant and collecting plants and seed of the best varieties, but that he was such a man, making very light of the times he was robbed and nearly murdered, able to apply his unique knowledge of the country, of the climate, of the language, and his study of these crafty and inscrutable people, who would betray him without a second thought if there was money in it or some advantage for them. And now he could use his inimitable experience, skill and judgment in advising how to make the most of

Eucalyptus deglupta – perhaps the most beautiful bark of all the eucalyptus.

the enormous lands in the Himalayas given over to tea growing.

Fortune and Jamison travelled on ponies, and Mrs Jamison who went with them was carried in a chair. The next plantation near Paorie was on a large tract of terraced land on the hillside and a most promising one, although suffering from hard plucking, that could be easily remedied; 'altogether' Fortune says 'the plantation is in a most satisfactory condition and shows how safe it is in matters of this kind to follow the example of the Chinese cultivator, who never makes plantations on *low rice land* and *never irrigates.*'

He finishes his report with these remarks: 'In my tour among the hills I have seen no place so well adapted for a central situation as Almorah or Hawulbaugh. Here the Government has already a large establishment, and tea lands are abundant in all directions. The climate is healthy and better suited to an European constitution than most other parts of India. Here plants from nearly all the temperate parts of the world are growing as if they were at home. As examples I may mention Myrtles, Pomegranates, and Tuberoses from the south of Europe; Dahlias, Potatoes, Aloes and Yuccas from America; *Melianthus major* and bulbs from the Cape; the Cypress and Deodar of the Himalayas; and the Lagerstraemias, Loquats, Roses and Tea of China.

In these days when tea has become almost a necessity of life in England and her wide-spreading colonies, its production upon a large and cheap scale is an object of no ordinary importance. But to the natives of India themselves the production of this article would be of the greatest value. The poor hill-peasant at present has scarcely the common necessaries of life, and certainly none of its luxuries. The common sorts of grain which his lands produce will scarcely pay the carriage to the nearest market town, far less yield such a profit as will enable him to purchase even a few of the necessary and simple luxuries of life. A common blanket has to serve him for his covering by day and for his bed at night, while his dwelling house is a mere mud hut capable of affording but little shelter from the inclemency of the weather. If part of these lands provided tea he would then have a healthy beverage to drink, besides a commodity which would be of great value in the market; being of small bulk compared with its value, the expense of carriage would be trifling and he would have the means of making himself and his family more comfortable and happy.'

Fortune compares him with his Chinese neighbour across the frontier, who never drinks anything but tea and considers cold water unhealthy: 'he drinks tea from morning to night, not mixed with milk and sugar but made from the essence of the herb drawn out in pure water. The Indian people are like the Chinese, the poor of both countries eat little animal food but exist on rice and other grains and vegetables; but for him to be able to afford tea it must be cheap enough, this can easily be done if he grows it on his own hills.'

Having completed his inspections, Fortune travelled back to Calcutta and once more stayed with Dr Falconer in the Botanic Gardens where he had the pleasure of seeing the *Victoria regia* flower for the first time in India, growing luxuriantly in one of the ponds. On the 29th August he sailed in the mail steamer which called at Calcutta to pick up her passengers for England.

In spite of Fortune's reports and the disagreements of Wallich and Griffiths, it was the tea planters in Assam who made the final decision to grow the tea plant that was under their noses. Within a span of three generations, learning by hard experience, they endured unspeakable hardships, made and lost fortunes, but carved tea plantations, literally out of jungles of India covering two million acres and employing over a million coolies. India at last took possession of the tea markets, monopolised by the Chinese for 200 years.

During the next few years Superintendents came and went in the Calcutta Gardens, but when Thomas Anderson took over in 1861, whatever he did or did not achieve was annihilated when the great cyclone of Calcutta – accompanied by a vast tidal wave from the Hooghli – laid the greater part of the garden under water, in some places to a depth of six of seven feet. Over a thousand trees, half the total number in the garden and innumerable shrubs were prostrated; of those that remained scarcely a leaf, flower or fruit was left.

From Anderson's report on the cyclone he says: 'three large breaches were formed in the river bank by the ships being blown into the garden with great violence; a larger and deeper breach was made by a French vessel being driven into the bank, the earth loosened by the weight of the vessels was washed away and at the distance of twenty feet from the western side of my house, a gap 50 feet long by 27 feet wide and about ten feet deep was formed. The gale at its height blew diagonally across the open surface of the river, and thus struck the garden with a force unbroken for the force of a mile, by any obstacle whatsoever. All the buildings and conservatories – many of them thatched – made of any other material than bricks and mortar were destroyed; in the nurseries about fourteen thousand plants in pots were buried under the ruins of the mahogany and mangoe groves, where the plants were kept for the sake of shade; all the plants of

Vanilla growing on the stems of mahogany trees were killed either by the falling of the trees, to which they were attached or by the violence of the wind.'

Anderson continues his tale of woe: 'All the damage to buildings, to rare plants in pots, and to the nursery stock are of small importance when compared with the wholesale destruction of trees: had the entire collections of plants in pots been lost the greater part could have been replaced in a comparatively short time, whereas even half a century will not be sufficient to restore the specimens of trees lost; many of them exist nowhere in cultivation except in this Garden and some are known to Botanists only by dried specimens and descriptions of those trees now lost. Many of the most picturesque parts of the Garden resulting from the grouping of trees no longer exist. In the teak avenue, sixty nine years old, only two mutilated specimens remain; thirty one of the sixty seven have been blown down, two of which had attained a circumference of thirteen feet six inches and had been sent to the Garden in 1796 by the East Indian Company. The Casuarina avenue, planted by Dr Wallich has suffered severely – only four much injured trees remain; the three gigantic specimens *Casuarina equisetifolia*, the oldest in the Garden and none of them less than 150 feet fell early in the storm and one was seen in the act of falling.'

The great Baobab of Africa described as '171 years old, the crown 1,100 feet in circumference, with about 666 aerial roots rooted in the ground and a girth of 51 feet' was uprooted and fell with a crash that caused vibrations in the earth which were felt at a distance of some hundred yards; this tree which had withstood the greatest force of the gale seemed to have at last given way from its roots having become loosened in the soil by the storm waves, whose waters rose to a height of four feet on the trunk of the tree.

Many trees, especially young specimens of teak were not uprooted but their stems were broken across fifteen or twenty feet above the ground, while every branch was wrenched off leaving nothing but bare poles without a leaf.'

This extract, from his description of the wreckage caused by the cyclone, ends by saying that 'nothing could convey the devastation than the loss of so many trees, many of the gigantic specimens prostrated, stripped of their branches without the vestige of a leaf or flower, the pride of the garden.'

Three years later, a less severe but still very destructive cyclone – in which 750 of the surviving trees were blown down – completed the ruin.

Anderson spent the next few years clearing up, but it wasn't until Dr George King appeared on the scene in 1871 that the garden began to recover.

His first sight of it must have been daunting; 'the vast area was completely without shade, coarse grass had taken over much of it and large parts of it were little better than swamps; what roads were left were narrow and subject to flooding, quite unfitted for carriage traffic and the ornamental lakes were now mostly unsightly channels and 'tanks'. Another calamity occurred about this time when the Curator of the Garden met with a fatal attack from a tigress, which, unnoticed by him, had swum across the river and was lurking in the shrubbery; six weeks later a black panther spent a night in the garden but was shot by King before it could do more damage.

King at least had liberal support from the Government of Bengal to whom control had now been transferred. The original scheme had been to treat the garden as a map of the world on Mercator's projection, the plants of India and Burma to occupy the central area of the large western part, this area being again subdivided in accordance with the subdivisions of the Indian Empire. Instead of continuing the formal systematic arrangement, King treated the entire garden for landscape effect. A series of lakes was excavated and the soil used to raise the level of the garden with attractive undulations; these lakes were connected by a system of underground channels, and a pumping engine kept the water level supplied from the river and the twenty-six irregular lakes — some of which were very large and with islands scattered throughout — designed with such skilful diversity of outline as greatly to enhance the overall beauty.

King made about 10 miles of carriage roads, all built on brick foundations, which stood up well to horse-carriage traffic, but were hard put to withstand the pressure of motor cars. Some of the roads he planted with magnificent avenues of single species trees, all (with the exception of some fine old mahoganies planted by Roxburgh about 120 years before) dating since the 1867 cyclone. Amongst the best were a half mile avenue of those exotic Palmyra palms and the large-leaved mahoganies — particularly beautiful when their bright green new leaves come out at the beginning of the hot season — and a fine avenue of Royal Palms, flanked by a double row of Mahoganies between the landing stage of the river bank and the Kyd monument, forming a truly regal grand entrance. Later in the spring when the Amherstias are in flower, the contrast between the lofty crown-spreading Albizzias, with their beech-like bark and delicate foliage, and the bushy Amherstias with their glorious pendant scarlet racemes of flowers, was particularly striking.

CHAPTER 8

The Botanic Gardens of Australia, Sydney

The interesting early history of the many botanic gardens in Australia begins in 1788 when Governor Phillip who – as Vice-Admiral Arthur Phillip commanded the First Fleet of convicts – arrived at Port Jackson in July of that year. He immediately set aside what became known as the Sydney Domain for his private reserve, which was the site of the future Royal Botanic Garden. At first it was used as a farm for growing grain, but this was soon moved to Parramatta a few miles inland, where the soil was better. Later Governors extended the gardens and built roads which enclosed the Government Domain with stone walls and paling fences, and helped to delineate the expanding gardens which now comprised three large plots and an extensive nursery. The day of its completion on June 13 1816 is celebrated as the foundation day of the Botanic Garden.

It had been discovered through Captain Cook's second voyage to the Antarctic that the climate was considerably colder in the Southern Hemisphere than at a comparable latitude of our own in the Northern Hemisphere. It was therefore necessary to apply a northerly correction of ten degrees which would put Botany Bay in latitude 33 degrees, similar to that of Toulouse in the south of France. It would be possible to grow all the fruits and vegetables native to that part of Europe, and the climate would suit the domestic animals including the fine woolled sheep of Spain, crucial as these turned out to be for the subsequent Australian economy.

Every ship that sailed back to England carried official despatches, private letters and specimens of natural history for Joseph Banks, with the first consignment from Captain Arthur Phillip, who clearly knew what would be of interest. This contained plants, seeds and gum, a stuffed kangaroo in a wooden case, a young kangaroo and the flying fox (or fox bat) shot on 27th June 1788 both in a keg of spirits, and among yet other items he sent was a case of the white clay used by the Aboriginals in marking their bodies, four tubs of flowering plants, an array of stuffed parakeets, two live parakeets and two live opossums. These interesting exchanges went on and the abiding influence of Joseph Banks ensured that the new colony would be a prime source of 'botanical novelties' for Kew and other grand gardens, and that a brisk traffic in seeds and plants developed.

Relishing with ever growing excitement the adventures of our intrepid explorers made me long to visit Australia myself, and having through various, nefarious means re-invented myself as a lecturer on my two favourite subjects, camellias and Sir Joseph Banks, I set about planning a 'Down Under' expedition to *Terra australis incognita* – as it was to me.

Banks is often referred to as 'the Father of Australia', so my lecture about him would be very suitable – my only fear being that my audience would know more about him than I did. My first engagement was in Perth, Western Australia, on the Swan River, named for its black swan inhabitants, which flowed past the old colonial house where I was invited to stay. This was practically in the Botanic Gardens, I was delighted to find, which had been opened in 1895 and named King's Park when Edward VII became King of England, and his son, George, Duke of Cornwall and Princess Mary came to visit.

Government House, where the garden had grown up, was situated in the main boulevard of the city, with panoramic views over the lake-like expanse of the river, and the 4 hectares of Government domain, created over the past 150 years. A copse of fine mature oaks and pine trees is believed to have been planted by the first Governor, Sir James Stirling, (1829-1838), as was an olive tree with the present girth of 3m. The garden is an example of informal landscape design, but with the existing drive in an elongated S shape, with the graceful curves adding an unexpected element of surprise.

The surrounding country is one of the most interesting botanical areas in the world, in which a primitive and ornamental flora has survived from an early geological era; it was on plants from this region that gardeners cast covetous eyes, and from the earliest days of the colony, enthusiastic amateurs had sent seed of the local wild flowers home. One of my greatest regrets is not to have seen this area, where these fabled collections of wonderful and unique wild flowers grow. I had not known about them until my arrival in Perth and the flowering season was over.

I was also disappointed to hear that the majority of the beautiful black swans, with their scarlet beaks and matching feet, have now moved to another part of the river where there are more tourists. There was very little spare time in Perth, but one other place I had to visit was the sea port, Fremantle, where the model of HMS *Endeavour* was being built; she was an exact replica, and later, on my visit to Sydney, I was invited to go aboard her for a day-sail round the harbour and under that wonderful bridge.

I shall not forget leaving Perth for Adelaide, especially my departure, when I discovered the difference between international and domestic airports. Too late as I saw my taxi disappear did I realise that the sole inhabitant of this vast

The striking Australian black swan with scarlet beak and matching feet.

airport besides myself was an elderly man, cigarette hanging out of his mouth, hoovering gloomily around the building. I had been hoping to catch the early flight to Adelaide for my next engagement and the horror of that moment threw me into panic mode; luckily the cleaner saved my life by summoning another taxi, and I reached the not too distant correct airport in time.

I was particularly interested to be flying over the Great Australian Bight imagining Matthew Flinders on his painstaking survey in HMS *Investigator* nearly 200 years before. Here he examined every inlet and gulf, hoping each time to find some big river from the north bisecting the huge continent. As we came down to land we flew round the city of Adelaide, which gave me the chance to look at Encounter Bay where Flinders overtook the French and found Captain Nicolas Baudin, who was in a bad way, having lost his consort ship *Naturaliste,* and with most of his crew sick with the scurvy fever – but Flinders did what he could to help and advised him to proceed towards Port Jackson, (Sydney). It must have been quite a moment when these two sailing ships, *Investigator* and *Geographe,* commanded by these intrepid young men met after their long, lonely and dangerous voyages into the unknown. Napoleon had personally ratified this expensively fitted out expedition, and one can imagine Josephine taking an interest and suggesting they bring her back some plants from this virgin continent.

The Oxford Companion to Australian Gardens tells us that Charles Fraser (1791-1831), botanist and botanic garden Superintendent, was born in Perthshire and became a gardener, probably for the extensive estates of the Duke of Atholl and subsequently for the botanic gardens of Edinburgh and Glasgow. He enlisted in a Foot Regiment in 1815 and arrived in Sydney in 1816, where Governor Macquarie quickly discovered this 'botanical soldier' and appointed him as colonial botanist, sending him off with Allan Cunningham – already plant hunting for Banks – to accompany surveyor John Oxley on a field trip to explore the Lachlan, Macquarie and Hastings river systems.

Fraser participated in two further major expeditions to make collections, one in 1827 with Captain James Stirling – later the first Governor in Western Australia to determine a site for the settlement. This he chose for the fresh water spring which had been noted by the first Europeans in the area in 1697 – Willem de Vlamingh and his party. The Swan River area had been visited by the French exploration under Captain Baudin in 1801, but according to Alice Coates' account, in her *Quest for Plants,* this voyage was ill-organised and unlucky and the boating party under M Heirisson reached no further up the river than Heirisson's Islands. Their naturalist Leschenault, however, had time to find the beautiful shrub named after him, and some living plants and seeds were collected for the Empress Josephine's garden at Malmaison.

When he was surveying the river Swan, Stirling named a feature near Heirisson Island in Fraser's honour, Point Fraser, and later – after his exploration – Fraser wrote a report titled *Observations on the soil &c, of the banks of Swan River,* followed by *Remarks on the Botany, &c of the Banks of Swan River, Isle of Buache, Baie Geographe and Cape Naturaliste,* these places being named by the French after their expedition's ships when they explored this coastal area.

Fraser's report is not exactly scintillating, but I quote a few extracts of what he found to be of interest in deciding where to place the settlement. He goes into great detail about The North and South Heads of the entrance to the Swan River which he says were 'formed of low rocks of fossil limestone in an advanced state of decomposition, presenting in many instances, apertures of the most fantastic form, in which are exposed to view masses of roots of trunks of trees of great size.' On the south bank he observed 'quantities of a species of brilliant sky blue *Brunonia* growing in great luxuriance on the margin of a salt marsh' as well as 'a magnificent species of *Melaleuca* with scarlet flowers and two species of *Metrosideros.'* The soil was of a fine light brown load containing a small proportion of sand, capable of producing any light garden crop, and here he found a brown snake, 'similar to that of Port Jackson, the only snake seen during the survey.'

There were vast springs under the rocks with fresh water, and the sandy soil improved as he climbed the hills, which he thought suitable for the site of a town, 'their elevated situation commanding a view of the whole of Canning sound.' He also considered this ground would make a splendid vineyard. At Point Fraser he found the first flat and, though no mangrove was to be seen, *Banksia grandis,* three feet in diameter, and the brome or Kangaroo grass was in great abundance.

Fraser was astonished at the 'vivid green of the eucalyptus and other trees and shrubs, so distinct from those of New South Wales', and he found the cause was the immense number of springs, 'the soil was quite moist though apparently at the end of an exceeding dry season'. He was amazed at the great luxuriance of the herbaceous plants on the banks, 'which exceed anything I ever saw on the eastern coast, some senecias reaching the height of nine feet and the beautiful species of Leptospermum which in habit resembles the weeping willow of Europe'.

The country beyond Pelican Point was covered with trees of richest green; 'here *Banksia grandis* appears in all its splendour, the Genus Eucalyptus forms the principal feature, but dryandra, hakea and grevillea richly clothed with yellow and crimson flowers – the dark green of the landscape being very striking to one long accustomed to the monotonous brown of the vegetation of Port Jackson.' His other observations included 'beds of tall thick rushes, about nine feet high' which he thinks are 'probably the rendezvous of the *dugong*, mentioned by M Peron (of Baudin's expedition) but of which we saw none.'

Fraser also reports hearing a species of *Psittacus* (Cockatoo): 'In large flocks, whose voice is more plaintive than that of the white cockatoo; it feeds on the roots of orchideous plants, to obtain which it scratches the ground to a considerable depth'. At the same time he listened to 'the bellowing of some huge animal, similar to that of an ox, proceeding from an extensive marsh farther up the river. Could this be the *dugong* of the French? '

Was the extraordinary dugong the source of the 'bellowing' recorded by M Peron on Baudin's expedition?

Here he was visited by 'three natives armed: they made signs for me to depart, but offered no violence and on hearing the voices of the party they retired into the woods.' He admired the *Zamia,* which reaches thirty feet, as does the *Xanthorrhoea arborea,* 'associated with the splendid *Banksias* imparted to a forest perfectly tropical.' He was baffled by ' the ridges on the banks, perforated with deep pits, the origin or cause of which we could not at first ascertain; they proved to be made by the natives for the purpose of catching land tortoises, with which these ridges abound.'

The climate was delightful, the thermometer seldom ranging above 85 degrees, the nights agreeably cool, and the sights remarkable: 'The quantity of black swans, (which gave the river its name), pelicans, and aquatic birds seen on the river was truly astonishing; without any exaggeration I have seen a number of black swans which could not be estimated at less than five hundred rise at once, exhibiting a spectacle which, if the colour and size of the bird be taken into account, and the noise and rustling occasioned by the flapping of their wings, previous to their rising, is quite unique in its kind. We frequently had from twelve to fifteen of them in the boats and the crews thought nothing of devouring eight roasted swans in a day'. He continues: 'The few natives which we saw were not disposed to behave ill; on the contrary they seemed alarmed much at first, but soon gained confidence; we gave them some black swans which they eagerly accepted; it is worthy of remark that these savages have no means of navigation, and rather show a horror of the water; their arms are the same as those of New South Wales, their clothing and appearance equally loathsome.'

Fraser sums up, pointing out the 'great ease with which a settler can bring his land into cultivation – the forests averaging not more than eight to ten trees to an acre, the great abundance of fresh water of the best quality, an advantage which NSW, east of the Blue Mountains does not possess, excepting on the immediate banks of the rivers and creeks. Such indeed were the attractions of the country that we all felt sorry on leaving it.'

Together with Stirling's effusive report on the naval, strategic and geological qualities of the area, these accounts were instrumental in convincing the British Colonial Office to establish the Swan River Colony, and provided the impetus to the period of excessively favourable publicity that has been labelled 'Swan River Mania'.

The Government therefore sent out a party of colonists under (now)

Admiral Sir John Stirling in the spring of 1829, which arrived in August of that year and set about founding Perth and Fremantle, which within four months had a population of 1,300. The first export from the colony was timber from the Jarrah tree, a species of Eucalyptus.

Charles Fraser was later severely criticised for the inaccuracy of his report; in reality the soils of the area were quite poor; it was shown that the party had only explored the narrow strip of rich alluvial soil that occurs near the Swan River and was thus unaware of the infertile grey sand that constitutes most of the sand plain. Fraser was to bear most of the blame from the Swan River Colonists for the misinformation they received. One, Eliza Shaw, wrote that: 'The man who reported this land to be good deserves hanging nine times over', and a naval officer stationed at the Swan River wrote that Fraser's report was so 'highly coloured' that it was inevitable people coming to the colony would be disappointed.

The party forming the settlement was either accompanied or immediately followed by James Drummond (1784-1863), who was required to lay out a botanic garden for the new colony. The Horticulture Society provided a collection of seeds, mostly of vegetables and fruit, but also including chrysanthemums and dahlias. Drummond had been the Curator of the Botanic Garden at Cork, Ireland, for twenty years before he embarked with his family on this adventure. He had been full of hope for his new career and was shattered by the blow when about a year after his arrival his post of Superintendent of Gardens was abolished and he was appointed Government Naturalist at the usual salary of £100 a year, especially as he had a number of children to support and times were hard. However, by 1835 he was farming a 3,000 acre grant of land in the Toodjay Valley, and by 1837 had begun work as an independent collector.

Drummond was another of the profuse correspondents, and wrote frequently to the editor of *Hooker's Journal of Botany* which published his letters under Botanical Information. The editor introduces a letter with: 'It is long since we have given any account of Mr James Drummond's excursions in Western Australia; we shall here and in our future numbers give occasional extracts from his many letters now before us, written during the year 1844, and since, from the Swan River Colony.'

Having just returned from an expedition to the country near the Beaufort and Gordon rivers, Drummond writes: 'Now that I have brought myself to live in the Bush as comfortably as in a house it would be a pity to relinquish collecting specimens for want of funds…let me travel in what direction I will. I cannot expect to collect more than 200 or 300 species to my store, and the sale of seven or eight sets of them does not defray half the necessary cost of collecting. However well the natives of this country are disposed to behave when unmolested it is impossible to venture among strange tribes without at least three persons well armed being of the party, with the necessary provisions, pack horses etc and this costs a great deal of money. My son, a servant and I have lived entirely in the bush for the last three months.'

The editor writes in another article: 'The friends of Botany will be glad to learn that fourteen sets of most interesting and well-preserved specimens of south-west Australian plants have been received by Mr Havard (Young St, Kensington) for distribution to the subscribers. Each collection consists of 550 species, including many entirely new, and of a most desirable character, others of the greatest rarity and very different from those sent by the same zealous and meritorious naturalist in his former transmissions.'

The price was £2 for the hundred species, with the share of freight. These plants were marked as a supplement to the 450 also sent, collected during the second Cape Riche journey, during which Mr Drummond suffered a dreadful attack of ophthalmia, making him quite blind for a fortnight and able only to travel by night, his eyes not being able to bear the light of day.

He describes some of these sensational flowers: a remarkable *Boronia* for instance with black flowers: 'it grows four or five feet, with drooping branches, the corollas are yellow inside, but this is not seen unless the branches are turned up, the black flowers are only fragrant at night.' While this plant may be rare and interesting, it does not sound very attractive and reminds me of a *Boronia megastima* I once bought mistaking it for the bright pink very scented one. It had dark brown flowers and no scent, (though I have to admit I did not test its scent at night), and I gave it away at once. Another much more desirable plant he names as *Gastrolobium Leakeanum*, which grows twelve to fifteen feet high, with opposite leaves three inches long by two broad, and bears clusters of large deep scarlet flowers in the axils of the leaves.

'During my late journey to the south', he relates, 'I gathered a most exquisite *Stylidium* in flower; for several years I have observed its foliage, but a careful examination of the plant in various situations leads me to the conclusions that the inflorescence is never produced in profusion except on the second year after the ground has been cleared by fire. The leaves, which shoot up very beautifully become hard and rigid in the course of two or three years and seem incapable of supplying the nutriment necessary to enable the plant to form its flowers and mature its seeds. I have named it *S. elegans.* The lanceolate leaves are 18 inches long, smooth and silky, the flowers rose-coloured and borne on stalks up to two ft high; on the whole I consider it the finest species of the genus.'

Another plant he mentions and that I covet is 'a *Banksia* with blood-red flowers compared with which the much vaunted *Banksia grandis* is but a pygmy.'

The second expedition Fraser accompanied was under Captain Patrick Logan in 1828 to the Moreton Bay area of Eastern Australia, where they ascended the ranges and he was charged to lay out a botanic garden for the four year old settlement of Brisbane. Allan Cunningham accompanied him,

Banksia coccinea – probably the Banksia with blood red flowers referred to by Drummond and much coveted by the author.

and they spent three weeks working on the garden and making more explorations in the neighbourhood. Some of the plants collected on this journey were planted out in the Sydney Botanic Gardens, notably *Araucaria cunninghamii* (Hoop Pine) and *Waterhousea floribunda* (Weeping Lilly Pilly) – now huge canopy trees at the southern end of the present palm grove.

It was in 1818 that Fraser took over the exotics in the Government Gardens, and over the next decade as Superintendent he organised the development of the Sydney Botanic Gardens, from its role as the Governor's kitchen garden to a world-renowned botanic garden, receiving and sending plants and seed to all the major horticultural centres as well as to penal settlements and gardens in New South Wales. Initially, food plants were grown – fruit trees, olives and grapes being especially successful – and liberally distributed among the settlers. As more economic and ornamental plants were given to him, he trialled, propagated and grew these under difficult conditions, with poor soil, inadequate water and no glasshouses. Being a skilled horticulturist he succeeded where others had failed and became respected by governors, botanists and explorers alike.

Fraser died of a stroke, at only forty three, when returning from another arduous expedition and was buried at Parramatta in 1831. His specimens are now principally in the herbaria at Kew and the Natural History Museum, London.

Sydney Botanic Gardens developed over the next few years under the care of various Superintendents and Allan Cunningham, until 1847 when Charles Moore succeeded to the post and worked there for over forty years. The scientific function languished during his time but he transformed the garden with extensive land reclamation, the addition of the Garden Palace Exhibition grounds with embellishments such as garden statuary and monuments. Moore tackled the problems of poor soil, inadequate water and shortage of funds, establishing much of the gardens as we see them today and replenished the trees, particularly with Moreton Bay Figs, one of the chief elements of his planting – in fact his signature tree. His successor was Joseph Henry Maiden, museum curator and botanic garden director from London University.

Maiden was born in London in 1859, and went on to gain the Fishmongers Scholarship at Cambridge, but did not take this up, preferring to study botany at the Science School of London University. But failing health encouraged him to take a sea voyage, and in 1880 he came out to Australia with a return ticket in his pocket. Arriving in Sydney he was so fascinated by the flora of the new country that when his health improved he decided to remain and try his fortune there.

The field was wide open and he found his feet at the Technological Museum where he lectured, and was invited to become its first Curator in 1881. He travelled all over New South Wales and formed the nucleus of the magnificent collection of technical material, a special feature of which was obtained from the native plants, particularly timbers that he found. Charles Moore, Government Botanist and Superintendent of the Sydney Botanic Gardens, also lectured at the Museum, where Maiden added much to his botanical knowledge.

In 1889 the Government took over the Museum and included it in the Sydney Technical College, of which Maiden was invited to be Superintendent. Here Maiden was a great success, and the College grew to be one of the most important branches of the Department of Public Instruction. When Charles Moore died Maiden was appointed Curator of the Sydney Botanic Gardens, and immense progress was made in these beautiful grounds, both in horticultural and scientific research work.

During twenty eight years as Director, Maiden greatly improved the arrangements and content of the living collections in the garden, establishing an outstanding herbarium, museum and library, making intensive studies of Eucalypts and Acacias and writing the massive *Flora of New South Wales (1904-1924)*. Other special interests included reduction of sand erosion, promotion of wattle cultivation for the tanning industry and control (or utilisation) of the prickly pear. Maiden's diverse interests also led him at different times to serve as Secretary to the Royal Geographical Society of Australasia, consulting botanist to the NSW Department of Agriculture, lecturer in botany and forestry at the University of Sydney and many others prestigious posts.

He became quite a legend among gardens and gardeners with his huge displays of native flowers in all his institutions, and by distributing thousands of plants to churches, hospitals, schools, cemeteries, war memorials, and police and railway stations to enhance their grounds.

When one of Maiden's staff left Sydney to work on forestation at Canberra, he readily co-operated by sending hundreds of trees and shrubs for the project. He visited personally to inspect the plantings and was able to comment on species likely to succeed, writing a report for the Commonwealth authorities. His name became well-known through the press, his public pronouncements and his correspondence, and one of his great achievements was to arrange the transfer from London to Sydney of many specimens collected in 1770 by Banks and Solander. He also wrote a biography of Sir Joseph Banks, and was awarded, among many other honours, the Linnean Medal by the Linnean Society of London for distinguished services to Australian Botany.

Maiden's strong sense of public duty was tempered by a gentle sense of humour, and he was devoted to his work and his family. He and his wife Eliza Jane suffered the terrible loss of their only son at sea but rejoiced in their four daughters, inevitably (and with reason) called 'the beautiful Maidens'.

He retired in 1924 and enjoyed a short time in his own garden despite increasing disability, and continued work on his *Critical Revision of the Genus Eucalyptus*. With this great work unfinished he died at his home in 1925 and was buried in the leafy churchyard of St John's, Gordon. The vast number and diversity of mourners attested to the breadth and depth of his interests and influence.

One must not forget that it was on Joseph Banks' judgment and recommendation where the First Fleet of convicts was based. When the Bunbury Commission was set up by Parliament to look into the possibility of creating a penal colony in New South Wales, it was Joseph Banks who was summoned to give his opinion; not only was he one of the only people who had ever been there, (when voyaging round the world with Captain Cook in HMS *Endeavour* 1768-1771) but he was also a botanist and, more importantly, an English farmer. The inspired way in which he assessed the Botany Bay region's potential to become a neo-Europe, and the way in which he equipped the first colonists to realise this, explains the central role he played in the first seventeen years of the colony's existence.

About twenty years before this, when the Government and the Royal Society joined forces to send a ship to the Pacific (with the scientific purpose of observing the transit of the planet Venus, and searching for a southern continent that was thought to exist) he seized the opportunity to go with them; this inspired him further with the idea of exchanging plants worldwide, even envisaging a day when there could be a network of botanic gardens.

It is not surprising that Joseph Banks took so much interest in the future of New South Wales. Sailing home in April 1770 from their discovery and circumnavigation of New Zealand, they had touched upon Tasmania before turning north, hoping to sight the *terra australis incognita,* and the excitement of these young Englishmen when land appeared on the horizon must have been acute. Banks put in his diary: 'The country this morn rose in gently sloping hills which had the appearance of the highest fertility, every hill seemed to be clothed with trees of no mean size.'

This was found to be the east coast of New Holland, later to be called Australia, which framed the new continent, of which only the west coast had been mapped at that time. No wonder Banks was longing to discover more about this vast and completely unknown land.

It was while continuing my research into how and when the first camellias had reached Australia that I unearthed the riveting story of John Macarthur, whose pioneering and determined behaviour was responsible for some of the early dramatic events of the colony. Digging into his origins I discovered that though he became a gardener of note, he started out as a sheep farmer – an intriguing beginning to a saga which led me to find out how he became involved with Joseph Banks and Bligh – all too good to be true.

John Macarthur was a Scotsman, whose parents had been forced to flee Scotland after the 1745 rebellion, and who was born in Plymouth in 1767. At 15 he joined the Army, but at 16 was retired on half pay and decided to learn sheep farming. Then at 21 he married a remarkable girl called Elizabeth Veale, and on being recalled to the colours as an officer, he found his next job to be taking part in the escort of the second fleet of convicts to New South Wales in 1788.

A graphic account of the voyage, with the second Fleet of Convicts, was found in Elizabeth Macarthur's Journal – in a torn condition – among the papers of her daughter, Lady Parker at Sheen, Surrey, and in the letters to her mother, Mrs Veale, from which I quote one or two extracts. John and Elizabeth had a very shaky start, when the Captain of their vessel the *Neptune* was replaced after a drunken brawl which took place while they were boarding at Plymouth. The new Captain turned out to be another hopeless character who refused to listen to Macarthur's complaint that their cabin was being divided off for the accommodation of female convicts.

Elizabeth relates: 'A slight partition was erected which was thought fully sufficient to separate us from the set of abandoned creatures that were to inhabit the other part.' Worse was to come – in the common passage, the only route to the stern gallery, where she would walk or sit with John on a fine evening – she recounts that this: 'was rendered impassable by being closely nailed up without their deigning to assign any reason for so doing…without a hope of relief, I was fain to content myself within the narrow limits of a wretched cabin, for to add to the horrors of the common passage to the deck, the Captain ordered it to be a hospital for the sick, the consequence of which was that I never left my cabin till I finally quitted the ship. Thus precluded from the general advantages that even the convicts enjoyed – air and exercise – no language can express, no imagination conceive the misery I experienced. Approaching near the equator (where the heat in the best of situations is almost insupportable), assailed with noisome stenches, surrounded with wretches whose dreadful imprecations and shocking discourses ever rang in my distracted ears, a sickly infant constantly claiming maternal cares, my spirits failing, my health forsaking me, nothing but the speedy change which took place could have prevented me from falling a helpless victim to the unheard of inhumanity of a set of monsters whose triumph and pleasure seemed to consist in aggravating my distresses.'

Luckily, soon after arriving at the Cape they managed to change ships and were well treated in the *Scarborough*, and after many more adventures, rows and illnesses they arrived safely in Port Jackson in June 1790 – the terrible journey had lasted seven months.

Macarthur was the first married military officer, and his wife the first educated woman to make the infant colony their home.

The Government policy in New South Wales was to give a grant of land and some stock to anyone who was willing to settle there. The young Macarthurs considered this a fine opportunity, and at Elizabeth Farm – their new home – they grew fruit and vegetables, corn and wheat and began to build up their livestock. They first had hairy Bengal ewes, which had come from India, to which were put a woolly Irish ram, and the resulting offspring bore mingled fleeces of hair and wool which gave Macarthur the idea of producing fine wool fleeces from his flocks. Ships were few and far between, but the next consignment from South Africa brought some of the much prized Spanish Merinos; from these he bred some of his finest sheep – and was then determined to improve the breed and keep it pure.

Macarthur was a colourful man, difficult and irascible, given to having rows with everyone, and after fighting a duel with his own Commanding Officer he was sent home to England to be court martialled. His capable wife Elizabeth carried on the farm while he was away and continued his marked success, carefully preserving the special breed.

Never one to miss an opportunity, Macarthur took some samples of his

John Macarthur, officer accompanying second fleet of convicts in 1788, became a pioneer sheep farmer and later a gardener of note.

fine fleeces from his sheep (which now numbered over 2,000), hoping to interest Lord Camden, Home Secretary of the day, and also to impress Joseph Banks with whom he had been corresponding.

Macarthur was lucky that his court martial papers were lost on the journey to England, and he was able on his arrival to persuade Banks to allow him to attend the public auction of the King's surplus Merino stock. The Spanish Merino breed was much sought after for improving the quality of fine wool in England, and it was at the King's request that Banks had managed to acquire some of them. As the Spanish did not allow their sheep to be exported, they had to be secretly smuggled via Lisbon; some of these had been over wintered on Banks's farm land in Lincolnshire, and it was necessary for these 44 precious Merino sheep to travel south to Kew where the sale was to take place. Sheep travel in 1804 meant walking with a drover over a distance of about 12 miles a day, quite an ordeal for the foot-weary little flock which took 11 days to reach their destination.

Macarthur was allowed to take his place among the distinguished and privileged buyers, and astonished everybody by buying ten animals – a quarter

Merino sheep – descended from the stock imported by Macarthur's to Camden Park Stud, and foundation of the mighty Australian wooltrade.

of all the available stock – and with some friends embarked at Portsmouth in his own whaling ship (suitably renamed *Argo* after the vessel in which Jason sought *The Golden Fleece*). They set sail in November 1804, and arrived triumphantly seven months later in Sydney. The five rams and one old ewe which survived this epic journey were bred with his original stock and formed the basis of the Camden Park stud, the first colonial stud of any consequence and the foundation of the mighty Australian wool trade.

Joseph Banks was intimately connected with everything to do with this 'infant colony' and deeply involved with the wool trade in England, so it had been inevitable that their paths would cross. Later Banks was also responsible for recommending Captain Bligh (of the Bounty) to be appointed Governor of New South Wales. Naturally it wasn't long before Macarthur fell out with Bligh (a man with a similar reputation), who had him locked up, and it was from prison that Macarthur organised the Rum Rebellion, staging a *coup d'état*, deposing Governor Bligh and running New South Wales as a military junta for two years. Surprisingly, none of the mutineers was hanged or even severely punished for this remarkable mutiny. Macarthur was, however, forced to return to England to defend his behaviour, and on this occasion he took two of his sons to be educated in England.

Banks, who had recommended Bligh for the job, could not have been too pleased by the reports he must have received of Bligh's conduct. Allowing for prejudice against him, there is a letter from Macarthur's wife in which she says: 'Our new Governor Bligh is a Cornishman by birth, Mrs Putland (his daughter) who accompanied him is a very accomplished person. The Governor has already shown the inhabitants of Sydney that he is violent, rash, tyrannical.'

On his journey out from England, Bligh had such a violent row with the Captain, the commander of the convoy, that the latter was in consequence court martialled. He was, however, honourably acquitted and recommended by the court to the favourable consideration of the Admiralty on account of the treatment he had received from Bligh.

Another letter from General Watkyn Tench, Royal Marines, who had travelled out with the First Fleet, to Macarthur's son Edward, (later Sir Edward, who had been the tiny baby travelling with his parents on that fearful first voyage) relates: 'I was firmly and decidedly of opinion that Governor Bligh by tyranny, oppression and rapacity has drawn upon himself the just resentment of the inhabitants of the colony and met with that spirited opposition and final defeat which I trust all unprincipled despots, whether in courts or cottages will always encounter...the concealment under the featherbed made me smile, but did not surprise me in the least, as I had long possessed the strongest testimony from a friend who had served with Governor Bligh that he was not only a tyrant but also a poltroon.'

He finishes by promising that when he is asked for information about New South Wales, 'which frequently happens at the tables of Generals and Admirals, I shall not fail to offer my undisguised opinion on proceedings which have excited so much public attention, and of my perfect conviction of the worth and integrity of your father, his defence will be an easy task'.

Much has been written about the 'starving years' and the terrible struggles that took place after the landing of the First Fleet of convicts; it is interesting to read how astonished were the French, when arriving at Port Jackson (helped on their way by Flinders) a few years later, to see 'the fine garden at Government House, Sydney where 'the Norfolk Island pine, the superb Columbia grows by the side of the bamboo from Asia; further on is the Portugal orange, and the Canary fig, ripening beneath the French apple trees. The cherry, pear, peach and apricot are interspersed among the Banksia, Metrosideros, Correa, Melaleuca, Casuarina, Eucalyptus and a great number of other indigenous trees.'

Even more amazing is John Macarthur's report home in 1794: 'From a state of desponding poverty and threatening famine, that this settlement should be raised to its present aspect in so short a time is scarcely credible. In my own farm of nearly 250 acres I have sold £400 of this year's produce, have more than 1,800 bushels of corn in my granaries and have 20 acres of fine wheat growing and 80 acres prepared for Indian corn and potatoes. My stock consists of a horse, two mares, 130 goats, and more than a hundred hogs, poultry of all kinds in abundance. With the assistance of one man and six greyhounds my table is constantly supplied with wild duck and kangaroos.'

He goes on to describe his excellent brick house with 'a large hall, closets, cellar etc; adjoining is a kitchen with servants apartments and other necessary offices. The house is surrounded by a vineyard and garden of about three acres.'

In the many letters written to each other, especially when John and Elizabeth were separated by his time spent in England, members of the family give fascinating pictures of their lives in the early days of the colony. The redoubtable Elizabeth also corresponds faithfully with a girlfriend in England, and these letters might have been something of a substitute for local friends as she says: 'having no female friend to unbend my mind to, nor a single woman with whom I could converse with any satisfaction to myself, the clergyman's wife being a person in whose society I could reap neither profit or pleasure.' One is tempted to continue quoting from all these articulate, intelligent, interesting and so-long-ago letters, but I will confine myself to just one more, written years later to her son, Edward, when staying with her daughter Elizabeth: 'We walked to the Botanic Gardens together...I believe we sauntered about three hours or more, looked at many things you had contributed to the collection....there is a new garden formed, laid out after the plan of the 'Glasgow Botanical Garden' of Dr Hooker, the introductions from Moreton Bay promise to be very ornamental, it assumes already a very tropical character, but as I intend this to be a short letter I must not let the Botanical Gardens run away with my pen'.

The Macarthur family had a great influence on the integrity in their sphere. John had his tremendous battles during the Bligh episode and others, but he came out of it all exonerated and his remarkable achievements in the fine wool trade were entirely due to his skill, perseverance and determination. His fine family of six children – two of his four sons knighted – says a great deal to his credit and that of Elizabeth, his remarkable wife.

It was in a letter written by John Macarthur junior, (one of the sons who had travelled with his father to be educated in England) that I found his description of *Camellia japonica [C j]*: 'the most magnificent flowering shrub that has ever been introduced into this country (England from Japan), the flower which is as red as the rose or white as the driven snow is the most perfectly beautiful that can be imagined.... They will flourish in the open air in New South Wales.' His first shipment arrived in Sydney in 1831, and Macarthur went on to establish a nursery for their propagation.

The first camellia material to reach Europe from China was sent by an English physician, James Cunningham, stationed at Chusan at the end of the 17th century. The English East India Company imported paintings of the exquisite formal double flowers which raised much excitement, and the grand gardens of Europe vied with each other to find the most exotic varieties.

A riveting account of one of these Camellias was sent to me by Min

Wood, Botanist and Garden Historian – based on information from the staff at Pillnitz. I quote a few lines from it: 'In 1720 Augustus 'The Strong', Elector of Saxony and King of Poland ordered the building of a summer palace at Pillnitz, 10 km from Dresden, which was to be designed in what was then called an 'Indian' manner; Popplemann, the architect, not having visited the East did his best from the sketches made by travellers and from the images on imported China ware. The result is one of the most enchanting and romantically sited palaces in Europe.

Augustus 'The Strong' was succeeded by his nephew Frederick Augustus 'The Just', who was a passionate gardener and botanist. Under his rule the hornbeam bosquets which lingered from an earlier house at Pillnitz would be joined by a pinetum, a Chinese garden, an extended Orangery, the then largest glasshouse in Continental Europe and an 'English' garden. It was into the 'English' garden in 1801, that a Camellia was planted in open ground. The story of that Camellia is every bit as exotic as the history of the Schloss Pillnitz itself. Dutch merchants were, in the 18 C, the only Westerners allowed to do business with Japan. (All others were banned due to their habit of arriving with missioneries), one of these was Carl Peter Thunberg, a Swedish student of Linnaeus. Thunberg was sent for three years to the Cape Colony to learn how to behave like a Dutchman'. Here he met and joined several plant hunting expeditions with Francis Masson who was the first of Joseph Banks' plant collectors commissioned by King George III. After this, Min continues: 'Thunberg then went as the East India Company doctor, to Nagasaki...Eventually he was asked to visit Tokyo and he made sure the journey took as long as possible so he could collect plants along the way. One of these was a Camellia japonica and it is not known whether it was a true wild species or a selection from a Japanese garden.

On his return to Europe he visited Sir Joseph Banks and presented to Kew four Camellia plants. Of these one was sent to Herrenhausen (Hanover), one to Schonbrunn (Vienna) and one to Pillnitz. Only the Pillnitz Camellia survives.

The planting of this Camellia in open ground in Saxony was a triumph of horticultural optimism over botanical wisdom. Tough though it is, Camellia japonica is not a plant that welcomes very low winter temperatures. At first it was protected by mats of straw and bark. By 1905, a wooden structure was being erected each year over the Camellia, but in January that year disaster struck. The stove in the building overheated, which was set ablaze and with temperatures at −20C, no water could be found to quench the fire. Whether from the heat or the exposure to the cold, later that night the plant was defoliated.' Camellias being the resilient plants they are, amazed everyone by producing new leaves the next spring and as Min recounts 'this German National Treasure has been tended with the greatest care ever since.'

This care was not delivered in half measures: after a succession of wooden houses to protect the multi-stemmed tree (now no longer a shrub), in 1992, a new metal framed greenhouse was built to house this indestructible plant, which at 212 years old had reached 9 metres high by 2.13 metres round the girth at ground level. 'This multifunctional glasshouse reached 13.2 m and weighing 54 tons was put in place from October to May. With 12 sides, four of which open out in pairs to allow the structure to move on rails four metres away from the tree in summer, the house provides automatic climate control to a minimum of 4-6C degrees in winter, variable ventilation, irrigation and shading on sunny days. Viewing platforms at two levels allow visitors to enjoy in comfort the carmine red single flowers from February to April and in a good year the plant is said to produce 35,000 blossoms.'

I am greatly honoured to have been entrusted by Min with a rooted cutting of this splendid historic plant, as a sort of 'cordon sanitaire', in case of further disaster – it is labelled 'Pillnitz'. I invited it as a lodger (free of course) and it lives in my cold greenhouse in winter, but enjoys its summer holidays outside, on the shady terrace. I repot it from time to time and although it is scarcely rivalling its ancient relative it has reached about 4 feet in height and after some harsh words and a dose of potash, three bright pink, miniature, single flowers bloomed this spring.

Sir Joseph Banks acquired *C Anemoniflora* and other named varieties for The Royal Gardens at Kew by 1804. Hundreds more, including the *C sinensis*, the tea plant and other species, were imported and grown particularly well in Italy, France and the Channel Islands, where much propagation took place. It soon arrived in America where its popularity resulted in many camellia societies being founded.

It was John Macarthur (junior) who had this passion for the genus, but it was his brother William (later Sir William) who took up the challenge in Camden Park, near Sydney, and writing some fifteen years later recounts: 'We have raised four or five hundred seedlings chiefly from seeds produced by the

Camellia japonica 'Anemoniflora', from Curtis's Botanical Magazine 1814.
Parent of many seedlings in New South Wales.

old *C j anemoniflora;* our largest plant has been planted out more than nine years and is of regular pyramidal form perfectly clothed with branches from the ground upwards and nearly twelve feet high'. This was *C j* 'Aspasia,' now known as 'Aspasia Macarthur'. He named 69 of the seedlings, issued printed catalogues of camellias, grapes and olives – despatching plants to nurserymen and private growers in New South Wales, Victoria, Tasmania and South Australia – and became their first great source within Australia. His father, John Macarthur, had brought grapes and olives from France when he took his two sons to England to be educated. He describes their travels in France and Switzerland in many letters written home to his wife Elizabeth.

There are still venerable old plants of his that Macarthur gave to Sydney Botanic Gardens; in 1852 he presented them with one of his seedlings, *C japonica* 'Imogen', which after a hundred years was still flourishing and flowering freely. Another amazing Australian specimen was *C j* 'The Czar', 12ft high and 16ft across and of such renown that in 1951 it was transplanted to the Melbourne Botanic Garden.

Mysteriously there are also very old camellias to be found in Vaucluse

House, near Sydney, which include one of the earliest known and most beautiful, *C j 'Anemoniflora'*, but there are no records of when it was planted or from where it came. The site was bought in 1803 by Sir Henry Brown Hayes, who arrived in Australia as a convict, transported for life for the crime of having abducted an heiress. It seems that money and social position were assets even to convicts, and the story goes that he travelled in special quarters in his transport ship and even dined at the Captain's table.

A description of the plant in the Sydney Botanic Gardens from a visitor later in the century says: 'Dark Norfolk Island pines serve as a background to large camellia trees, literally one blaze of blossom, pink, white, crimson and variegated. These grow in such rank profusion wherever they receive the slightest care that we marvel to find them in so comparatively few gardens.'

My next lecture engagement – suitably on camellias – was destined to take place in the beautiful city of Sydney. I was staying in the RAC Club which I was pleased to find opened up from the basement lift on to Circular Quay, that unforgettable landing place of the First Fleet of convicts. From here I found my way to join the exact replica of HMS *Endeavour*, sailing under the magical and famous bridge – one of the highlights of my visit to Australia. I explored in depth the Botanic Gardens and the magnificent Botanic Library with its marvellous modern equipment. I also visited the mysterious Blue

Campbell's Wharf, The Circular Quay, Sydney – landing place of the First Fleet of Convicts in 1788. Painted by Conrad Martens, official visual recorder on the voyage of HMS *Beagle*.

Three Sisters, Katoomba, The Blue Mountains, New South Wales.

Mountains and took some memorable photographs.

But I had one more important date in Sydney, which was to visit the home of the late Professor EG Waterhouse (1881-1977) whom I had met when he came to England aged 94 to receive an award from the Queen Mother. He was one of the foremost authorities on the camellia, his particular interest for the genus being for its history and nomenclature, and he was internationally known for his botanical accomplishments. When the camellia became unfashionable at the end of the 19th C, Waterhouse made determined efforts to save it and to quote one of his friends: 'he rescued it from neglect, restored it to the princedom of the garden and is acclaimed throughout the world as the leader of its adherents'.

As a superb linguist who taught French, German and Italian at the highest level, lecturing at the University of Sydney, Waterhouse was fascinated by the origin of the camellia and at the age of eighty started to learn Japanese especially to be able to read camellia texts in that language. He wrote several books *Camellia Quest, Camellia Trail,* and *The Magic of Camellias* – now collectors' items – and eventually worked on the remarkable publication *The International Camellia Register* with Tom Savige, (I come to him in the chapter on Melbourne) who took the project over and finished it after Professor Waterhouse died.

I found the Professor's house in Gordon, part of Sydney, which had been romantically named 'Eryldene' after his wife Janet's home in Scotland. It was now a sort of camellia shrine and held one of the largest private collections of these beautiful plants in Australia. As a camellia addict myself, it was a pleasure to wander slowly, enjoying this romantic garden, full of all the most desirable varieties, many of them his own excellent hybrids, which I grow in my own garden at home. One could feel the lifelong passion for these plants, lovingly arranged to show off their elegance.

Camellia x 'E G Waterhouse' – named after the eminent camellia authority Professor Waterhouse (1881-1977). Painted by Paul Jones.

CHAPTER 9

The Melbourne Botanic Garden

Standing on the edge of Encounter Bay, Adelaide, next stop Antarctica, I imagined Flinders and Baudin at their historic meeting, I could also envisage another hopeful young man who landed in Adelaide in 1847 from Germany, and who was to make his mark in Australia. Ferdinand von Mueller, botanist and explorer, was born in the Baltic city of Rostock in 1825; his father had been an officer in the Prussian army and all the family links appear to have been German. At the age of fifteen he was already carrying out botanical research, and later he took up an apprenticeship in pharmacy, and when he was not studying he was out in the countryside collecting plants for the herbarium his work required. At twenty-one, after completing his apprenticeship, he graduated at the University of Kiel.

His reason for migrating was the threat of tuberculosis; he had lived through his boyhood in the shadow of both his parents' and his favourite sister's terrible illness and subsequent death; there is a photograph of him when he was eighteen, looking doubtful, anxious, unhappy, as if he had turned his back on human beings and the disease and death that infected them. Work and study were what mattered; he had to learn to stand alone, and this became a habit and determined the course of every human relationship he attempted throughout the rest of his life.

And so, leaving behind the anguished atmosphere and unhealthy climate, he gathered his two remaining sisters with him and set out to try his luck in a warmer and drier environment. There seem to have been quite a few German young men eager to investigate this brand new continent of Australia, and Mueller must have read of some of the discoveries already made in this fresh and exciting land: the wonderful variety of unknown plants found by Joseph Banks (with Cook) and Robert Brown (with Flinders), and the extraordinary animals, unique to the country, from the kangaroo – which must have seemed eccentric enough – to the duck billed platypus (its present habitat is now called a 'platypussery') – the latter, to my mind, the most original creature of the natural world, described as 'fur covered, venomous, beaver-tailed mammal with its beak and webbed feet, its nest under water among the roots of trees, and its habit of laying eggs and suckling its young'. Mueller must have longed to be able to make his own discoveries.

Among the Germans already there was a naturalist, Dr Preiss, working in Western Australia. Another German, Ludwig Leichhardt had set sail for Sydney in 1841 and was to play an important part in the exploration of Australia; Leichhardt wrote many letters and journals describing in the most lively and vivid way all that he saw which interested him. On his arrival he wrote: 'I can't tell you with what excitement I leapt ashore, with what delight I greeted every botanical novelty, or how new impressions came crowding in from all sides until I felt positively dizzy.' He described one of his friend's imaginative inventions suitable for exploring the unknown – a hat which would expand into an umbrella, three feet in diameter, when he pulled a string!

Leichhardt's adventurous expeditions had made him a hero, and he was awarded gold medals by the geographical societies of London and Paris. He was determined to be the first man to cross the northern part of the continent from east to west, and then travel down the coast to Perth. He made several attempts which failed, and this, his last expedition, was also ill fated: he and his pioneering friends left from the Darling Downs early in 1848 and after a last letter written on 4th April of that year, he disappeared and was never heard of again; this was just as Mueller was arriving with his sisters in Adelaide and it seems to have started a lifelong hero worship, an obsession to emulate Leichhardt and a deep resentment for what he felt was the unconcern of the Government for his fate.

Adelaide was clearly the best choice for Mueller's destination, the capital of Southern Australia, founded in 1836. There were two thriving settlements of Prussians beyond the town, and because south Australia had never received convicts from Britain, the tone of the place was highly moral, with many churches and chapels, Sunday schools and temperance movements. Perhaps Mueller was influenced by the Head Gardener of the Kiel Botanic Garden,

Ludwig Fischer, who was also emigrating and by a lucky chance travelling in the same ship as the Muellers.

After a gruelling journey of five and a half months, they landed more dead than alive in a most uninviting looking landscape. There had been days when the ship pitched and rolled and tossed, and the timbers creaked and groaned, and others when she sat motionless on an oil-smooth sea without a breath of wind, when the sails flopped and fluttered. Nine passengers had died during the voyage and three babies were born.

On landing they had a stroke of luck; Samuel Davenport, a recent immigrant himself invited the Muellers to stay until they could find suitable accommodation, and his friend who had a chemist's shop in the town offered Ferdinand work. Samuel's wife took to the girls, and soon they were happily settled.

Adelaide lay to the north of the estuary of the 1,600 mile long river Murray. Mueller immediately started to explore the lower reaches and found the variety of flowering eucalypts and exotic plants utterly absorbing and rewarding - there is evidence to prove that he began collecting plants within a few hours of his arrival. A contemporary botanist wrote of him that, 'the year 1847 must for all time be looked upon as the beginning of a great epoch in Australian botany, for it is due to Mueller's zeal and indefatigable labour that the way of the botanist at the present time is so plain and easy'.

Mueller started to explore further afield, to the Mount Lofty Ranges behind Adelaide, climbing both Mount Brown and Mount Arden, then north across the plains to the salty mud-flats of Lake Torrens, 130 miles long by thirty miles wide, the second largest salt lake in Australia. All his early expeditions were made on foot and alone, and as he was a prodigious walker, he thought nothing of covering hundreds of miles. He learnt to be a survivor and his scientific training made him a good navigator, later finding out how to manage horses, repair harness and make hobbles.

Mueller spent five years in South Australia, extending his botanical experience widely, and in 1850 began to publish papers on his work, first in Australia and then in England and Germany. For example, *Flora of South Australia displayed in its fundamental features* was published in Sir William Hooker's Kew Journal in 1853. Among professional botanists his work began to be noticed with interest – it was always of the highest quality.

In 1851, gold was discovered in Australia and there was hectic excitement everywhere. The largest, most accessible goldfield was between Ballarat and Bendigo in Victoria, and in three fenzied months (says Edward Kynaston in his book *A Man on Edge*) almost 10,000 men settled down in tents and makeshift bark huts to make their fortunes. Strikes of gold followed in other areas and thousands more people poured out from Melbourne, leaving the town half deserted. Suddenly Melbourne and Victoria had become the golden hub of the Australian wheel of fortune. To be a 'digger' was to throw one's hat over the moon and abandon the dull routine of daily work for glorious irresponsible freedom – and the chance of becoming a millionaire.

In the chemist's shop in Adelaide 500 miles away, Mueller's two doctor friends – one of them Dr Wehl, who was later to marry his sister Clara – asked Mueller to join them as pharmacist in their venture to practise medicine in the Victorian goldfields. Mueller wanted more leisure for botany, and money made quickly could give him the independence he sought. He moved to Melbourne in 1852 where Hobson's Bay was crowded with tall ships from every part of the world, and where in this one year 100,000 immigrants had arrived with gold fever. Most of these ships were abandoned by their crews who had deserted and rushed up country to the diggings.

Melbourne is now, of course, the venue of the most important event in Australia, the Melbourne Cup. It was my misfortune to arrive by air just in time for this. The rain poured down and it felt rather cold, so I enquired my way on a Sunday evening where I could buy some warmer clothes, then to my surprise walking towards the shops I began to feel rather hot and decided perhaps I did not need warm clothes after all. It was a surprise to find shops open and I was directed to a huge store which seemed to be a sort of Japanese Harrods. My dilemma was that going to the races in Melbourne is as smart an occasion as Ascot, but as the forecast was for more rain it seemed gumboots would be more suitable than Coco Chanel. I decided to take a bet on the race, look at it on telly and join any frivolities I was invited to afterwards, in the dry.

Next day my tour of the Botanic Garden was stunning, and I revelled in the wonderful collections and brilliant colours of so many plants unknown to me. My most vivid recollections are of the huge bushes of gardenias, which I had once grown in Singapore and certainly couldn't grow at home. There was also the little house in which Captain Cook was born, brought over from near Whitby in England lock stock and barrel and reassembled in these beautiful gardens.

My next port of call was to stay a few days with Tom Savige, the co-author of the *International Camellia Register* published in 1993. It was a remarkable achievement to include the details of origin, history and synonymy – as well as succinct descriptions of 32,000 cultivar names and 9,000 oriental names – in the appendix. Savige took over this challenge from Professor EG Waterhouse as I mentioned, and it took him nearly thirty years of dedication, enthusiasm and careful scholarship. I was thrilled to be going to meet him at last.

He lived in Albury, almost halfway to Sydney, and I was looking forward to a train journey for a change and seeing more of the countryside. Tom and his wife were brilliant hosts and after showing me his collection of camellias they took me to see a particularly lovely garden called, appropriately, 'The Diggings' – as this was very much a gold digging area. We saw where the huge river Murray was dammed and explored in a nearby gold town which reminded me of Wild West films. Then it was on to the next journey by rail for Sydney.

I was very impressed with the train which was not expensive even travelling first class; I had hardly taken my seat when I was offered a Cornish clotted cream tea, which was a great surprise, especially as it was about ten in the morning. Then a cricket team came on board, and as time went by and they finished the supplies in the bar, the ticket collector came round and warned them to behave. To my amazement – as they seemed not to pay much attention to his words – at the next stop they were all thrown off the train and told they would not be allowed to travel again.

After the relative sedateness of Adelaide, Melbourne must have seemed to Mueller like a nightmare of noise and debauchery, but in the end he never joined the frantic pandemonium of the gold rush as he had intended, because soon after his arrival he was introduced to the Governor, CJ La Trobe – an amateur botanist, geologist, painter and musician, a man who had travelled all over Europe, Mexico and the United States and had written four books about his travels. La Trobe wrote to his botanist friend R C Gunn in Tasmania, who was also a friend of Joseph Hooker, (son of Sir William) at Kew: 'There is an honest looking German here, Dr Mueller, who as far as I can judge seems to be more of a botanist than any man I have hitherto met with in the colony, and I shall give him every encouragement. He has punished me with the description of the genus *Latrobe* of Meisner... he tells me that an exceedingly pretty dwarf acacia flowering most abundantly in its native soil at Jolimont has been distinguished by my name also…'

Mueller had arrived in the right place at the right time. The position of Government Botanist was being created and La Trobe thought he knew who might fill it. Approval of the appointment rested with Sir William Hooker, and Mueller was officially gazetted Government Botanist of the Colony of Victoria on 2nd February 1853. La Trobe had established the Botanic Gardens across the river Yarra on an undulating site of eighty three acres in 1846; with the same farsighted vision he had also planned the Carlton and Fitzroy gardens, city parks of beauty and inestimable value, in the grounds of the Royal Melbourne Hospital, the University of Melbourne and the Public Library of Victoria. Mueller had played his cards well and won himself a prize plum. He was, in time, to become a collector, exhibitor, explorer, scientist and a famous controversial public figure.

He couldn't wait to begin making explorations of the north-eastern ranges of Victoria, this time using riding horse and pack horse, and duly climbed Mounts Buller and Buffalo – the first white man to do so – then struck across the Upper Goulburn to Mount Disappointment – the La Trobe watershed, Port Albert and Wilson Promontory and so back to Melbourne by the coast. Mueller covered 1,500 miles during this pioneering expedition, adding almost 1,000 species to the list of Victoria plants and in less than three years the young Mueller had managed to travel over 5,000 miles of wild forest, desert, swamp and alpine range. No botanist has accomplished so much in so short a time, and with his well-informed mind and thorough disposition, he was brilliantly successful and left little for others to discover in any area he had visited. Between journeys he worked tirelessly classifying the vast amount of material collected – leaves, seeds, flowers and bark, throwing himself into the work with enthusiasm because of a love of plants and knowledge that was part of his nature.

He largely ignored the feverish search for gold that was going on all around him, but his solitary journeys through primitive country, virgin forests and virtually unknown territory certainly attracted the attention of other explorers, many of whom would have read Mueller's article on Australian exploration that he carefully distributed to the right people, Sir William Hooker of Kew among them. He was now asked to join an important party travelling across the Northern Territories, down through the sub-interior of the present state of Queensland, led by two brothers, AC and HC Gregory, acting with the approval of the Colonial Office in London. They planned to trace the Victoria River to its source, and then follow north flowing rivers continuing to Brisbane. A secondary aim was to seek traces of Ludwig Leichhardt and his party, of great interest to Mueller. The group was to consist of eighteen men, fifty horses, 200 sheep and provisions for two years, 1855-1857.

Hooker recommended Mueller as botanist to the expedition, and Mueller obtained leave to carry out botanical work, without pay, for the next eighteen months. He longed to extend the researches of his great predecessors, Joseph Banks and Robert Brown, and arrived at Sydney with a few days to spare. But he was also obsessed that Leichhardt might still be alive, captive among the natives, deprived of the means of returning to his friends and waiting day to day, year to year, hoping for his rescue.

Right from the beginning the expedition was dogged with disaster; the Gregory brothers started successfully enough, in two ships at Sydney – the *Monarch*, a barque, and *Tom Tough*, a schooner – embarking the sheep and horses at Brisbane River in Moreton Bay. But the pilot then managed to run the *Monarch* aground, and the ship engaged to tow her off struck a rock and sank. Yet another ship now picked up the tow, steamed at full speed ahead and snapped the hawser – then to the dismay and astonishment of the passengers vanished over the horizon without a word of explanation. The party finally got away sailing north from Moreton Bay, rounded the tip of Cape York, sailing through oily, tropical seas teeming with brightly-coloured fish, and sea wasps with tentacles a yard long; there were also Portuguese man-o'-war jelly fish with even longer tentacles, as well as sharks, dugong and turtles. Eventually crossing the mouth of the Gulf of Carpentaria they came to the shoals and sandbanks of the sixteen mile wide mouth of the Victoria River. Here further calamities occurred. The *Monarch* had once more stuck fast on a rocky reef at the top of the spring tide, and for eight days her crew sweated and swore as they tried to warp her off. At low tide she settled on her side so the horses were thrown about, and two died from their injuries with the remainder having to swim two miles to the landing place – during which two drowned, one was sucked down into the mud and one went mad and bolted into the bush.

The river was navigable for about sixty miles, so Gregory sent the *Tom Tough* upstream with instructions to make camp at the highest point they could reach. He and his brother, Mueller, and seven others rode beside the river on horseback. The thermometer showed 114 degrees in the shade as they moved slowly at eight to ten miles a day. The horses suffered severely: they strayed, ate poisonous plants, collapsed from exhaustion and could not get up again and were attacked by crocodiles. Amazingly the men remained in good health, but had great difficulty in finding the schooner, which had in the meantime become a wreck, with four feet of water in the hold.

The expedition was now in disarray, most of the sheep and too many of the horses had been lost, the schooner was badly holed and in need of major repairs and much of the stores were damaged or destroyed by salt-water. On top of all this, the party was attacked several times by Aboriginals who stole supplies from the camp and then set it alight. Gregory, however, was determined to follow the Victoria River to its source, and arranged for half the party to remain with the schooner and the exploration party to set off for an expedition for twenty days. Even this plan was thwarted by an accidental firing of a gun from the boat just as they were leaving, which stampeded all the horses – whose packs were torn off against trees and scattered with their saddles damaged. The party finally left two days later.

Mueller found plenty to occupy him and would wander off on his botanical quests, frequently getting lost and having to be searched for. Sometimes he would be left behind in charge of the camp, and for several days would botanise happily undisturbed.

The whole expedition lasted two years and for Mueller it was the great adventure of his life. They had travelled 5,000 miles and in spite of the early bad luck at sea, the intense heat, and attacks by Aboriginals, not a man had been lost. Botany was well served, and Mueller had collected 1,500 specimens. Thanks to the Gregory brothers, exceptionally tough men of unusual ability, the expedition had turned out to be a remarkable success. Mueller was very lucky to have taken part; the real dangers and hardships he had experienced made him realise his own solitary travels through the Victorian Alps had been more like Sunday afternoon rambles. After this, hardly a single major expedition in Australia, the Antarctic, or New Guinea during the remainder of his life was set up without his being in some way involved.

Mueller wrote to a great many people, keeping them all in touch with his adventures and botanical discoveries. Somehow, finding time in his extremely busy life to write about three thousand letters a year – always signed 'regardfully yours'. These are published in three large volumes and (with a good deal of skipping) make rather solid but interesting reading. His greatest secret ambition was to write the *Australiana Floriensis* for which – if he had played his cards right – he would be the only contender, but because this last expedition was an official one, backed by the Government, all the botanical specimens had to be despatched to England via the Colonial Office.

During the expedition Mueller must have been thinking about his proposed visit to England. Before he left he had received the letter from Hooker making it quite clear that he was more than anxious that Mueller should come to England: 'to do what nobody but yourself can do, towards the publication of your treasures, let alone all you have collected in the South. A visit to our Kew Herbarium and Libraries and our Botanists would refresh you and strengthen you for further labours. It will be a great disappointment to us if you should not find it needful to come to Europe.' The opportunity was now within his grasp.

And yet? Immediately after the expedition he spent time arranging and dealing with the specimens he had brought back, but still seemed set on travelling to London to gain the experience at Kew that was indispensable if he were to undertake the *Flora Australiensis*. It remains inexplicable that for no convincing or obvious reason he changed his mind and did not go. Mueller wrote to Sir William Hooker on 15th January 1857: 'I found it uncombinable with my position here to leave for home at present and that I am thus yet for a year or two deprived of the anticipated pleasure of seeing you.' He wrote again making many unconvincing excuses about his health, (he had never been fitter), the state of his finances, ingratitude to the Government colonists 'to leave instantly again my adopted home when I have been so kindfully and flatteringly remembered'. Another letter from Sir William's son, Dr Joseph Hooker this time: 'I cannot therefore too strongly advise if there be any possibility of avoiding it, to refrain from publishing your Victorian plants until you have compared them in England. Come to Kew. No one is now nearly so well qualified as you are to publish an Australian Flora, and nobody else can do it at all'. There it was in black and white, his dearest wish promised to him, and yet he would not go.

On his return to Melbourne his first concern was the Botanical Garden. While he had been away, the Government had extended the scope to include a zoo and required Mueller to undertake the work of Director and Curator as well as official botanist, and he intended to make the gardens more educational and attractive to visitors. They were beautifully situated on ground sloping down to the river Yarra, and included a large lake. Mueller increased the number of gravel walks and made ornamental plantations, using metal labels for the more important plants. He planned a new conservatory, and a proper building was put up to house the herbarium where the dried plants could be kept free of insects and in proper conditions, and also set aside three acres for demonstrating native ferns and trees and facilitating the study of their mutual botanical alliances. There were many native birds on the lake and in the woods, and Mueller encouraged the introduction of foreign birds.

Seeds were exchanged with gardens at Kew, Hobart, Brisbane, Sydney, Adelaide, Paris, Mauritius, Capetown, Calcutta, Boston and Hamburg. More than 5,000 packets of seeds were sent out all over Australia and to other British colonies. The exchange of plants was much facilitated by the introduction of Wardian cases and the use of steamships which reduced the long journey home to only two months. His improvements in the garden continued with fast-growing shade trees planted along the walks and between the lawns, with seats and resting places more suitably sited, and where the ferryman had rowed people across the river, Mueller had a footbridge built which greatly increased the number of visitors – 200,000 came during that year.

In defiance of the need for a comparison with the plants in England, Mueller now started to write his *Australiensis Floriensis,* naming it *Fragmenta Phytographiae Australiae.* This recorded and described new Australian plants, and was written entirely in Latin and published like a serial as each volume was completed. There were eventually eleven volumes with a twelfth uncompleted.

Meanwhile Mueller still hoped to persuade Hooker that the *Flora Australiensis* could be completed only by himself without consulting the material at Kew, but a letter he received from Hooker – as he was finishing his annual report on the Botanical Gardens in 1862 contained, in a single paragraph, news which proved the end of his highest hopes. This said: 'The publication of a universal work on the Australian Flora is contemplated by Mr G Bentham, the President of the Linnean Society of London, whose phytological labours, continued since the last forty years, have raised him to the highest rank in botanical science. For this work the treasures of plants accumulated in Britain since the time of Sir Joseph Banks will form the foundation. I felt it incumbent on me to share in so important a task, and tender to it all the support which could be derived from the use of our vast collections, and from the manuscripts therewith connected. Accordingly arrangements have been made for the temporary transmission to Kew of such fascicles of our herbarium as require to be consulted for the elaboration of each particular volume. This universal Australia Flora, to which the Governments of several of the Australian colonies have given generous encouragement and support, is likely to extend over eight or ten volumes, and will probably require as many years' labour for its completion.'

Here I must digress to give some background information about the distinguished and learned Mr George Bentham, (1800-1884). He was a British botanist whose classification of seed plants *(Spermatophyta)*, based on an exhaustive study of all known species, served as a foundation for modern systems of vascular plant taxonomy. Bentham was impressed by the French naturalist Pyrame de Candolle's analytic tables of French flora, and began to study botany while managing his father's estate near Montpellier in France. He served as secretary to his uncle, the British philosopher and jurist Jeremy Bentham, and in 1833 when he inherited the wealth of both his father and uncle, he turned his full attention to botany. Afterwards he donated his herbarium of more than 100,000 specimens to the Royal Botanical Gardens at Kew. In 1854, Sir William Hooker, the then Director, invited him to establish permanent quarters there and the latter writes of George Bentham: 'I cannot omit a passing reference to the unobtrusive but splendid and indeed inestimable services to the State of this gentleman, who for a quarter of a century has been, though unpaid, virtually a member of the Kew staff, and has contributed not a little by his unparalleled series of botanical writings to the scientific reputation which Kew now bears. After Sir William Hooker's death, his herbarium and library were purchased for the nation in 1867, and the Hooker and Bentham herbaria and libraries, being then completely fused, became the foundation of these departments at Kew. Bentham, in collaboration with Hooker's son, Sir Joseph, spent twenty seven years in research and examination of specimens for the *Genera Plantarum* which included 97,200 species'.

Mueller, as you can imagine, could not compete, and had thus given up his undoubted right to become the author of the *Flora*; he had fought long and hard for the privilege and been defeated, in the last resort, by himself. The essential condition of the writing of the Flora remained: comparison of Australian species with the great collections in England. Mueller was unable to bring himself to leave Australia, so Bentham had won the argument. But Mueller could not quite let go and, ignoring his defeat, had one last go at getting the *Flora* for himself with a letter which shocked both the Hookers and Bentham. Once more Hooker wrote back, 'you seem to think the *Australian Flora* ought to be left entirely to you…could you come over to this country for the purpose? No-one could nearly so well as yourself, prepare the general flora that is so much wanted. Yet at the same time, that to be satisfactory to the botanical world it must be done in this country…my father and I are much concerned that we are now again at cross purposes with you…with regard to the authorship of the work our only desire is to see that it is well done…it must surely be evident to you that to work out the *Australian Flora* without references to the collections of Banks, Solander, Brown, Cunningham, Drummond and the Paris Herbaria would be a proceeding that no botanist could approve.'

Hooker was sick of buttering up this tiresome, opinionated, unreliable foreigner, and so finished off with another broadside: 'It would be of little use to point out to you the difficulty of the efficient construction of so gigantic a Flora as that of Australia, how much talk it requires to seize prominent characters, to make diagnoses, both brief, diagnostic and accurate, in doing which Bentham has forty years' experience, and you none; and how much advice and council the wisest and best botanists among us take of one another in all these matters, before arranging a plan that is to include 8,000 species, so arranged and described as to be really useful and not troublesome. All this I affirm requires work of a very different character from that you have been accustomed to, and hence for systematic methodising that you have never felt called upon to exercise. Let me assure you as a friend that in the opinion of your best friends here, circumstances are against you undertaking the *Australian Flora* far more than against mine even, and I had for many years set my heart on it, too, but I have abandoned it long ago in favour of Bentham, because I have no time to do it justice and because it would be a public calamity if it were taken out of his hands.'

Hooker may have thought he had overdone it by inferring Mueller was a 'public calamity' and in his next letter he sounds more kindly, congratulating Mueller on his election to the Royal Society.

Mueller at last surrendered, and it was not much consolation that he was to be involved in the enormous task of sending over 100,000 of his plants to England over the years. The last letter from Hooker ends: 'By the way, we cannot allow you to be at the expense of sending your Herbaria backward and forward, we shall pay one way at any rate.'

Mueller's complicated character did not fit into the new Australian philosophy, although he probably would not have noticed this. Perhaps it had something to do with the first settlers – mainly convicts. What mattered to them was money. If you had it you were somebody, and if you didn't it did not matter if you were a Baron with the distinguished German 'von' in your name, or had honours from the Queen of England – she had recently made him a Knight Commander of St Michael and St John. If you were not rich you were still nobody. In fact Mueller ended up with three other knighthoods, a decoration from the Czar of Russia, three commanderships, five university doctorates. He was still rather despised for these honours and especially the 'von' which was not accepted in Australia. But Mueller collected and loved them, especially the Barony which he seems to have actually solicited – they all made him feel more secure. He was a very lonely man and the disappointment of his dearest ambition made him cling to the adulation and recognition of which he dreamed. He was also a complete loner, and at thirty six his achievements in his scientific sphere mattered more than anything else to him, and he wore these medals with such pride, on every possible occasion, never mind that they were pinned on to his most shabby, untidy, and often not even very clean, sort of clothes.

1863 had been a bad year for him. As always, he took on far more work than any normal man, and the frustrations with London, his work as Botanical Director, his journeys and his daily struggles with Government departments had all combined to make him depressed and lonely. Furthermore, he had never been able to enter into close personal relationships, having always kept a polite and impersonal distance from people, a habit which suited him; he sublimated what personal needs he had with the sheer unremitting intensity of work. Although he gave the impression of being terrified of women it was at this stage of his life that he began to behave rather uncharacteristically. Outwardly he was a mature man, a famous explorer, a celebrated botanist, a highly honoured figure of modern science; inside he was an immature, insecure adolescent.

When making one of his tours of inspection in the Botanical Gardens he had come upon a Miss Euphemia Henderson painting flowers near the river. In her day, a spinster of uncertain age would have no real place in a society composed of respectable wives and mothers, and she would have had to find a meaningful life for herself under the irksome authority of some of these ladies, usually as unpaid aunt or a rather despised governess. But, Miss Henderson had not done too badly, as she had emigrated with her married sister Georgiana and her husband Mr McHaffie from Jersey in the Channel Islands, and lived with them on Phillip Island about seventy miles from Melbourne, where her brother-in-law ran the Victorian Acclimatization Society, which used it as a bird and animal sanctuary.

A photograph of Euphemia shows a typical Victorian unsmiling woman, dressed in black bombazine, her hair scraped back under her unattractive hat and with a rather grim expression. One can imagine the scene and how it all came about: Mueller was a well-known figure, the Director of the Botanic Gardens, with his guttural accent and flowery conversation. He would have known who she was – as McHaffie's sister-in-law – and would have made himself known to her where she sat in the garden at her painting. Her pulse must have quickened when he approached her, recognising him and instantly summing him up as a 'catch' as she observed him, wondering if she could play her part well enough, so that even now in her forties, she might be reprieved from permanent spinsterhood. It does not sound as if either of them was ever remotely in love, but they do sound as if they could have been soulmates, blindly searching for each other.

Euphemia ingratiated herself with Mueller by asking his opinion on her collection of algae, thus enticing him to show off his expertise, and thanks to her adroit behaviour, a romance blossomed.

The McHaffies, husband and wife, were certainly hopeful; a permanent spinster sister living in the house was something of a mill-stone, also a powerful friend on the Council of the Acclimatisation Society would be no bad thing. His visits continued.

Mueller was so completely inexperienced in this sort of situation – in the hands of a determined family plot as one might call it – that he began to feel alarmed, so he wrote a letter intimating that he was contemplating a visit to Europe for several years to complete his studies. Christmas was imminent and the plan moved faster, and when Mueller was invited to stay with the McHaffies he accepted with alacrity. One can imagine the exchange of gifts, the musical evenings, the botanical excursions and the growing intimacy. Mueller even spoke of alterations to his house, including a 'gracious balcony', which if he had any imagination at all, he would guess Euphemia would take as a matrimonial enticement. He could hardly have whetted her appetite more. He wrote long, fulsome letters, sending her presents and telling her of his progress with botanical writings, he even named a flower after her. He was, in fact, at bay and over Christmas could not resist the beguiling atmosphere. He proposed, was accepted, and immediately regretted the whole thing. He was now trapped and committed to marriage with a woman with whom he had almost nothing in common; he could no longer pretend to a passion he had never felt, and as a genuine if simple minded Lutheran, this intensified his guilt. He had wanted friendship and had been deceived into a marriage that he could not contemplate; somehow he must get out of it, but how? He could not go through with the engagement; a way must be found for committing the most heinous crime of respectable Victorian society – the jilting of a fiancée.

Mueller's dilemma was acute; he minded intensely about his image which he had spent years building up; he was a man of distinction in the world and was determined not to spoil his reputation. He saw rearing a family as fundamental to married life, and was now aware that from a physiological point of view Euphemia was past child-bearing age. He consulted his medical friends and decided his only possible course of action was to say that he could not continue the engagement into marriage because his health made it impossible for him to consummate it – he was, he claimed, impotent. He could not bring himself to deliver this blighting blow personally, but sent a doctor friend to transmit the solemn message. 'Their union', he wrote in the letter in which he sought his release from the commitment, 'offered no prospect of family happiness'. He continued: 'I shall never cease to admire your talents blended as they are by a gentle disposition, qualities which carried me away in enthusiasm. But unfortunately I noticed that destiny had brought us together years too late for matrimonial life.' In fact, he was only thirty-seven, and in robust health.

Euphemia's reply is not available to quote from, but she must have told Mueller his reasons were absurd, because he replies 'I can only say they are purely based on the laws of life and nature, and were ladies aware of the doctrines of medicine many matrimonial engagements in advanced life would never be carried out.' The letter goes on for pages and is a remarkable document – indeed it needed to be – he desperately wants to give her the opportunity to withdraw 'from an engagement which opens only a gloomy future'; he wishes her to 'after the first emotions of grief…lessen your censure…exchange your love for friendship.' He then adds what could be construed as an unforgivable pun on her name, 'O! You never should build an ephemarious and delusive happiness, and glittering worthless grandeur on the ruin of my own tranquillity.' He promises she will 'anon view with melancholic pleasure the events of the earlier parts of this year as a beautiful dream.' Euphemia, after the first furious shock, amazingly did forgive him and maintained friendly relations with him. The McHaffies huffed and puffed a good deal but eventually, dreading any further scandal, resigned themselves to the inevitable.

Not visibly daunted, two years later at the age of forty, Mueller became engaged again. This time his intended was only seventeen, but again nothing came of it and the story goes that she was repelled by Mueller's reluctance to risk a chest infection by bathing more than once a week! His third foray into potential matrimony – it hardly seems possible – was when he referred to another probable engagement as he wrote to his friend von Krauss in Stuttgart, who was negotiating on his behalf for his title of Baron: 'This high hereditary title which is of great value to the lady of my choice, will contribute considerably to the establishment of my domestic happiness, and that within the next few months…'. Sadly, Mueller was not third time lucky – that romance never came to anything either.

But Mueller, besides his personal problems, also had enemies in the Government who meant to bring him down. His achievements in the Botanic Garden seemed enough to make his position unassailable; he had created a garden that was famous throughout the world, had planted 30,000 trees, created a magnificent library from his own nucleus of over 1,000 botanical books, laid out twenty five miles of walks, set up a herbarium and laboratory based on his own collections of 350,000 specimens, and distributed over 500,000 plants throughout the colony. In addition he had for years supplied all the flowers required by the public – both officially and unofficially – and maintained an exchange programme with gardens in every part of the world, as well as researching industriously the uses of plants of economic value to the young colony. All this was quite apart from his work on Australian plants, his own explorations, his publications, and his work with Bentham on the *Flora Australiensis*; not surprisingly he was at the time the most internationally decorated and honoured man in Australia.

Criticisms of Mueller's administration of the garden began to be heard in

1862 when forty of Victoria's horticulturists and florists petitioned the Government, protesting that his large scale distribution of plants from the garden was 'very injurious' to their trade. The wider community supported what Mueller was doing, and he himself was not much interested in trade. The Government response was to restrict Mueller's distributions to private individuals, but positively instruct him to continue to provide plants, cuttings and seeds to public institutions and to supply cut flowers for 'benevolent or artistic purposes or for public festivals.' But the hostility increased and the first step in his downfall was when William Ferguson, Inspector of Forests – a gardener by trade – was appointed Manager of the Garden by no less a person than the Prime Minister, Sir James McCulloch – this without even informing Mueller officially. Mueller's budget was also greatly reduced, and although he remained nominally in charge of the Garden, Ferguson refused to take orders from him. After a complaint from the Chief Secretary that the Garden was ill maintained, Mueller was blamed. He was desperately upset and wrote: 'This is the first time in seventeen years of administration and thirty years of Directorship that a letter of censure has been sent to me; it has given me very much pain, as it seems to imply , as if it was through my administration, that the want of order arose…my authority is seriously impaired by the Inspector of Forests, who utterly disregards my position of Director, who withdraws himself utterly from my control, who usurpates (sic) largely my directional power…it will be known to Sir James McCulloch that I am the main founder of the Botanic Garden in all its branches…it is therefore unnecessary to add that I do take a deep interest in the work of my own creation, and would soon set the disorderly state of the grounds right if I was not impeded in my authority'.

There was really nothing he could do. A board of enquiry was now set up with his enemies in charge. Mueller and the Botanic Gardens were in the news and letters to the press winged their way to and fro. Mueller had quite a lot of support, but not enough. He wrote to Joseph Hooker: 'God knows how it will end. You have no idea of the meanness and lowness existing in Victoria, among much people of really high principle'. Venomous attacks were launched against him in Parliament where the attitude to him was spiteful and mean. It had the power to torment him and used it ruthlessly. Somehow Mueller miraculously managed to carry on with all his departmental work, his co-operation with Bentham on the *Flora Australiensis* and his own writing.

The long difficult and acrimonious collaboration was almost at an end.

Despite everything, Bentham had kept a deep respect for Mueller which showed itself in his invitation to him to round off the Flora with a supplementary volume in which he could have his say. Bentham says : ' I had once intended putting in to the last volume some general remarks about the geographical distribution of the Australian flora....but I have been obliged to give up the idea.... It would however, I think, be of much interest if you, with your experience, would give us a general view of the character and extent of the different floras more or less spread over Australia. This you could well do, and take the opportunity of completing the list of Australian plants with references to where you have published the species not contained in my flora, and rearranging the whole systematically according to your views of genera and species where they differ from mine.' This must have been soothing balm to his much injured soul.

Mueller fought on with enormous courage. In truth, the charges against him were quite ridiculous when you consider that around 300,000 people visited the Gardens because they enjoyed them; it is true there were no statues and not enough fountains but the public had not seemed to mind. For what they were, the Botanical Gardens were pleasant enough and had never been intended as a landscaped public park.

The Board's report was an astonishing document. The worst it could find to complain about was that: 'the Gardens had not been managed so as to give general satisfaction', that the Director's views were 'entirely different from those of the public' and that the Director was not a landscape gardener, also that Mueller had used the money available to create a Botanic Garden instead of a public park, that he had planted too many plants and trees, and that he had neglected the soil.

The Board's recommendation was a foregone conclusion. Mueller was to revert to his position of Government Botanist, devoting himself to science, leaving the gardens severely alone. A Curator was now to be appointed to take charge of and run the gardens.

The press came down heavily on Mueller's side, pointing out the well known prejudices of the men on the board. But for Mueller it was a devastating blow, and worse was to come when he was expelled from the Director's house in the garden at short notice, forced to take refuge in a hotel, and then denied access to his laboratory which was converted into a storeroom. He was even allocated a niggardly £300 a year to maintain his department which had to be compressed into a building too small for it. Mueller retaliated by removing his whole library without permission, ignoring a series of demands to return it and continuing with his work – never giving up his endless letters of complaint about his treatment – but reputedly never visiting the gardens again.

The young man appointed as Curator to the Gardens, William Guilfoyle, had been a protégé of Mueller's and had collected specimens for him in the Pacific Islands and in northern NSW where his father cultivated plants for the family's nursery in Sydney. Some nepotism had influenced his appointment, but he was in fact a brilliant choice and managed to remain friends with Mueller. He relocated many of the trees planted by Mueller and in so doing creating splendid vistas that have remained a feature of the garden ever since. Over the next twenty-five years he made the site into a place of 'wondrous beauty in the style of the great English country gardens of the previous century.' Guilfoyle made no attempt to give the garden a scientific character such as Mueller had sought to, and neither he, nor anybody else, cared to acknowledge that much of his work was based directly on the engineering work undertaken during Mueller's period as Director, and on the vast range of plants Mueller had brought in from all over the world.

In spite of everything he went on busily writing, no matter how despairing he felt. In 1879 he published the first part of an atlas on Australian eucalypts, and the first part of a book on Victorian native plants with an appendix about the care and maintenance of the native forests. He was ahead of his time in foreseeing how easily this might be destroyed and how difficult it would be to replace.

The wear and tear of Mueller's workload and the constant vigilance against his opponents were making him feel old. His enemies were succeeding in his demoralisation if not in his defeat. Although he never stopped complaining, his last years were spent in comparative comfort in a small house in South Yarra, where he had a manservant to look after him. He wrote far into the night, every night, but in September 1896 he suffered a stroke and died soon after. His funeral, a proper Victorian send-off with a pomp and panoply even he would have rejoiced in and felt was appropriate to his baronial dignity.

It is interesting to compare the intelligent opinion of someone like Charles Darwin, who, travelling about thirty years before Mueller, describes how he found the character of the new inhabitants of Australia. 'Before arriving here' Darwin says, 'the three things which interested me most were – the state of society amongst the higher classes, the condition of the convicts, and the degree of attraction, sufficient to induce persons to emigrate. On the whole, from what I heard more than from what I saw, I was disappointed in the state of society. The whole community is rancorously divided into parties on almost every subject. Among those who from their station in life, ought to be the best, many live in such open profligacy that respectable people cannot associate with them. The whole population, poor or rich are bent on acquiring wealth; among the higher orders, wool and sheep grazing form the constant subject of conversation. There are many serious drawbacks to the comfort of a family, the chief of which, perhaps, is being surrounded by convict servants. How thoroughly odious to every feeling to be waited on by a man, who the day before was perhaps flogged, from your representation, for some trifling misdemeanour. The female servants are of course much worse, hence children learn the vilest expressions, and it is fortunate, if not equally vile ideas.

On the other hand, the capital of a person, without any trouble on his part, produces him treble interest to what it will in England and with care he is bound to grow rich. The luxuries of life are in abundance and very little dearer than in England, and most articles of food are cheaper. The climate is splendid and perfectly healthy. Settlers possess a great advantage in finding their sons of service when very young; at the age from sixteen to twenty they frequently take charge of distant farming stations. This however must happen at the expense of their boys associating entirely with convict servants. I am not aware that the tone of society has assumed any peculiar character, but with such habits and without intellectual pursuits it can hardly fail to deteriorate. My opinion is such that nothing but rather sharp necessity should compel me to emigrate'.

When contemplating the fate of the convicts he says: 'As to a sense of shame, such a feeling does not appear to be known and of this I witnessed some very singular proofs......On the whole, as a place of punishment, the object is scarcely gained; as a real system of reform it has failed as perhaps would every other plan; but as a means of making men outwardly honest – of converting vagabonds, most useless in one hemisphere, into active citizens of another, and thus giving birth to a new and splendid country – a grand centre of civilisation – it has succeeded to a degree perhaps unparalleled in history.'

CHAPTER 10

The Botanic Gardens of Canberra

The Botanic Gardens of Canberra are very remarkable and unusual in their history; an international competition had been launched in 1911 by the Commonwealth Government for a design for the Australian national capital and it was won by the American architect Walter Burley Griffin, an ardent nature lover and pupil of the great Frank Lloyd Wright. In his plan for Canberra he provided for botanic gardens surrounding an artificial lake, and envisaged a plant collection from all parts of the world set out in continental groups, but as the city developed the concept changed and the collection has been confined to Australian species from all the States and some of the Territories of Australia itself.

The competing planners were invited to introduce the latest English and American ideas for a garden city, so it is not surprising that nobody suggested that the garden should be reserved exclusively for the study and cultivation of Australian flora; Walter Griffin in his winning design envisaged a large scale continental arboretum, a new idea in which separate areas would be planted with species from Europe, Asia, Africa, North and South America on the north side of the lake, with Australia and New Zealand represented on the southern shores. The gardens were to extend from the lower slopes of Black Mountain to the lake's edge. When describing this area in his Report Explanatory of the Preliminary General Plan (October 1913), Griffin made a bitter comment which has endeared him to nature-lovers ever since. In a plea that part of this reserve should be protected from any alteration, his closing comment was '...perpetuating there the only remnant of primeval luxuriance on the city site'.

Peter Vicar, Minister for the Interior, wrote in a short history of the garden: 'It was not for Burley Griffin, an American, to intrude any suggestion that Australians should be more concerned about the study and cultivation of their unique flora by the establishment of a national garden of Australian plants, but he left the poignant hint that it would not be incompatible for inclusion in his vision of the city beautiful.'

It was intended from the beginning that Canberra should be a garden city, and one has to remember that the city was being created at the same time as the Garden. In 1911 a nursery, in anticipation of future needs, was established (where Canberra Hospital now stands) and thousands of seedlings of trees, shrubs and smaller plants – mostly exotics – were planted.

The Superintendent of Nurseries, TC Weston, found it necessary to extend the nurseries, and thousands more seedlings were raised for future requirements. Weston was concerned that too much of the planting was of exotica, and appealed to JH Maiden, Director of the Sydney Botanic Gardens, for a supply of 'such native trees and shrubs as are likely to prove suitable for the climate of the proposed Federal Capital.' Maiden, a world authority on eucalypts, sent 1,300 miscellaneous plants, many of them exotic, because he thought that if the plantings were confined to 'native plants suitable to the district, they would be very bare for the next five years.' In October 1912, the Director of Commonwealth Lands and Surveys, anticipating an early decision on the design of the city and the location of its principal features, recommended that Weston should devote 'his whole energies in the direction of planting within the Federal area, especially about the principal buildings.' So in 1913 while the first roads were being marked out and the foundations constructed for the building sites – Weston planted the first trees.

In December 1915, Burley Griffin, now appointed Federal Capital Director of Design and Construction to supervise the implementing of his own design, showed his keen interest in Australian trees by asking Weston to make sure that seeds of *Syncarpia laurifolia* – a small genus of evergreen eucalypt-like trees – are obtained from specially hardy specimens, 'in the Blue Mountains at our altitude.' Griffin became more and more interested in the use of Australian native varieties, but must have been seriously daunted when Maiden paid a visit from Sydney and made a seven page report to the Surveyor General in which he highly praised Weston while castigating Griffin with crushing eloquence: 'No one impugns the ability of the Federal Director of Design and Construction in regard to matters of architecture and its related engineering problems, but problems affecting planting in Australia, in which Australian indigenous species are concerned and also questions of meteorology, drainage and soil, in so far as they affect plant welfare, belong to a different category.'

Maiden continues: 'The Director of Design and Construction, in addition to his many accomplishments, has not yet had time and perhaps opportunity, to obtain more than a superficial knowledge of Australian plants, their requirements and acclimatisation, and therefore work of that kind should in my view be placed in the hands of a man whose knowledge and experience will reduce the anxiety of the Government to a minimum.'

Maiden can't resist a further dig: 'The Director of Design is to be commended for his desire to cultivate native trees, but his sentiment must not be translated into actual practice. The list that he submits is inadequate and even erroneous as a whole and the adoption of it can only result in disaster...' Maiden certainly had the last word and poor Burley Griffin must have felt rebuffed at the way his imaginative plan to include a National Garden of Australian Flora was so fiercely rejected – and that was in 1919.

In 1927 when visitors arrived for the opening of Parliament, Canberra's avenues were tree lined with conifers, and the parks had their poplars, oaks and Chinese elms contrasting against a background of native acacias and eucalypts, making the city 'one vast botanic garden.' Cattle grazed on Burley Griffin's 'only remnant of primeval luxuriance on the city site' and nobody seemed to mind.

But in 1933 a number of local enthusiasts, under the leadership of Councillor TM Shakespeare, unanimously recommended that 'a start be made with laying out a portion of the site set apart for the Botanical Gardens and of planting same with native and exotic trees and shrubs and plants of economic and medicinal value as distinct from those grown for ornamental purposes only.' For more than a year Dr Dickson and Superintendent AE Bruce of Parks and Gardens gathered information from botanic gardens throughout the world, and in 1936 the Dickson report was presented. Dr Dickson went much further than the Advisory Council had suggested, indeed right back to Burley Griffin's original proposal, endorsing it warmly and specially commending the choice of the Black Mountain area.

Then the Second World War broke out and everything was shelved. At the time of the Dickson Report in 1936, Lindsay Dixon Pryor had come to Canberra as a researcher in forestry and made a special study of the vegetation of the Australian Capital Territory and the genetics and breeding of eucalypts. On his appointment as Superintendent of Parks and Gardens in 1944, a list of post-war projects was prepared and approved. Then on September 21st 1945, less than three weeks after the war in the Pacific ended, Pryor laid a claim for an immediate start on the Botanic Gardens, his number one post-war project.

His moderate request for £1,000 to cover definition of the boundaries, a survey and base plans, some small items of meteorological equipment, fencing the area and removal of stumps was approved, and though it took some time to implement, the order was at last given to the fencing contractor.

The British Commonwealth Conference in Agriculture was to take place in Canberra in September 1949, and this gave a splendid opportunity to raise interest in the project at top level. How this was wangled or arranged is not known, but on September 13th the Canberra Times ran as its headline 'First Tree Planting in Botanical Garden Area' and reported that, in the presence of the delegates, 'the Prime Minister, Mr Chifley planted a small gum tree and Sir Edward Salisbury, Director of the Royal Botanic Gardens, Kew, a small oak.'

When the idea for Canberra to be a Garden City had first been thought of, advice was sought from all the State Botanic Gardens, and the enthusiasm of professional colleagues throughout Australia for the establishment of the Canberra Gardens and specifically for the study and culture of native plants – this convinced the planners that their decision to specialise was not only practical but very popular too. They said: 'The Lake Scheme has been a means of transforming the attitudes of the small scattered community of pioneers into unity and harmony and drawing them into a focal point of interest for Australians where the desire is to stay and foster appreciation of those things that are uniquely Australian.'

During Dr Pryor's fourteen-year term as Superintendent, a Viennese botanist, Erwin Gauba, had been his close collaborator in research on the genetics of eucalypts and the flora indigenous to the Capital Territory. Between them they had amassed and classified a large amount of material and a significant herbarium had been created, while planting and landscaping had transformed the gardens on Black Mountain. By 1966 the early plantings of Dr Pryor had grown to a substantial size and maturity, and his forays into the country – as far away as Western Australia and Tasmania – had been most rewarding.

By the next year public interest was generated by radio and television, and it was decided to open the gardens for eight hours daily from September 1967.

The great moment was the formal opening of the Canberra Botanic Gardens which took place in 1970, when it hosted the International Congress of Parks.

As the new capital city of a new nation that is becoming more and more aware of the vast potential of its national resources, Canberra is expected to encourage appreciation of those things which are uniquely Australian. Nobody today would think of asking why its Botanic Garden is exclusively for the study and culture of Australian native flora – it is so obvious, so fitting and exactly what one would expect.

I much regret that I never got to Canberra on my lecture tour 'down under'. I would have been thrilled to explore it, especially as I try to grow some of its singularly characteristic plants myself. I have two yellow bottle brushes, *Callistemon pallidus* and *C.sieberi,* as well as a *Hibbertia aspera* which I am very proud of – though the latter did not enjoy this winter's January frost. My *Billardiera longiflora*, grown for its spectacular purple fruits, is very decorative and I am still looking for a *Eucalyptus ficifolia,* a small red flowered eucalypt, which I intend to try in my greenhouse.

POSTSCRIPT

Botanical Enterprise

It was in 1880 that William Thistleton-Dyer (son in law of Sir Joseph Hooker) read a paper at the Colonial Institute in London – titled *'The Botanical Enterprise of the Empire'* – which tells us that what his predecessors had planned about 130 years before was still going strong in the capital of each colonial botanical garden all of which were animated with the entire spirit of Kew and worthy of comparison with it. 'We make a special point,' he says, 'to grow at Kew every plant which is known to have any useful application, and these we yearly distribute, as they are wanted to the different Indian and Colonial gardens with which we are in correspondence. And if it is enquired why operations of this kind are carried out by a Government establishment, the answer may at once be given that no private establishment could attempt anything of the kind. No horticulturist could afford to maintain such a stock of plants of purely botanical interest on the chance that one day or other they might prove to meet an unexpected demand.' He adds that only such an institution as Kew would have the command of obtaining such plants from foreign countries: 'It seems always to be a pleasure if not a point of honour for scientific men to be of use to Kew, where we pride ourselves on being a sort of botanical clearing house or exchange for the Empire.'

A practical result of this work comes, he says, in a letter from Mr Walter Hill, of the Brisbane Botanic Gardens, who sends him seeds of the Wine Palm of Brazil, which Sir William Hooker had sent him some thirty years before: 'The fruit is much relished by our colonists and we are planting it on many of the islands that lie between Brisbane and Thursday Island in the hope that it may afford the means of sustenance for castaway sailors' (the coast near the

Great Barrier Reef) 'being especially dangerous to small coasters who are unlikely to have up to date charts.'

Even twenty years earlier than this, the Duke of Newcastle, Secretary of State for the Colonies, had instructed William Hooker to 'draw up a plan for the publication of Colonial floras in an inexpensive form and in the English language'. This was to be produced with every feature of scientific accuracy, but 'as far as possible in such a lucid and intelligible way, that it would be possible for persons of average capacity, with very little practise and attention, to name their plants from them.' Now, twenty-two volumes have been issued, with many others in active preparation.

Thistleton-Dyer remarked that 'the most important of these is the *Flora Australiensis* prepared at Kew by Mr Bentham, with the co-operation of Baron Ferdinand von Mueller in Australia; so far seven volumes have been completed.' (Mueller would have been gratified that his work had not been in vain). He illustrates the value of this work from a practical point of view: where for example, about 300 distinct kinds of Acacias have been discriminated by Mr Bentham, and the distinctive characters pointed out by which they may be recognised, and 135 Gum Trees (Eucalyptus) similarly characterised, and to show how useful this may be he gives this example: 'if a purchaser wants a 'White Gum' – its useful qualities are quite various – but does not realise that under this name are 12 quite distinct trees, eight of which are known as 'Red Gum', while the names of 'Blue Gum', 'Stringy Bark' and 'Iron Bark' each represent seven distinct species, the chances of his getting what he wants are about eleven to one against. If, however, he knows its proper scientific name, with the help of one of the Australian botanic gardens he may expect with some certainty to get it.'

Thistleton-Dyer describes another of Kew's official duties – public correspondence. He records: 'It is of course a great compliment to Kew and an impressive acknowledgement of its efficiency that from all parts of our British possessions, letters should continually pour in on all subjects in any way connected with botany, and upon some, such as 'sponge fisheries', which are not even remotely so.' What he hopes will happen is that when the local botanical departments are better known and trusted, 'an immense amount of work now done at Kew could be carried out at such places as Jamaica and Ceylon, where some of our correspondents reside and which have admirable botanical equipment and highly competent scientific men. The work then reserved for Kew which would still be considerable, should be that of appeal in last resort. Kew could therefore confine its expertise to plants that had been overlooked and are difficult to determine, or to find new plants for cultivation from obscure sources, or to help in dire cases where diseases were ravaging crops.'

To help interested garden visitors identify local plants, he suggests that a collection of the smaller or herbaceous plants of the colony should be kept arranged growing in beds in systematic order so that the residents can identify them, also that there should be a named collection of economic plants. He also recommends a reference library of botanical books and a named herbarium, the specimens of which shall be securely fastened on paper, 'poisoned' to secure them from insect attacks and kept on shelves in neat cabinets. The plan he suggests is to dry the specimens in duplicate, carefully number them and send one of each to Kew.

He does not mention another invaluable capacity of the Royal Gardens of Kew which was to handpick and recommend trained and suitable young men to be employed in the many botanic gardens. In the archives of Kew Library there are hundreds of letters written by Government officers, not only from our own colonial gardens but from those worldwide, dating from the early 1800s and requesting botanists, gardeners or highly qualified men trained at Kew to be employed in gardens such as those in Mauritius, Java, Jamaica and elsewhere. The salary offered might be £300 a year rising to nearly twice that amount for a scientific botanist, and only sometimes would accommodation be offered as well. What was more, applicants might even have to have paid their own fares, and this for the several month's long journey by sea, occasionally accompanied by their family.

This correspondence, often extended over several years, and with each letter taken by slow boats under sail, to and fro, seemed endlessly to be asking for a replacement for one of these valuable young men whose health had been ruined in tropical climes or who had died – probably of malaria – years before his time.

From the days when Sir Joseph Banks looked for likely lads to send abroad to hunt for plants in far off countries, there seems to have been a sort of underground grapevine which pointed the way to Soho Square (Banks's London house) – even for 'unlikely lads' such as George Caley, for whom no-one ever had a good word, yet it was Banks who spotted his talent. They were nearly all chosen either from qualified doctors, often with army experience – part of whose training would be to know about plants – or from gardeners already at Kew who might have started as schoolboy naturalists. There has never been a shortage of keen young hopefuls who found their dreams come true when they were chosen to work in some far-flung country. The calibre of these enterprising young men was remarkable, and from among them would come future the Curators or Superintendents of the Colonial botanic gardens – chosen either by Banks or by the Hooker dynasty. Their characters were as important as their ability to distinguish one plant from another. They nearly always travelled alone, (no modern luxury of picking up a mobile phone to ask advice). Always short of money, usually exploring completely unknown territory and trusted to start up some enterprising venture – they had to learn fast and be prepared to take the right decisions. What was also impressive was their articulacy and erudite handwriting and spelling. You would be hard pressed to find many young men as well educated in this field today. They could not wait to write back to their mentor at Kew in the mother country and tell of the plants they had found, or of their good fortune and adventures. The detailed and informative reports – sometimes written annually from the Directors of the Botanic Gardens – give a vivid picture of their aims and ambitions and problems as do the revealing communications from the botanists and gardeners to each other, accompanied by many plants and objects of natural history either as gifts or for exchange.

From the random selection of people I have chosen to write about, and who created the gardens in my collection, their one common denominator, besides a passion for botany, was their desire to find something new, go somewhere no-one had ever been before, and to hunt for plants that no-one had yet seen – unconsciously, or perhaps consciously, inspired by the example of Sir Joseph Banks who had somehow left a legacy for young men seeking scientific knowledge both for its own sake and for passing it on to anyone who would listen.

Young Lieutenant William Parry, newly accepted as volunteer for a command on a Banks inspired expedition to the Arctic, writes to his parents after his briefing at Soho Square: 'It is impossible in the compass of a letter, to repeat to you half of what Sir Joseph Banks said to me upon the subject – much less to give you any idea of his very affable, communicative manner; he desired that I would come to him as often as I pleased (the oftener the better) and read or take away any books I could find in his library that might be of service to me...Having obtained *carte blanche* from Sir J, I shall of course go to his library without any ceremony whenever I have occasions, for his invitations are not those of fashionable life but are given from a real desire to do everything which can in the smallest degree tend to the advancement of science'.

'This Infant Adventure' does not end here - indeed I hope it will never end. Sir Joseph Banks' original concept of botanic gardens branching out worldwide, and linked together by the umbilical cord from Kew continues to flower and flourish. Gardens may come and go, but there will always be naturalists and botanists to follow in the footsteps of the intrepid pioneers, some of whose stories have been the bedrock of my collection in this book, and who will inevitably continue unearthing hitherto undiscovered plants to keep us avid gardeners enthralled.

INDEX